TOWEL SNAPPING THE PRESS

Communication, Media, and Politics

Series Editor
Robert E. Denton, Jr., Virginia Tech

This series features a range of work dealing with the role and function of communication in the realm of politics, broadly defined. Including general academic books and texts for use in graduate and advanced undergraduate courses, the series encompasses humanistic, critical, historical, and empirical studies in political communication in the United States. Primary subject areas include campaigns and elections, media, and political institutions. *Communication, Media, and Politics* books will be of interest to students, teachers, and scholars of political communication from the disciplines of communication, rhetorical studies, political science, journalism, and political sociology.

Recent Titles in the Series

Political Campaign Communication: Principles and Practices, Fifth Edition
Judith S. Trent and Robert V. Friedenberg
The Rhetoric of Redemption: Kenneth Burke's Redemption Drama and Martin Luther King, Jr.'s "I Have a Dream" Speech
David A. Bobbitt
Reelpolitik II: Political Ideologies in '50s and '60s Films
Beverly Merrill Kelley
New Frontiers in International Communication Theory
Edited by Mehdi Semati
News Narratives and News Framing: Constructing Political Reality
Karen S. Johnson-Cartee
Leading Ladies of the White House: Communication Strategies of Notable Twentieth-Century First Ladies
Edited by Molly Meijer Wertheimer
Entertaining Politics: New Political Television and Civic Culture
Jeffrey P. Jones
Presidential Candidate Images
Edited by Kenneth L. Hacker
Bring 'Em On: Media and Politics in the Iraq War
Edited by Lee Artz and Yahya R. Kamalipour
The Talk of the Party: Political Labels, Symbolic Capital, and American Life
Sharon E. Jarvis
The 2004 Presidential Campaign: A Communication Perspective
Edited by Robert E. Denton, Jr.
Women's Political Discourse: A 21st-Century Perspective
Molly A. Mayhead and Brenda DeVore Marshall
Making Sense of Political Ideology: The Power of Language in Democracy
Bernard L. Brock, Mark E. Huglen, James F. Klumpp, and Sharon Howell
Transforming Conflict: Communication and Ethnopolitical Conflict
Donald G. Ellis
Towel Snapping the Press: Bush's Journey from Locker-Room Antics to Message Control
James E. Mueller
The Internet Election: Perspectives on the Web in Campaign 2004
Edited by Andrew Paul Williams and John C. Tedesco

TOWEL SNAPPING THE PRESS

Bush's Journey from Locker-Room Antics to Message Control

James E. Mueller

ROWMAN & LITTLEFIELD PUBLISHERS, INC.
Lanham • Boulder • New York • Toronto • Oxford

ROWMAN & LITTLEFIELD PUBLISHERS, INC.

Published in the United States of America
by Rowman & Littlefield Publishers, Inc.
A wholly owned subsidiary of
The Rowman & Littlefield Publishing Group, Inc.
4501 Forbes Boulevard, Suite 200, Lanham, Maryland 20706
www.rowmanlittlefield.com

P.O. Box 317, Oxford OX2 9RU, UK

British Library Cataloguing in Publication Information Available

Library of Congress Cataloging-in-Publication Data

Mueller, James E., 1960–
Towel snapping the press : Bush's journey from locker-room antics to message control / James E. Mueller.
p. cm. — (Communication, media, and politics)
Includes bibliographical references and index.
ISBN-13: 978-0-7425-3850-4 (cloth : alk. paper)
ISBN-10: 0-7425-3850-8 (cloth : alk. paper)
ISBN-13: 978-0-7425-3851-1 (pbk. : alk. paper)
ISBN-10: 0-7425-3851-6 (pbk. : alk. paper)
1. Bush, George W. (George Walker), 1946– —Relations with journalists. 2. Presidents—United States—Press coverage. 3. Journalism—Political aspects—United States. 4. Press and politics—United States. 5. Mass media—Political aspects—United States. 6. United States—Politics and government—2001– I. Title. II. Series.
E903.3M84 2006
973.931092—dc22

2005035628

∞™ The paper used in this publication meets the minimum requirements of American National Standard for Information Sciences—Permanence of Paper for Printed Library Materials, ANSI/NISO Z39.48-1992.
Manufactured in the United States of America.

For Catherine, David and Sarah

CONTENTS

ACKNOWLEDGMENTS

The idea for this book came from listening to sports talk radio. In the fall of 2000 I was listening to Randy Galloway's radio show for a dissection of the Dallas Cowboys latest misadventures when he made an offhand comment about the presidential debates. Galloway said George W. Bush looked stiff and not at all like the George that he and the other sportswriters used to joke with when he owned the Texas Rangers. Galloway and his "Einsteins," as he joking called his sports panel, agreed that presidential candidate George was not the George they knew.

Their discussion made me wonder. What was Bush like with the sports press? Did he learn anything from dealing with the sportswriters in a market like Dallas, where a lot of people take sports more seriously than politics? Galloway graciously sat for an extensive interview on the subject and directed me to other sources. I wrote an academic paper on Bush and the sports press. The more I studied Bush and his press relations, the more I became convinced his attitude and experience was unlike that of any other president and was worthy of a book.

The book was made possible by the cooperation of Galloway and many other sources who agreed to be interviewed. Other journalists who were extraordinarily helpful in the amount of time they gave for interviews and the insight they provided were Wayne Slater of the *Dallas Morning News*; Arnold Garcia and Dave McNeely of the *Austin American-Statesman*; Ron Hutcheson, president of the White House Correspondents' Association; and freelance photographer Chris Usher. Helen Thomas demonstrated that in her case, the more famous you are, the nicer you are. She returned my phone message immediately and spoke candidly. Bob Schieffer, although quite busy taking over for Dan Rather, showed an equal graciousness. Their attitude toward a fledgling author was remarkable considering several reporters of lesser stature ignored interview requests or set up interviews and then stood me up.

Unfortunately, space does not permit me to list all of the other people I interviewed for this project, but I sincerely thank them for their time and candor.

I also want to thank Tonia J. Wood, archivist for the Texas State Library and Archives Commission, who helped guide me through Bush's governor's records.

All of the people at Rowman & Littlefield have been tremendously helpful, especially Jenn Nemec, Bess Vanrenen, and Brenda Hadenfeldt. Brenda's ideas about the organizing the book greatly improved my original concept.

I am deeply indebted to Marvin Olasky, who was my dissertation adviser at the University of Texas, for writing the forward. Professor Olasky has been one of my intellectual role models, and I hope this work reflects that.

Lastly, this book would not have been written without the enthusiasm and intelligence of my wife, Catherine Lynn Mueller, who helped research, edit, and proof the text and inspires me in everything I do.

FOREWORD

Towel Snapping the Press is an informative book that's also fun to read. That's because Jim Mueller interviewed 29 journalists, recorded their often-amusing anecdotes, and then put present practice into historical perspective. What comes out is a dual portrait of the president and the press.

Some of the best stories come from Wayne Slater, Austin bureau chief of the *Dallas Morning News*. For example, Slater recalls that his wife was prepared to dislike Bush since he had beaten Democratic governor Ann Richards, but at the press Christmas party he "talked to her casually while he was eating a muffin, crumbs dripping on the governor's mansion carpet, and she was struck by how genuine he was." Slater's quote captures Bush well: "He was not this type of pretentious, aloof figure but a regular person."

Towel Snapping the Press shows how the regular person learned that being regular wasn't enough. When Bush was a Texas Rangers owner, he could talk with sportswriters and garble his syntax. As sports columnist Randy Galloway puts it in this book, "If he would misspeak, so what? We were probably doing the same. It wasn't that big a deal." Bush could even be caught picking his nose during a televised game without having it noted in a newspaper. Even when he was governor, no one worried that his word usage wasn't perfect—but when Bush became president, reporters became picky.

I sometimes wonder how much the abnormal environment inhabited by White House reporters contributes to press nastiness. This book describes it well: "The life of a White House reporter is indeed a strange one. . . . Television viewers are used to seeing reporters gravely doing their stand-ups with the White House in the background, the implication being that they are intimately familiar with what goes on inside the mansion. In contrast, the press quarters are cramped, the hours are bad, and the traveling schedule is too hectic to allow them to see much of the dramatic sites they visit."

But Jim Mueller goes deeper, writing that some of the press animus results from the journalists' sense that they are cramped not only in their offices but in the stories they produce: the cult of "objectivity" does not allow them to be forthrightly honest about what they really think. He asks why this is so: "Defenders of objectivity say people need neutral views, and if they get their news only from sources that cater to their own biases, they will be uninformed. But who says in an information society with myriad satellite television channels, websites, and print and Internet newspapers, people will not look at multiple sources to test the accuracy of their favorite view?"

That's an important question, and it got me thinking about how readers and viewers find out what George W. Bush is like. Sure, they can watch his speeches, but people also like to hear about him from someone who's seen him up close over a long period of time. Say you could listen in on a discussion of a half-dozen journalists who have covered the president. You wouldn't expect each to offer, in carefully tailored tones, a "balanced" account. You'd expect each to tell you what he had seen and his assessment of the meaning of what he'd seen. You could then evaluate the information, taking into account both the specific detail offered and the reliability of each informant.

The argument of some newspaper or television news editors is that few people subscribe to multiple newspapers or watch multiple broadcasts concerning the same event, so they won't be able to get a half-dozen varied assessments; therefore, newspapers or television stations should be careful not to tilt their coverage one way or the other. But the assumption of one-source reliance by readers or viewers is rapidly becoming outmoded. With the rapid development of new websites and blogs, millions of people—and the number grows each month—are trading in old, one-stop information shopping for the freedom to read multiple views for themselves.

There is thus no longer a need for a newspaper to be even-handed: It can present one sharply angled assessment with the knowledge that readers can readily access other perspectives. Similarly, the "fairness doctrine" in broadcasting is outmoded: It's not unfair or socially irresponsible to present one point of view when viewers or listeners can instantly move to dozens of others.

The Bush terms have been the 21st century's first chronologically, of course, but they've also been the first in which online news and views figure prominently. How soon will White House reporters and, more importantly, their editors and producers, understand the change and move toward greater frankness and honesty in reporting? As Jim Mueller concludes in his final chapter: "With each news source stating its political slant, the consumer could disagree with a news source while at the same time respecting its honesty. In the current environment, news consumers are taught to not only question the accuracy of the news but also the honesty of the individual journalist who reports it."

George W. Bush is of course a politician, but he's also a person who prefers short, frank accounts rather than dithering. Most news consumers are the same. This book tells interesting stories but also suggests a way for journalists to be more helpful to the president, his critics, the nation, and themselves.

Marvin Olasky
Professor of Journalism, The University of Texas at Austin
Editor-in-Chief, *World*

PREFACE

George W. Bush has reached a new level not only in terms of his relationship with individual reporters but also in terms of the broader historical context of presidential press relations. Bush entered the White House with more experience dealing with the press than any previous president. What's more, he has used this experience to manage press relations through a combination of personal charm (and sometimes pressure), message discipline, and the rigid control of both press access to administration sources and control of leaks coming from sources within his administration. While most presidents have used some of these tactics with varying degrees of success, Bush has managed press relations by combining all of them in a way that few, if any, of his predecessors could equal, and in a way that his successors will likely try to emulate.

In this book, I have not tried to measure Bush's success at managing press relations by examining the press coverage itself. Researchers have already done numerous studies of the coverage of Bush and his administration. These studies typically create a definition of the tone of a story and then count stories and calculate the ratio of positive to negative stories. The authors then usually conclude based on the statistics whether the coverage favored one side or the other. Such studies have their place, and I even cowrote one about the 2000 campaign coverage in youth-oriented magazines that showed coverage favored Vice President Al Gore over Bush.[1]

The problem with the statistical approach is that journalism is not a mathematical endeavor. Journalism is a field that is based largely on human relationships; how a reporter and a source interact. The end product of these relationships—news stories—is dominated by events. The president, simply because he is president, can influence the media's news agenda by discussing one issue over another. But the smoothest source in the world cannot make bad news good. In presidential politics, particularly in the partisan Clinton-Bush era, the effectiveness of the press relations of the opposition party also plays a role in the president's success. Bill Clinton, for example, owed some of his success in his mid-1990s budget battles with Congress to the inept way his Republican rivals handled the government shutdown.[2] All of these outside factors make it difficult to pin down cause and effect when evaluating presidential press relations by examining what has been written or broadcast about the administration.

Nevertheless, we do know that a tremendous amount of the president's job is communicating his goals to the public and persuading the people to follow his leadership. The president must do much of this through the media. We can get an idea of the effectiveness of a president's press relations by looking at elections and accomplishments. Bush has succeeded at both. Bush won two presidential elections against long odds, and he campaigned so extensively for his party in the 2002 midterm elections that many observers credited him with making the difference for his party in a surprising triumph in that contest.[3] In terms of accomplishing goals, Bush persuaded Congress to approve a large tax cut and education reform early in his first term despite the fact he had entered office in a controversial election that saw his opponent actually win the popular vote total. Perhaps most notably, he persuaded the public to support his war against Iraq at a time when there was significant national and international opposition.[4] But again, electoral and policy success are not by themselves proof of success in managing press relations. Disastrous events will drive a president out of office regardless of favorable press coverage, and good news can make up for poor communication skills.

This book, rather than an analysis of his press coverage, is a narrative of Bush's lifelong association with the press and how he has learned and adapted his press tactics to his various circumstances. It is based largely on what reporters who have covered Bush have said and written about him as a news source. Most journalists have found him to be charming even if they decry his refusal to go "off message" or his attempts to control information. And even those who criticize the administration for being too restrictive on reporters' access admit that it is a successful tactic from the president's vantage point. The tactics Bush has applied in the White House were honed over long years of dealing with reporters at all levels of the media.

1

FRIENDS FOR A LONG TIME

Wayne Slater realized his relationship with George W. Bush had changed when the president tried to choke him in the White House and no one laughed.

The president wasn't really trying to kill a troublesome reporter. It was just the kind of horseplay that the two men, who had been part of a similar fraternity culture at their respective colleges, had engaged in when Slater had been the Austin bureau chief of the *Dallas Morning News* and Bush had been the governor of Texas. Slater knew Bush about as well as any reporter did, having covered him regularly since he first ran for governor in 1994 and spending almost every day with him during the 2000 presidential campaign. But after the election, Slater had returned to his Austin job rather than join the White House press corps, an assignment he felt would involve too much sifting through presidential news releases rather than investigative work. In addition to his duties with the *Morning News*, Slater had written with James Moore a book called *Bush's Brain*, in which Bush political strategist Karl Rove has the title role as the mastermind of the president's political career. At the time of the mock choking, the book had not been published. But prepublicity for the book had started, and Bush asked Slater, who was at a White House Christmas party, "What's this I hear about you writing that Karl Rove is my mentor?"

Slater said, "No, sir, Mr. President, I didn't write that he was your mentor, I just wrote that he was smarter than you are."

Bush laughed. Slater grabbed his arm, and Bush grabbed Slater around the neck as if he would choke him. It was, Slater thought, just like when Bush was governor and would sometimes act goofy with reporters. But at the same time, Slater noticed that the people surrounding Bush in the White House looked shocked.

"And then I realized . . . wait a minute . . . I'm in the White House," Slater recalled. "People with guns are here . . . he's the president of the United States. On the one hand he's the same old guy, but on the other hand, he's at a new level."[1]

Bush's dealings with the sports press when he owned a share of the baseball Texas Rangers is one example of his preparation for handling the political press. It might seem quite a jump from sports to politics, but the two professions have some strong similarities. Wally Haas, owner of the Oakland A's, said that although sports doesn't involve life-and-death issues, it's a very public business. "What other business, other than running for president, is your business in the paper every day?" Haas said. "It's really black and white: if you win, you're great, and if you lose, you're a bum."[2]

Just as politicians require media coverage to promote their campaigns and their politics, professional sports teams need publicity to sell tickets. Perhaps no baseball team was in more dire need of publicity in 1989 than the Texas Rangers. The club had suffered a number of losing seasons in a row and local interest was so low that Eddie Chiles, the elderly owner who planned to sell the team, was entertaining offers from people who wanted to move the franchise to a more hospitable market than the Dallas–Fort Worth metroplex. Bush, a lifelong baseball fan, wanted to buy the team—but although Bush had the desire, he didn't have the money. Bush, then 42, had an undistinguished career in the energy business and was best known for being the son of the president of the United States.

Being a member of such a powerful family led to connections that could provide the partners to help Bush buy the team. Unfortunately, the wealthy people Bush knew did not want to be under the media scrutiny that comes from owning a professional sports franchise. Bush told them not to worry, "I know how to handle the press."[3] The other owners took him at his word. Although Bush had the least amount of money invested in the franchise, the other owners in the partnership appointed him the managing general partner, which meant he became the public face of the ownership group.

To the person with casual knowledge of journalism, this might seem a fairly easy task. Sportswriters, the common assumption goes, are the least sophisticated of journalists and the easiest for sources to manipulate. After all, the thinking goes, sportswriters are largely fans who have been lucky enough to make their hobby their job. But Tracy Ringolsby, who covered the Rangers for the *Dallas Morning News* in 1989 when Bush owned the team, said the future president was not dealing with unsophisticated journalists. "I never found covering politics to be brain surgery," Ringolsby said. "You're still in journalism. . . . I would say for sports you have to be better versed because you're dealing with finances, you're dealing with labor organizations, you're dealing with racial issues. . . . Here I'm covering a ballgame and labor relations. Labor writers don't cover labor relations and a ballgame."[4]

And the sportswriters in the sports-crazy Dallas–Fort Worth metroplex were competing at a fever pitch to scoop each other because there were three competing metropolitan dailies—the *Dallas Morning News*, the *Dallas Times Herald*, and the *Fort Worth Star-Telegram*—in addition to broadcast stations and smaller papers. Bush entered this cauldron of journalists with the added handicap that he was perceived by many to be a spoiled rich kid who was able to buy a share of the franchise only because his daddy was the president of the United States. Randy Galloway, a columnist who has worked for both the *Star-Telegram* and the *Morning News* in addition to hosting his own radio show, said he resented Bush almost immediately because he thought the franchise should have been sold to a more deserving owner.[5] Galloway was not alone in his skepticism.

But Bush threw himself into his new job, attending most of the games while mixing with the fans, making public appearances, and, most importantly, cultivating reporters. Phil Rogers, who at the time covered the Rangers for the *Dallas Times-Herald*, first interviewed Bush by phone. Rogers was shocked later when Bush hollered a greeting to him across the infield at a minor league game in Oklahoma City before the pair had ever met face to face. "That doesn't happen by accident," Rogers said. "He had someone giving him good advice—who was who and how to get off to a good start with people."[6]

According to Rogers, Bush got on well with all of the sportswriters, which Rogers said was unusual for a source to do with such a diverse and competitive group. Bush gained their confidence through his honesty, his accessibility, and his friendliness. It also helped that the franchise was extraordinarily successful under his tenure, which included the construction of a beautiful new stadium and improvement in the team's play. As late as 2003, sportswriters still referred to the Bush era as the glory years of the franchise.[7] Although the team was a contender in its division again in 2004 and 2005, the problems between the team's management and players and the media were a definite contrast to the atmosphere during the Bush era. During the 2005 season, pitching ace Kenny Rogers was suspended for striking a cameraman. General Manager John Hart suggested Rogers was mad over media reports that the pitcher had faked an injury to avoid starting against some good teams. Reporters claimed the story came from Rangers management, but Hart denied that and instead blamed the media for being too intrusive and irritating the players. Team owner Tom Hicks also blamed the press, chastising a roomful of reporters: "You guys are a tough group at times with people."[8]

Bush knew reporters could be a tough group, but he and Tom Schieffer, the club president during the Bush years, made a point of getting along with them. Schieffer's brother is CBS anchor Bob Schieffer, who has covered Bush for years and first knew him through the connection with his brother Tom. "I've heard my brother say, many, many times, there are two kinds of baseball owners: there are the guys that sit up in the press box and talk about what a bunch of jerks the press is, and then there are the other group who go down on the field and stand there behind the batting cage during batting practice and let the press have at 'em," Bob Schieffer said. "Bush and my brother always believed that you had to come down there and talk to the press every day, and they always did."[9]

Bush's press relations eventually won over even Galloway, with whom he would occasionally argue vehemently about stories. Galloway wrote a farewell column when Bush sold his shares in the franchise, saying he was sorry to see him go.[10]

Jim Reeves, a *Fort Worth Star-Telegram* sports columnist, was, like Galloway, initially skeptical of Bush. Reeves said Bush sensed that skepticism and made an effort to win him over by inviting him to play golf. Reeves accepted the invitation and had a good time. Years later Reeves asked Tom Schieffer if the golf match had been designed to sway him, but Schieffer denied it. At any rate, Reeves grew to like Bush.[11] "When you are around George . . . he has a way of making you feel comfortable and that you and he have been friends for a long, long time," Reeves said.[12]

In fact, Bush and the press have been, if not friends, certainly familiar acquaintances for a very long time—since he was a child. Bush's family, because of its prominence in business, has been familiar with the media going back to at least the days of his great-grandfather, Samuel P. Bush, who made his fortune as head of Buckeye Steel Castings in Columbus, Ohio, around the turn of the 20th century. The family was famous enough in Columbus that when Prescott Bush, Bush's grandfather, wrote home a prank letter during his World War I service that he had personally saved three allied generals from an artillery shelling, the local paper took the letter from his parents for a front-page story. (The paper later ran an embarrassing correction.)[13]

Samuel P. Bush, unlike his own father and his famous political descendants, did not attend Yale but instead studied management and engineering at the Stevens Institute of Technology. He brought those scientific concepts to the management of Buckeye Steel, where he was adept at communicating with the workers in what would now be considered corporate communications. Concerned about employee morale, he organized a Thrift Committee to encourage savings by the workers, and a company flyer defined the topic and argued its importance.[14]

The future 43rd president was not around to witness those nascent public relations efforts, but he was raised in a family used to being in the public eye. When he was four, Bush likely absorbed—if not intellectually, at least by observing the reactions of his elders—his first lesson about the press during his grandfather Prescott Bush's 1950 campaign for the U.S. Senate in Connecticut. A family photo shows Prescott's grandchildren (who are not identified) selling orangeade to "Help Send Gampy to Washington." The orangeade was not enough to overcome an erroneous radio story by Walter Winchell linking Prescott Bush to the Birth Control League, a damaging accusation in a state in which it was illegal to sell condoms. Gampy Bush lost by just over a thousand votes, which the family blamed on Winchell.[15] But Prescott, like his son and grandson would later do, learned from his first campaign and won his second, this time a special 1952 election to fill the Connecticut Senate seat left vacant by the death of Brien McMahon.

Back in Midland, grandson George W. Bush was observing his father become a mover and shaker as a civic activist. In *First Son*, the most thorough and balanced biography of Bush to date, author Bill Minutaglio noted that one of the future president's first media appearances was in a photograph that appeared in the *Midland Reporter-Telegram* that showed him competing in the eight-year-old age division of a YMCA electric train race.[16] By itself, appearing in the newspaper as a child is not unique; countless Americans have thus earned a smattering of fame, because a principle of American newspapers is that local faces sell local papers. But this picture included another future U.S. president, George H. W. Bush, who had befriended *Reporter-Telegram* publisher Jimmy Allison. The publisher would later become a trusted adviser and booster of George H. W. Bush's political career. Young George may have been a cute kid, but it is equally likely his picture was taken because of who he was rather than what he was. At any rate, well before he was 10 years old, George W. Bush was interacting with the press, getting the idea that it was a natural occurrence to be photographed and interviewed—and that this was part of the process of running for office in the United States.

"You can't underestimate that he grew up in a family where the father was a member of Congress, then was a high-ranking member of both the RNC [Republican National Committee] and Republican administrations," Wayne Slater said. "And so even if he is away at prep school, and later at college or in the military, he is a person who understands that at some point, people will be looking at you. You're the child of somebody—maybe not a movie star—but you're still the child of somebody who from time to time is interviewed and talked to."[17]

As he got older, Bush experienced this lesson firsthand in his father's campaigns. Sometimes American politicians have to deal with embarrassing family members—witness Jimmy Carter's brother Billy and Bill Clinton's brother Roger. But whenever possible, politicians use their relatives in publicity appearances as shorthand messages that they have a nice family and are thus upstanding citizens. If the family members are particularly articulate, they can campaign as surrogates—giving speeches and interviews in place of the candidate and allowing the candidate's campaign to cover more territory with personal appearances.

Some members of political families are reluctant participants. George W. Bush's own daughters, for example, did not campaign in 2000 and volunteered for the 2004 campaign only after Jenna had a nightmare that her Dad lost the election.[18] Jenna's father had no such hesitation when he was her age. Bush participated actively in all of his father's numerous campaigns, beginning with making public appearances on stage during his failed run for a U.S. Senate seat from Texas in 1964. By 1970, when his father was a congressman trying once again for a Senate seat, Bush, 24, was a full-fledged surrogate candidate, traveling through Texas giving interviews to local media and answering questions on his father's behalf with ease.[19] The young man enjoyed politics so much that he volunteered on other campaigns as well, continuing to hone his media skills. During Edward Gurney's successful 1968 campaign for a U.S. Senate seat from Florida, Bush served as a press wrangler, escorting journalists to their hotel rooms, transportation, and meals.[20] Bush had a higher-profile job as a paid political director for Winton M. "Red" Blount's 1972 campaign for a U.S. Senate seat from Alabama. Blount lost the race, but Bush gained valuable experience traveling across the state doing advance work for the candidate.[21]

Bush also used his media skills outside the family business of politics. When Bush's Yale fraternity was investigated in 1967 for abusing pledges with branding during initiation, it was Bush who the *New York Times* quoted as a key source defending Delta Kappa Epsilon.[22] After graduation, Bush enlisted in the Texas Air National Guard, embarking on a brief military career that has been analyzed by political opponents with the zeal that Kennedy assassination fanatics devote to the Zapruder film. In the futile search for the smoking gun that could reveal whether Bush gained his slot through family connections or shirked his duties, observers miss the interesting fact that in yet another aspect of his life, Bush had dealt with the media. In the case of the National Guard, Bush was featured in a press release as an example of an enthusiastic young flyer. Perhaps the Guard featured Bush because he was the son of a congressman. But the Guard was filled with famous sons during the Vietnam War—Bush's outfit was known as the "Champagne unit" because of the rich and famous on the roster.[23] However, Bush was an experienced interview subject who was able to give the press officer the quotes needed for the story. In any case, his interview for the press release was just more of the same type of thing Bush was doing in the Gurney and Blount campaigns, both of which he worked on while he was in the Guard.

After his discharge from the Guard in 1973, Bush entered Harvard Business School and earned an MBA in 1975. He returned to Midland to start a career in the oil business as his father had done almost 30 years earlier. But the younger Bush's talents were always in representing the organization rather than in the nuts and bolts of the business. Bush was successful at raising money for his various oil companies; getting investors to buy into the company and then serving as the public face of the business. In fact, Bush's roles with Arbusto Energy, later Bush Oil, later Bush Exploration, later Spectrum Seven, and finally Harken Energy, presaged his role with the Rangers, which was not setting ticket prices or making player trades but rather representing the ownership of the business to the public and the press.

During this time period, Bush continued to develop his press skills. Radio journalist Ed Clements, who at that time was news and sports director of KCRS in Midland, got to know Bush as a news source but also became a friend through their joint work on civic groups such as the United Way.[24]

Bush was always accessible to the local media to promote the United Way and even appeared several years in a row on Clements's sports show to talk about the Harvard–Yale football game, a topic of some interest in Midland because many residents either came from the East to work in the oil business or sent their kids to Ivy League schools when they struck it rich. "He was always good with the media then, and just like I think he does now, put them in a position where they did not feel intimidated," Clements said.[25]

Bush unsuccessfully ran for Congress in 1978, but Clements recalled that although it was his first campaign, Bush "was not a political novice by any means" and knew how to deal with the press. "He was anxious to get interviews," Clements noted. "He was anxious to be on your radio station because of just the nature of running a political campaign. He wanted the attention at that time. He wanted the *free* attention with the radio interviews."[26]

In fact, the president who now is regularly criticized for avoiding the media had some trouble attracting attention in 1978. Mel Tittle, who was city editor of the *Lubbock Avalanche-Journal* that year, recalled that Bush's visit to the newspaper generated little interest. "He was a nonentity at that time," Tittle said. "I remember him sitting in a room and having to scour the building to find someone to interview him."[27]

But whether he was cooling his heels in a newspaper office or chatting about Ivy League football on a sports show, Bush could mold his relations with journalists depending upon the need. When he was a surrogate candidate and later when he was the candidate himself, he was charming with individual reporters in most cases. But during his father's 1988 presidential campaign, the younger Bush was the self-described "enforcer"—monitoring the loyalty of campaign staffers and getting them to do what the candidate needed done. He also was the gatekeeper for press interviews and the one who gave a terse "No comment, asshole," to reporters he didn't like or administered a tongue-lashing over what he considered an unfair piece.[28] Nevertheless, he could work the press when he wanted to. During the 1988 Republican convention, Bush and a campaign worker were standing on the convention floor, looking up at the press boxes on the upper floor that literally circled the building. Bush decided to do interviews and went up to the press floor and proceeded to go from booth to booth until he had covered all the media.[29] A person doesn't do that without being well practiced with the media.

Bush was learning about the media, but still growing. Slater recalled seeing an interview of Bush on C-SPAN in the late 1980s. The interview, while certainly not the adversarial kind a candidate would get on the campaign trail, was interesting because it showed facets of "this young George Bush, who on the one hand was quite skilled at dealing with the interview . . . but on the other hand still had that aspect of a smart-aleck, young guy."[30]

Bush's father won the election in 1988, and the younger son bought his share of the Rangers the following year. He was more than ready to take on his role as chief spokesman for the franchise. The Rangers public relations director, John Blake, said Bush was the most media-savvy owner he had worked with in his more than 20 years in the sports information field.[31]

"He was great," Blake said. "I mean, he was one of the easiest people I've ever had to work with because he did have an understanding of what you had to do. He realized early on you had to face the music on things that weren't popular whether it be a ticket price increase or whatever it is; firing a team president. Those were the kinds of things we had to face the music on. He was very good at it. Having that understanding made it much easier for me because he would go on a talk show and talk about an unpopular issue, and I've always felt that's the best way to do it. You can't run and hide from things."[32]

Bush brought that same level of public relations skill to his political career. A number of people have argued that Bush is by nature a salesman, and that in his various jobs and government offices he has sold the company or administration policy more than developed them. When he first ran for president, Bush himself said: "Nobody needs to tell me what I believe. But I do need somebody to tell me where Kosovo is. I know how to ask."[33] Part of this is dictated by the nature of the two elected offices he has held. The Texas government has a weak-governor structure, in which the lieutenant governor is in many ways more powerful than the governor, whose greatest influence comes by using the bully pulpit. The presidency in comparison has much more power under the U.S. Constitution, but it is still just one of three branches of the federal government and fulfills an important symbolic role as well as recommending legislation and nominating judges. The president must persuade Congress and the public to follow him.

Persuasion, salesmanship, charm—whatever you want to call it—is certainly one of Bush's natural talents. But by his lifelong experience he has also learned how to communicate ideas to the public through the media.

Because of his family background and his own intense interest in the family business—politics—dealing with the media is as natural to Bush as acrobatics is to a child of the Flying Wallendas. His education at the Harvard Business School helped Bush develop a professional attitude toward management and business. When you combine media knowledge, business education, and interpersonal skills, you get someone who is extraordinarily adept at media relations. In fact, it is not a stretch to say that George W. Bush is the first president who by experience and inclination is what we call in journalism education a public relations practitioner. Bush may have the natural skills of a salesman, but his work experience has been public relations. To use the Texas Rangers as an example, someone working at an ad agency would write advertisements for the team and buy space to run them in the local media. A public relations practitioner would represent the organization to the press and the public, and that was one of Bush's main roles as managing general partner of the Rangers—and a role he often fulfilled later as governor and president.

Other presidents, of course, have been skilled at press relations. Certainly in America's media-saturated culture no person could even mount a serious run for the office without some knowledge of journalism. In fact, all serious candidates have had enough public service before running that they have encountered the press in a variety of capacities. Bill Clinton, for example, was governor of Arkansas and thus had to deal with that state's capital press corps. Bush's father had encountered the press in such high-profile jobs as director of the CIA, chairman of the Republican National Committee, and ambassador to the United Nations, in addition to his own campaigns for Congress. And Al Gore, the man who almost won the 2000 election, had even been a newspaper reporter himself.

Yet none of these men had the lifelong intense exposure to the press that George W. Bush has. Ronald Reagan, whose main career was entertainment but who also spent years as a spokesman for General Electric, comes closest to matching Bush's experience. But Reagan's profession was acting, and he certainly wasn't raised in a political family. Bush, on the other hand, had encountered the political press from childhood on and also dealt with the business and sports press. Throughout his various careers, Bush was invariably the spokesman representing a candidate, a fraternity, a military unit, a business, a sports team, and ultimately, his own administrations.

"I think his attitude toward us was shaped in large part by what he watched of his father's administration," said CBS White House correspondent Bill Plante, who has covered every president since Reagan. "People tend to forget that when his father was president, he was used for sort of special missions. He was the hatchet man when his father decided to fire his chief of staff, John Sununu. So he had an insider's view of how the presidency worked. That's the kind of training that no other modern president has ever had—being that close to the decision maker on the inside."[34]

Of course, it is important not to place too much emphasis on experience alone, because all politicians—even county commissioners—have to deal with reporters at some point. In addition to experience, Bush is blessed with a natural charm that many, but not all, politicians possess. Arnold Garcia, editorial page editor of the *Austin American-Statesman*, is fascinated with John F. Kennedy and has done extensive reading on his presidency. He believes the two men are very similar. "Bush is borrowing the Kennedy playbook. . . . They were both kind of scions of New England wealth and prestige, but they both come across as a guy I would like to have beer with. *But they're not like us.* Unless your granddaddy was a senator and your daddy was a president—mine certainly wasn't—they're not like us at all. But they work on cultivating that air."[35]

Some politicians, like Gore, for example, can have extensive—in Gore's case, even firsthand—experience with the media, yet their interpersonal skills fail them in handling reporters. Slater, who covered both Gore and Bush during the 2000 campaign, said Gore never developed a friendly relationship with reporters, and consequently reporters saw him as a "guy who is kind of tetchy; he fills out the caricature the Bush people offered up" of a serial exaggerator who claims to have invented the Internet. Nonjournalists would be surprised, Slater said, at how many politicians are afraid of reporters or simply don't know how to interact with them.[36]

This lack of sophistication is particularly true in Texas, and Bush, who in general had good relations with most of the Austin capital press while he was governor, may have benefited from his polished manner in contrast to the limited skills of many of the state legislators. Jay Root, who covered Bush as governor for the *Fort Worth Star-Telegram*, said Bush was extremely professional and accessible, especially compared to other Texas pols, one of whom literally ran away from Root rather than submit to a few questions.[37]

This surprising naïveté extends to the highest levels. Clinton, who is generally regarded as charismatic and one of the most intelligent men to occupy the White House, was charming with reporters one on one, but never understood the press. Slater, who interviewed Clinton when he made a campaign trip through Texas, said the then Arkansas governor was the best politician he's ever seen at connecting with reporters on a personal level.[38] But Clinton often didn't bother to do that at the White House, despite the constant pleadings of his staff. Howard Kurtz, the *Washington Post* media critic, detailed Clinton's problems in *Spin Cycle*, a masterly account of coverage of the various Clinton scandals. Clinton's media advisers, Kurtz wrote, constantly urged Clinton to use his considerable charm on important reporters, some of whom were Clinton fans and eager to be given some positive news to write about. But Clinton rarely consented to do that kind of schmoozing, and when reporters he had courted wrote tough pieces, he felt betrayed. Clinton never grasped that presidents have to be cautious of every word they say to reporters, and that no matter how you court them, the journalists' ultimate loyalty is to the story.[39]

Bush was never under such an illusion. He could be almost as charming as Clinton, but he understood the limited benefits the charm would bring because he understood the nature of journalism. Slater said that Bush would charm reporters in an attempt to "work the refs" much like a basketball coach will try to cajole and hassle referees in order to influence calls.[40] Coaches know such influence is limited, although it can help in a call or two later on, and that's about the best politicians can hope for—that the press will be fair and will give the politician the benefit of the doubt.

Bush's working of the refs and his high public approval ratings in the aftermath of 9/11 led some to infer that Bush had the White House press under control because he had charmed them, that—to use the phrase for which this book it titled—he had a towel-snapping relationship with reporters. Robert Reno used that phrase to describe Bush's press relations in a *Newsday* column that was critical of the White House press corps.[41] Bush observers seem drawn to using sports clichés to describe him, perhaps appropriately since the president made a name for himself by owning a baseball team. Towel snapping seems particularly accurate because Bush enjoys the rough give-and-take humor that one might associate with a group of ballplayers who get along well together.

But upon closer reflection, the phrase doesn't work if it is meant to suggest that the president and the White House press corps share the carefree camaraderie and loyalty of a championship team. Although Bush had a friendly, sociable, and in some cases almost intimate relationship with reporters when he was a sports executive, a governor, and a presidential candidate, that relationship ended as dramatically and as finally as a sudden-death playoff game when he became president. The very nature of the job, the security level, and the huge number of people in the press corps preclude any kind of intimate, towel-snapping relationships. No president can cajole good coverage out of the large, diverse group of competitive reporters who make up the White House press corps. The "presidential bubble" makes an intimate bond between president and journalist almost impossible.

Ron Hutcheson, a Knight-Ridder White House reporter and president of the White House Correspondents' Association, said simply, "I think that's crap," when asked his opinion of the "towel-snapping" description. Hutcheson said Bush did charm reporters during the 2000 campaign but has not since he was elected president. "It's a lot harder to be charmed by a guy you don't interact with."[42]

Nevertheless, towel snapping works as a description of Bush's press relations if you think of the president as being in control rather than being the reporters' buddy. Bush, in this sense, is the star of the locker room, the power pitcher on the baseball team, the unquestioned leader who might smack another player on the rear end but would not tolerate being smacked in turn. There is an element of fun, of humor, but also of establishing who is on top of the pecking order.

Bush's use of nicknames is an example of this type of towel snapping. Bush became famous during the 2000 campaign for giving reporters nicknames almost immediately upon meeting them. It harkened back to his fraternity days and seemed part of the boyish charm that many reporters wrote about during the campaign. It even became a sort of status symbol among some of the reporters to be noticed enough by Bush to get a nickname.[43] Others didn't like it.

Plante, the CBS White House correspondent, said he thought Bush didn't give him a nickname because he was older than most of the other reporters. He said he would have resented a nickname in any case because it would have implied a relationship between them when he was trying to be objective. Plante also saw it as a subtle way of establishing power.[44] "This puts the reporter, I think, at a bit of a disadvantage," Plante said. "It makes the reporter look as though he or she is friendly with or beholden to the president, and I think that's one of the ways that he keeps . . . the advantage in the relationship with the press; by holding us at arm's length, by making us appear, even in a small way, complicit with him."[45]

At the White House, there's no question who is snapping the towel. Although Bush's first term included a bloody insurgency in Iraq, an economic recovery marred by slow job growth, and a political opposition so rabid that "Bush-hater" became a common term, the president won re-election with a three-million-vote margin. The White House press corps turned on itself like a dog snapping at its shadow. Some reporters criticized themselves and their colleagues for not holding the president to account.

When asked to assess the press corps' coverage of Bush, Helen Thomas, longtime UPI White House correspondent and in 2005 a columnist for Hearst, summed it up in one word: "Lousy."[46]

The George W. Bush who could joke with Slater after the reporter had teased him about his intelligence merely smiles and snaps the towel in the face of such criticism. In his first press conference following his reelection, he joked that he was going to hold each reporter to one question. The denial of follow-up questions is a serious business for journalists. A reporter can't get any depth with just one answer. Reporters, who are, after all, human, also bridle under such restrictions.

Nevertheless, it certainly seemed that Bush was joking. He teased one reporter that he couldn't have a follow-up because Bush had denied the privilege to another reporter, and it would hurt the first scribe's feelings. "He is a sensitive guy," Bush said.[47]

In fact, several reporters did ask follow-up questions. Hutcheson pointed out that a president can't really stop the reporters from asking multiple-part questions, and he had taken Bush's comment as a joke, albeit one with an element of truth. "You know, he would love nothing better than to do that, but he's been trying to do that for four years and he's failed, and he knows that he can't; he knows he's going to fail again."[48]

But the frustration among both reporters covering the White House and administration critics that Bush has gotten the upper hand led others to question whether Bush was really joking. "I don't think he was joking, but I wish he was," Thomas said.[49]

Was it a joke? Or a new policy dreamed up by Karl Rove? Was it a devious, inscrutable, seemingly off-hand remark that had been carefully crafted to get into the reporters' heads? Bush let the one-question remark stand for itself. The reporters, if they wanted to, could agonize over its meaning.

The president concluded the press conference on an upbeat note. "Listen, thank you all. I look forward to working with you. I've got a question for you. How many of you are going to be here for a second term? Please raise your hand," Bush said. After surveying the crowd, he added, "Good. Gosh, we're going to have a lot of fun, then."[50]

2

NOT HIS FATHER'S (OR GRANDFATHER'S) PRESS RELATIONS

When Neal Spelce was a young television reporter covering Lyndon Johnson, there were certain unwritten rules about when you conducted interviews. Spelce discovered that fact, to his embarrassment, when he asked LBJ a question during a barbecue at the president's Texas ranch. LBJ had held a press conference, and when it finished, the cocktails and the steaks came out. In recalling the episode some 40 years later, Spelce had forgotten the question he'd posed, but he easily remembered Johnson's response.

"You're off base, kid," Spelce recalled Johnson telling him. "You didn't follow the rules here. We're having a good time. It's not the time to talk about those sorts of things. You had your chance, why didn't you do it?" The dressing down was noteworthy enough that another reporter wrote a story about it.[1]

That was an era when a president or presidential candidate could stroll up to chat with reporters in a hotel lobby, as John F. Kennedy did at the New York Waldorf during the 1960 campaign, and feel confident his conversation would not be reported. "In the code of that simpler era, it went without saying that the chat was off the record, not an interview or an occasion for newsmen to question the candidate," longtime Associated Press reporter Walter Mears recalled of the incident in his memoir.[2] But now presidents are on the clock all the time. They can no longer share a private moment with a small group of White House reporters and be sure it will remain private.

In a broadcasting career that dates back to the 1950s, Spelce has interviewed every president since Harry Truman except Ronald Reagan. Spelce, who took time out from journalism to work in public relations and marketing, has seen both sides of the news business and thus offers a unique perspective on covering presidents. His viewpoint also differs from that of White House correspondents because although he has traveled for some interviews, he has, as he said, observed the presidents largely "from the hinterlands" as a reporter for the CBS affiliate in Austin. Spelce said relations between the press and the presidency have changed too much over the last 50 years to be able to fairly compare the press relations of presidents who have served in the last 25 years with those who served between World War II and Watergate.[3]

"I'm exaggerating to make a point," Spelce said. "It's almost as if there were a partnership between the president and press. As an example, the press would fly free on airplanes provided by the government to go cover stories. Then, later, the press said, 'We're going to pay our own way—we're not going to be beholden.' Well, that's a different time. I think that era is a different mind-set as well as a different time. Now, if you try to compare those presidents that we knew in our lifetime, it might be unfair because of the chasm that's there now between the press corps and the White House that was not there to such an extent—it was there—now it's Grand Canyon sized. Before it was just a creek or brook you could jump across."[4]

That chasm deepened and widened to a gulf that was hazardous to presidents who were unmindful of it. The Bush family has been in politics since George W. Bush's grandfather, Prescott Bush, was in the U.S. Senate in the 1950s. Both Prescott and George H. W. Bush started their political careers in the "partnership" era that Spelce referred to. Prescott Bush's U.S. Senate career ended before Watergate and Vietnam had soured presidential press relations. George H. W. Bush's career spanned the two eras, but he never quite managed the change in the relationship and suffered the humiliation of being a one-term president. His son, on the other hand, witnessed and absorbed lessons from those changes. George W. Bush was reelected with a three-million-popular-vote margin and the most popular votes ever received by a presidential candidate.

George W. Bush's reelection did not mean he had bridged the chasm. No matter the era, it is natural that there will be a creek, a chasm, or some kind of divide between all presidents and reporters, because the two want different things. Presidents want publicity and to communicate their ideas to the public, and they want to emphasize positive news. Reporters just want news, and because American journalists define news as the unusual and the dramatic, that often means they are interested in stories that don't necessarily reflect well on presidents. Consequently, one account of the history of presidential press relations from George Washington to Ronald Reagan asserted that although every administration starts with "mutual protestations of good will," the presidential press relationship always ends badly because "no president has escaped press criticism, and no president has considered himself fairly treated."[5] The history, entitled *The Press and the Presidency*, argued that the relationship had been steadily trending toward an "imperial" presidency that could manipulate press coverage so effectively that the First Amendment might be nullified.[6]

The Press and the Presidency, however, was published before the Iran-Contra scandal reduced Reagan's ability to dominate the press and the news cycle. George H. W. Bush was brought low by bad economic news, and Bill Clinton's administration was mired for almost its entire second term in sexual and financial scandals. By that point, the relationship between the press and the presidency had reached an all-time low with even the mainstream press reporting graphic details about Clinton's sexual relations. Louis W. Liebovich wrote in *The Press and the Modern Presidency*: "Balance in reporting was largely replaced by antagonism and unstinting criticism. Prying into the personal affairs of the president and his family took precedent over analyses of issues and political initiatives."[7]

Liebovich satirized that if the Civil War press was distrustful of the chief executive as today's reporters, they would have written about the Gettysburg address as an attempt by Abraham Lincoln to bolster his sagging poll numbers by drawing attention from bad publicity caused by his wife's gaffes. Modern journalists, Liebovich wrote, probably would not recognize a historic speech because they would not want to be seen as public relations shills for the president.[8]

Liebovich's satire became reality when Bush gave a speech on June 1, 2002, at West Point outlining his new doctrine of preemptive war. Chief speechwriter Michael Gerson told a reporter that the speech was important and would "be quoted for a long time." The reporter, however, missed the big picture and told Gerson the speech wasn't newsworthy because it didn't use the word *Iraq*.[9]

The consensus of journalism historians is that the turning point in presidential press relations, indeed of press relations with government and industry in general, was the twin-headed monster of the Vietnam War and the Watergate scandal. The lies of the Johnson and Nixon administrations exacerbated the natural cynicism and mistrust of journalists. Reporters became skeptical of anything presidents said or did. The presidents following Richard Nixon—Gerald Ford and Jimmy Carter—professed openness and friendly press relations as an antidote to the problem. But they set standards of openness that a chief executive cannot hope to meet, and when they fell short, they were pilloried. Ford and Carter also ceded the role of controlling the news agenda, allowing reporters to frame their presidencies any way they chose.[10] The press portrayed both as overwhelmed and incompetent, and a majority of the voting public agreed.

Ronald Reagan reversed that trend, at least for his first term. He did not promise open press relations, and he did not deliver them. Instead, the Reagan administration tightly managed the news. His press advisers took special care in selecting the venues in which he appeared so he always seemed positive and presidential. And perhaps more important, they fed the reporters a steady stream of stories and a theme for the day.[11] The results are self-evident. Although the Iran-Contra scandal kept Reagan's second term from accomplishing as much as he wanted, he left office as one of the most popular presidents in history. His passing in 2004 was met with sincere national mourning and widespread recognition for his accomplishments, even from his one-time political enemies.

George H. W. Bush had a tough act to follow. He decided to set his own style of press relations, and it turned out to contribute to his undoing. He was more comfortable with the earlier, pre-Watergate press relations where the press and the president were more partners than adversaries.[12] In that sense, the first President Bush's press relations were closer in style to Prescott Bush's press relations than to George W. Bush's.

Mickey Herskowitz, Prescott Bush's biographer, wrote that the eldest Bush politician's Senate career was overlooked by historians precisely because he did not seek media attention and noted that he had an "ice" personality compared to his grandson's "fire." George H. W. Bush told Herskowitz that Prescott "wasn't a media darling. He was more the prototype of the distinguished senator. He looked the part and he acted the part."[13]

Prescott Bush was an austere, serious man who insisted on the family dressing for dinner. His wealthy, New England, Ivy League background was suited to the view of the politician's relationship with the press as being part of a gentlemen's club. When he had a dispute with press coverage, he liked to work it out man to man. During the 1952 Senate campaign, Bush ran against Abe Ribicoff, who was Jewish. Ribicoff used the campaign slogan, "You're better off with Ribicoff." Bush, using a line his wife,

Dorothy, came up with, mocked Ribicoff's slogan in a speech saying, "You'll be in a jam with Abraham." Opponents accused Bush of anti-Semitism by emphasizing "Abraham." Bush recalled that a local newspaper editor, who was Jewish, came by his house to ask him about the charges. Bush's description sounds very clubby in the language and the attitude of how things can be solved simply among the gentlemanly ruling class: "So they dropped by to get the whole story. I told them exactly what had happened. They left perfectly satisfied. It was a one-day story, here today and gone tomorrow, because it should have been obvious that the remark was not meant to reflect some Jewish bias."[14]

Prescott got along well with John F. Kennedy, with whom he served in the U.S. Senate. In 1959 Bush spoke at the University of Virginia, where Ted Kennedy was then a student and president of the law school forum, as a favor to Jack Kennedy.[15] Nevertheless, Prescott didn't think much of the way the Kennedy family tried to cultivate the media. Nancy Bush Ellis, Prescott's daughter, said in an interview that Prescott "thought that old Joe Kennedy was unseemly in the way he courted the media. The sort of imagery around Camelot, he just thought it was ridiculous."[16]

Connections, not imagery, were important to Prescott Bush, whose Yale friendships helped launch his business career. When Prescott was senator, he befriended Oveta Culp Hobby, a Houston newspaper publisher whom Dwight Eisenhower appointed secretary of health, education, and welfare. Prescott believed her paper gave George H. W. Bush a break during his 1964 Senate campaign: "Mrs. Hobby's paper was very fair to him, in an area where Democrats are predominant."[17]

In Prescott's time, politics was often conducted out of the reporters' earshot, and if reporters did hear something, they were expected to give politicians some privacy. Prescott became a confidant of President Eisenhower's and an important figure in the national Republican party, brokering deals between the liberal and conservative wings of the party and more specifically between Eisenhower's administration and critical Republican congressmen. Prescott, like most of the Bush family, was an avid sportsman, and many of his conversations with Eisenhower occurred over a game of golf. A reporter once asked him what they talked about. Prescott replied, "Nobody who plays golf with the president ever talks about it."[18] Indeed, reporters became leery of even asking him his golf scores.[19]

Yet Prescott was aware of the power of the media. As was mentioned in chapter 1, his first campaign for Senate in 1950 had been derailed by a false story linking him to the then unpopular topic of birth control. The news hit the Sunday before the election, and Bush family lore blames the story for tipping an election that was decided by about 1,000 votes.[20] In subsequent campaigns, Prescott stayed close to the media. During the 1952 and 1956 campaigns, the Bushes kept an apartment in a hotel in Hartford, which in addition to being the political center of the state, was conveniently located near Connecticut's largest newspapers and wire services such as the Associated Press.[21]

Prescott also saw the power of the media in the way it covered one of the biggest news stories of the 1950s: McCarthyism. Bush had been on a bipartisan committee of six senators that conducted hearings to determine whether Senator Joseph McCarthy's witch-hunting tactics should be censured. The committee report, which Bush endorsed, supported the censure of McCarthy. Bush voted for censure despite warnings from some Republican operatives that it would hurt his 1956 campaign.[22] When Time Inc. president Jim Linen asked Bush over dinner why the Senate hadn't done something sooner, Bush retorted that it was hard to do something when the media, including a *Time* cover, reported how powerful McCarthy was.[23]

Herskowitz described Prescott Bush as "media savvy" for his use of weekly telecasts to voters.[24] His interest in broadcast dated to 1932, when as an investment banker he helped William Paley buy half of CBS at a time when the medium was still in its infancy. Bush eventually served on the board of CBS and "came to understand the power of television, as did few politicians of his era."[25]

Nevertheless, Prescott Bush was of a different era, and so was George H. W. Bush. As George W. Bush biographer Bill Minutaglio noted, the two older Bushes "were accustomed to knocking back drinks with selected members of the media, pitching horseshoes with writers such as George Plimpton, inviting writers on trips to China, to dinner, on tours of Kennebunkport."[26]

According to Spelce, the partnership era of press relations ended with LBJ.[27] Still, the change was gradual, and factors other than the duplicity of Nixon and Johnson complicated the relationship. Assassination attempts on presidents and other political figures necessitated tighter security, limiting casual access to the president. The advent of the 24-hour cable networks and later the Internet made the press corps so huge that even if the presidents who succeeded Nixon had wanted to establish personal relations with reporters, they would have had difficulty getting to know individual reporters without appearing to show favoritism. The size of the press corps and the 24-hour deadlines also made competition for scoops fiercer and ensured that anything embarrassing a president said in casual conversation would likely be reported by somebody.

"Gotcha" journalism—where reporters try to trick a source into saying something controversial or report any careless slip of the tongue—has become so prevalent that all sources have to be careful what they say, according to Chris Black, who covered Democratic presidential nominee George McGovern in 1972 and was spokeswoman for Teresa Heinz Kerry during John Kerry's 2004 presidential campaign. Black said reporters want to make their name by writing an exposé, so that in 2004 there was no understanding, as there was 32 years earlier, that reporters wouldn't "pound" the candidate at the end of a hard day.[28]

Prescott Bush served in the era before the 24-hour pounding, but his grandson entered politics when, as Spelce said, a Grand Canyon had been eroded between reporters and presidents. George H. W. Bush's career spanned the two eras, but in his attitude toward journalists he remained in the "kinder, gentler" era when personal relations dominated the relationship.

Dave McNeely, who has covered the Bush family for various Texas broadcast and print media since the early 1960s, said George H. W. Bush was gracious and personable. In 1965 McNeely was working at the *Houston Chronicle* when Bush visited the newsroom. McNeely mentioned he had written his master's thesis about Bush's 1964 Senate race, and Bush borrowed a copy and read it. Bush traveled with an aide who took pictures of Bush talking with people. Later he would send the person an autographed copy. "It doesn't necessarily buy him any favor with me, but it doesn't hurt," McNeely said of George H. W. Bush's tactics. "And as a sort of political drama critic, you think, that's pretty good; that guy's thinking."[29]

Bush was able to preserve that type of relationship through the 1980 presidential campaign. Roger Simon, political editor of *U.S. News & World Report*, recalled that in 1980 "the press would congregate in the candidate's motel room at night with Bush and a bucket of beer" for friendly conversation.[30] But the media world was changing around him. During that same 1980 campaign, Reagan told an ethnic joke insulting to Italians and Poles when he thought it would be confined to the campaign bus. It was reported on ABC, which Mears noted provided a good lesson for modern candidates: "Don't say anything you don't want to see in the newspaper or on TV."[31]

But Marlin Fitzwater, who served as presidential press secretary for both Reagan and George H. W. Bush, wrote that Bush never understood he could not be friends with reporters or that they would write negative stories despite his attempts to establish personal relationships. Fitzwater's philosophy was that reporters did not like overtures of friendship because it offended their sense of independence. He advised Bush to treat reporters as professionals.[32]

Bush instead tried to win them over through casual accessibility. He held 280 press conferences and invited them to the White House residence, the Oval Office, and even his Kennebunkport home for informal conversations.[33] Bush ordered the press office to compile a list of reporters and their favorite hobbies, such as jogging or movies, so he could invite them to participate with him.[34] After one large 1989 party for the press at his Kennebunkport home, an observer told Bush the he didn't have to do this sort of thing anymore because he was president. Bush smiled and replied, "How do you think I got here?"[35]

Whether friendly reporters helped Bush to the White House was certainly debatable–and they may have helped him leave with relentlessly negative coverage during the 1992 campaign. In fact, Bush's relationship with the press deteriorated during his term. Historian John Robert Greene, who wrote one of the first assessments of Bush's presidency, asserted that the relationship "soured" after the failed 1989 coup in Panama. Some stories recalled the "wimp" criticism Bush had received during the 1988 campaign, and Bush was so upset with leakers in his administration that he angrily told reporters on Air Force One there would be "a whole new relationship."[36] The press was tightly controlled during the subsequent invasion of Panama and the first Gulf War, and the restrictions naturally antagonized journalists. By the 1992 campaign, "George Bush truly seemed to hate the press, and, in many journalism quarters, the feeling was mutual," Greene concluded.[37]

Bush biographer Herbert S. Parmet agreed, writing that Bush's long public service and dealings with the press "didn't make them easier to stomach" and that, although he knew he shouldn't let press criticism bother him, "it just cut him in the gut."[38] In truth, Bush had a long suspicion of the press that was informed by his father's experience in the 1950 Senate campaign and his own dealings with reporters going back to the 1960s. For example, when Bush was a congressman from Texas, he traveled to Vietnam to see firsthand the progress of the war. He returned angry over what he thought was unfair coverage of the war. A minor shelling attack that he slept through was reported as if it were "the Bataan siege, for heaven sakes," Bush recalled. Bush also thought the press unfairly portrayed the South Vietnamese army as corrupt and cowardly.[39]

But the media story that irritated Bush the most, according to remarks he made in 2001 at a conference on the media, was the *Newsweek* cover story headlined "The Wimp Factor," which appeared when he was running for president in 1988. Bush said the thing that most bothered him was that the reporters involved told him the story was going to be a broad profile about him and his family. He gave the magazine access to his family, including his 89-year-old mother, and was hit with what he thought was an unfair political story. "I thought the reporter grossly misled us–the whole family–and I was furious about it," Bush said. He was so furious, in fact, that he cut access to other *Newsweek* reporters who were writing a book about the campaign.[40]

But Bush's press relationship philosophy remained the same. "And while they never responded to friendship, the president's yardstick for judging the press never changed," Fitzwater recalled. "It was 'I like him or her, or I don't.' I urged him time and again to mitigate that feeling to say 'I don't like him but he's fair' or I do like her, but she can be critical.'"[41]

And the media *was* critical of Bush. Research shows the media was tougher on George H. W. Bush than Bill Clinton during the 1992 election, in part because journalists believed they had been too easy on Bush in the 1988 campaign. The consensus among journalists was that the press corps had succumbed to "antiliberal bias"–the fear of being perceived as liberal–so they did not hit him hard on issues like the ethics of the Willie Horton political ads. Those attack ads, which spotlighted a black Massachusetts convict who had committed further crimes while on a furlough, targeted opponent Michael Dukakis's effectiveness as governor, but some observers saw the ads as race baiting.[42] Influential journalists, including Tim Russert of NBC, Jon Alter of *Newsweek*, Ken Bode of CNN, and David Broder of the *Washington Post*, urged their comrades "to ensure fair and informative campaign practices by taking the news agenda away from the politicians and telling the truth rather than just the facts about the election process."[43]

Researchers at the American Enterprise Institute, a conservative think tank, reported during the campaign that economic reporters slanted business news to make Republicans look bad and Democrats look good. They compared headlines over economic stories for the George H. W. Bush, Bill Clinton, and George W. Bush administrations and found that after adjusting for differences in economic performance under the presidents, the Republicans received 20 to 30 percent fewer positive headlines on average. Although the *New York Times* reported the story, it spent more than half the space on quotes attacking the results and the researchers, concluding with a quote that to base a news story on such research "is to demonstrate a pronounced bias toward right-wing hacks." The quote was from Brad DeLong, described by the *Times* as "a liberal-leaning economist at the University of California at Berkeley,"[44] not as, to use DeLong's terms, a left-wing hack.

One specific example of biased coverage was the famous story about Bush being amazed at seeing a grocery store scanner at a trade show convention. A cash register official showed Bush a new scanner that could read a product code that had been ripped. Bush later said he was "amazed" at some of the new technology at the convention. A *New York Times* reporter who was not at the convention wrote from press pool reports a story that implied Bush didn't know how a scanner worked and was out of touch with the average consumer, a damaging assessment during an economic downturn. The AP's Mears called the story a "cheap shot" at Bush and noted that the reporters who actually toured the convention with Bush didn't write the piece the way it appeared in the *Times*.[45] But the influence of the *Times* was such that many media outlets picked up its version and the story became, according to Fitzwater, "one of those stories where the truth never catches up with the lie."[46] Bush was so enraged by the episode that he wrote what he said was the only letter to the editor he sent as president.[47] *Times* CEO Arthur Ochs Sulzberger sent a letter of apology, acknowledging the article was "just a teeny-weeny bit naughty," but as Fitzwater noted, an apology doesn't make a president feel any better, especially when it doesn't include a correction in the paper.[48]

But in other cases Bush would oddly refuse to try to set the record straight. Fitzwater wrote that Bush "had a curious code of media discipline" where he would take hits if he thought he was doing the right thing. He cited as an example that Bush refused to gloat publicly when the Berlin Wall came down because he was worried it would irritate the Russians when the two countries still needed to negotiate. When a newscaster prompted him at a press conference, saying, "You don't seem elated" over the news, Bush replied, "I am not an emotional guy." The most dramatic thing he would say was, "I'm very pleased." The reporter, Lesley Stahl of CBS, then went on air saying Bush seemed distracted and disinterested, and other reporters picked up the same theme.[49]

Bush was furious, but the final straw, according to Fitzwater, occurred when Bush was grilled during the 1992 campaign about a rumored affair with a staffer. It was old news that had been investigated years before and been "dismissed as gossip." But a reporter asked Bush about it during a 1992 press conference with new Israeli prime minister Yitzhak Rabin. Bush brushed the question aside, saying, "It's a lie," but the question was deeply embarrassing because it was asked at his home in front of his mother, wife, daughter, and grandchildren, one of whom started crying because of the tension. "The Bush family attitude toward the media hardened that day to granite, and I didn't blame them," recalled Fitzwater, who wrote that it was based on one quote from a source who had died, but was picked up by the media after Clinton media aide James Carville kept faxing it to reporters.[50] Of course, reporters would ask even more aggressive and embarrassing questions of Clinton during his administration, but his adulterous behavior was well documented and extensive, whereas Bush's rumored affair seemed little more than a campaign-generated smear.

The media had changed drastically from the days when a politician like Prescott Bush could chide reporters for asking about his golf conversations with Eisenhower or George H. W. Bush could kick back with a handful of reporters in a hotel room. Prescott Bush never lived to see the change, and George H. W. Bush could never adjust to the new cynical, confrontational nature of the relationship. During a 1992 press availability in the White House to discuss relief efforts for Hurricane Andrew victims in Florida, a reporter asked how Bush's actions would be viewed by the electorate. Bush said he wasn't thinking about the politics but helping people. "I see a bunch of people running around interviewing people who have been thrown out of their homes by a natural disaster, saying how do the politics work," Bush replied. "Good heavens, isn't there any honor here? Can't we help people without having somebody trying to put a political interpretation on it?"[51]

After he left the White House, Bush criticized the media in a number of appearances and interviews, although usually in a joking way. In a 1996 speech he said, "When I was president, I defended freedom of the press; now I rejoice in freedom from the press."[52] When asked in a 1998 interview with historian Greene if he hated the press when he was president, Bush smiled and said, "Well, not the whole time."[53]

The elder Bush generally refused to comment on press coverage of George W. Bush when the latter began running for president, saying that his comments would hurt his son more than help him. "They got the last word," he said of the press. "And besides, you might feel good for a moment, but it would be a loser. And these are people that have different political views—these editors and writers—and who am I to say they shouldn't say it the way they think it is?"[54]

Nevertheless, he decried the intrusion by the press into the personal life of politicians. "In the old days it didn't happen at all. . . . The ethic in the press corps has changed about these things. On the other hand, when you have a legitimate interference with a person's job, or something that directly affects what he said, credibility, lying to people—then I think the press has an obligation to look into it. Hard to draw a distinct line on paper."[55]

In fact, in a confessional culture dominated by talks shows exemplified by Oprah Winfrey's eponymous program, there is no line. Americans expect all the details of a president and presidential candidate to be reported. During the 2004 campaign, John Kerry's supposed Botox treatments for forehead wrinkles and Bush's weight gain were the subject of news reports. In addition to details about the president's personal habits, the public expects the president to show emotions, to "share his feelings." This is a concept that is alien to men of a pre–Baby Boom generation, like George H. W. Bush, but which his son had no trouble adapting to—one trait that he shares with Bill Clinton.

While George H. W. Bush said he was not an emotional guy, his son wears his emotions on his sleeve. One of the most often cited examples of Bush's sensitive side as revealed to the press came shortly after 9/11, when he allowed journalists to witness his phone call from the White House to New York mayor Rudy Giuliani. When a reporter asked Bush if he thought the terrorists were trying to assassinate him and what he was thinking, Bush teared up and said he was not thinking about himself but the families of the victims. "I am a loving guy," he said. The *New York Times*'s Frank Bruni, ever the political reporter, noted in his book that it made Bush look like his campaign slogan—compassionate. But Bruni acknowledged that an observer could dismiss the moment "as meaninglessly theatrical, but theater is an integral part of the presidency, and Bush, in any case had never been much of an actor. The expressions that flashed across his face could be trusted as accurate reflections of what he was really thinking and feeling."[56]

Reporter Wayne Slater called George W. Bush "the most transparent politician" he'd ever met. He said that reporters could always tell what Bush was thinking by looking in his eyes and noticing his mannerisms.[57]

And Bush was not afraid to show emotions to reporters. Dave McNeely lost his wife, Carole, to breast cancer in 1998 while Bush was governor. The day after she died, McNeely was walking along a lake in Austin. "All of a sudden somebody was coming the other way; skids to a halt. And it's Bush. And he comes up and comes over and gives me a hug and says, 'I just wanted to tell you how sorry Laura and I were about Carol.'"[58]

Bush also relates well to children, which is extremely important for a politician in an age of "soccer moms" and "security moms" as key demographics. Older politicians like Prescott Bush and George H. W. Bush were raised at a time when most women stayed at home to raise their families. Fathers were concerned with earning a living, and presidents were concerned with the economy and foreign policy. During one of the 1992 debates, a woman asked George H. W. Bush how the national debt affected him personally. He didn't pick up on the fact that she meant the recession, not the debt, but Bill Clinton knew what she meant and gave an empathetic response. Bush did not do well answering personal questions from the crowd; in fact, at one point he was caught looking at his watch while third-party candidate Ross Perot was talking.[59]

In contrast, George W. Bush is comfortable with this new style of family politics and talking about kids and feelings, even though he cultivates a cowboy persona and sometimes will tell reporters he doesn't want to be psychoanalyzed.[60] But his actions and stories he tells about himself are often at odds with this professed gruffness. One of his often-repeated stories to the press to explain his beliefs about crime describes a visit to a juvenile facility in which one of the young inmates asked Bush, who was then governor, what he thought of him. Bush told the boy that he had made a mistake but that if he worked hard, he could turn his life around. He told media advisor Karen Hughes that it was "a powerful moment" and symbolized why they had to fix the education system so kids don't get shuffled through and wind up in jail.[61]

Bush showed this tender side with reporters' kids as well. Among the governor's files at the Texas State Archives is a box of photographs from the various press Christmas parties. By all accounts, Bush was very charming at these parties and made a real effort to please the reporters. McNeely contrasted the parties with those held by Bush's successor, Rick Perry, who barely made an appearance at the events.[62] Bush worked the room, wooing spouses and children of the scribes who covered him. A highlight of the event was getting a photograph with the governor. The archives box is filled with photographs of Bush and reporters, many who are holding a drink or look like they've just finished one, posing with Bush with their arms draped casually over each others' shoulders. Even Molly Ivins, the liberal columnist generally credited with nicknaming Bush "Shrub" and coauthor of two polemical books about him, is included in a photo that belies the acidity of her political commentary on Bush. Other photographs show the adults acting like kids, making goofy poses with the Christmas decorations and one man even having a press pass or some other identification plastered to his forehead for the amusement of Bush and others in the photograph.[63]

But more often Bush is pictured with reporters and their children. In many of the photos, Bush is seen holding or hugging a toddler or a baby. In one picture, a boy is chewing on a wallet, perhaps Bush's. In another, a girl's face is smeared with chocolate while she is holding a piece of dripping candy menacingly close to Bush's tie. Bush is holding her mindless of the mess and mugs at her with an expression that conveys he thinks she is the cutest kid in the world. When looking through a couple of boxes of these photos, one is reminded not so much of an office party but of a family gathering, albeit one where the participants are dressed in their best clothes. The warmth of expression in the photographs is that good.

Spelce said Bush's behavior with children in general is a good indicator of his personality. Spelce recalled that at one party, a girl about four years old, who obviously had met Bush before, spotted the governor and ran up to him to give him a hug. Instead of reaching down to hug her, Bush held his arms straight out as if he were going to hug an adult. The girl ran under his arms and hugged his legs. Both kid and governor laughed at the joke. "From my perspective," Spelce said, "that's not turning on the charm; that's who he is."[64]

The charm worked on adults, too. Slater, for example, recalled that his wife went to Bush's press Christmas party with a negative attitude because she had been a big Ann Richards supporter. But Bush talked to her casually while he was eating a muffin, crumbs falling on the governor's mansion carpet. Bush impressed her with his genuineness. "He was not this type of pretentious, aloof figure but a regular person," Slater said. "And he really demonstrated this sort of regularness as part of his political signature. And when we left, she said, 'I like that guy a lot,' and she became a big fan of George Bush."[65]

But Bush's folksy ways with the Texas press were not duplicated with the Washington press corps. He would still joke with reporters as president, but the old intimacy of the Texas days would be gone when he occupied the White House. George W. Bush understood the new adversarial relationship between presidents and the Washington press corps even if that lesson came too late for his father. Indeed, Bush, so often denigrated for being a mediocre student, absorbed his father's presidential press relations as if he were a public relations graduate student attending a seminar on how to handle the media. Even as a governor who was only considering a presidential run, Bush had a keen understanding of the Washington media. In an interview with C-SPAN's Brian Lamb, Bush analyzed the difference between the Washington and Texas press and said competitive pressures had spurred the poor relationship between the White House and the press.[66]

Bush used his natural charm on the campaign trail during the 2000 election when it stood him in good contrast to the stiff, unfriendly Al Gore. Bush even ramped up his "charm offensive"—doing things like serving drinks to reporters on his campaign plane—when John McCain, his main rival for the Republican nomination, appeared to be getting favorable press coverage by his openness with reporters aboard his campaign bus called the "Straight Talk Express."[67]

Chris Usher, a freelance photographer who covered both Gore and Bush in 2000 for major newsmagazines such as *Time* and *Newsweek*, said Gore never seemed to be a very nice guy. Bush, on the other hand, was skilled at working the press, but was very aware of who he needed to work. Bush would spend a whole three-hour flight with the press corps, chatting with reporters. When he worked his way to the very back, where the photographers and the technical crew—the people Usher jokingly called the "riff-raff of the press corps"—were seated, Bush's demeanor would be friendly, but not as intimate. "He just quits making it a personal appearance and just like, 'Hey, how you doing? Hey. Hey. Hey. And he just runs through there like a rope line at an event. . . . I wanted to chat him up and see what's going on, but see, we have no purpose in that capacity so he didn't waste his time with us; all we're going to do is shoot pictures."[68]

Once Bush reached the White House, the relationship was completely different. Bush would still be friendly and "joke and jab" with the reporters, but he did not seem to want a personal relationship. Usher, who has continued to cover Bush off and on through his second term, said Bush recognizes him but does not know who he is. Clinton, on the other hand, seemed interested in getting to know all the journalists. Clinton was frequently late for events because he would always stop to chat with everyone behind the scenes, whether they were busboys or photojournalists. Bush, in contrast, will sometimes wink at Usher or another journalist "to keep you in his playing field" but the relationship goes no deeper than that. Usher was once invited with a group of journalists for snacks at Bush's Crawford ranch. It was a very informal affair, but Usher and some of the other journalists spent most of the time sitting on Bush's couch, examining the house. "You know, he pretty much spent his time with the John Kings and the whoever, the on-air people and writers, and, you know, you don't want to butt in, so the rest of us just kind of hang out in a corner and have some coffee and some finger food and get 20 minutes in there and then we're off." Usher didn't make a point of trying to approach Bush because he believed it just didn't seem worth it, he recalled.[69]

But Bush's very adaptability—the knowledge of what kind of press relations are needed at what level and how to execute those relations—demonstrates his expertise. Bush is a chameleon with the press. With sportswriters, he was particularly earthy and adopted the personality of an athlete. With the Texas press, he was friendly and accessible. But when he got to Washington, he knew there was no advantage in trying to schmooze the White House press corps. He knew the intense competition and the elite bias of the Eastern press toward a conservative from Texas could not be overcome by joking.

As an aide on his father's 1992 campaign, Bush had suspected media bias, telling others in the organization that the campaign was "running into a 90-mile-an-hour headwind."[70] The people who worked in the campaign never forgave the media for what they perceived as biased coverage of the 1992 conventions. Republicans were portrayed as strident and extreme; Democrats were not, even though some speakers politicized AIDS and the party would not allow pro-life Democrats to speak at its convention. Republicans learned that they could not trust the media to cover the conventions fairly and that they therefore had to be scripted tightly.[71] The fact that Bush's judgment was confirmed by independent analysts[72] shows his deep understanding of the media.

Bush uses personal charm when he thinks it's appropriate, but he understands its limitations and doesn't rely on it. For George W. Bush, the president and the reporters are not members of the same gentlemen's club who together are running the country.

Adam Clymer, the retired chief Washington correspondent of the *New York Times* who covered both Bushes, said George H. W. Bush could take a joke or criticism. Clymer pointed out that even after Bush lost the presidency, he invited to the White House Dana Carvey, a comedian perhaps most famous for his less-than-flattering imitation of Bush on the television show *Saturday Night Live*. "I can't imagine the son doing that," Clymer said.[73]

The first president Bush was always a gentleman, even with those who wrote unfavorable stories, Clymer said. "I think the old man had a respect for the position of the press, the position and responsibility and importance of the press—not that he liked everything we did, but he thought the press was a significant institution in America," Clymer said. "I don't know that his son agrees."[74]

Clymer experienced George W. Bush's attitude toward the press firsthand at a campaign rally in 2000. Then-candidate Bush called Clymer a "major league asshole" in an aside to his running mate, Dick Cheney, that was picked up by a microphone Bush thought was turned off. More detail on the incident will come in a later chapter, but Clymer basically shrugged off the remark as something that happens occasionally between sources and reporters, although rarely in such a public setting.[75]

George H. W. Bush may have had similar feeling toward reporters, but he was more circumspect in expressing them. The *American-Statesman*'s McNeely described the elder Bush as less cocky, more gracious, and more accommodating of the press than his son. "I think that H. W. was charming cvcn if hc didn't particularly likc you or trust you," McNccly said. "I mean, he realized that you needed to do this, and he also suffered more [political] defeats than W."[76]

Father and son approached the press from the differing perspectives of their generations. "One of the things is that the landscape has changed vastly during their tenures," McNeely said. "Bush was a World War II veteran, and . . . journalism changed when you had a generation of reporters who came out of World War II who referred to the government as 'we.' And then following the Vietnam War/Watergate it spawned a generation—at least a decade, maybe a little bit more—of reporters who referred to the government as 'they.' And I think that W. cut his teeth more in the latter period, and so he is adjusting more to the situation as it is now."[77]

3

MESSAGE DISCIPLINE BEFORE IT WAS COOL

It's hard to beat photographers at creativity, but the Bush administration has tried to do just that in an effort to get their news photos to illustrate the message Bush wants to send to the public. Chris Usher, a freelancer who has covered Bush for the major newsmagazines, pointed out that the background for Bush campaign speeches usually included a banner behind the president that would state the message of the day in some punchy slogan like "Jobs and Opportunities" or "Tax Relief." The administration's plan was that the next day's news would show a photograph of Bush with the slogan behind him, emphasizing the point he made in his speech.

But the photojournalists wanted something that would be more than an advertisement for Bush's campaign. They would take tight shots of his face, trying to eliminate the banner, or else focus on Bush's face and one word, like "relief." One wag even shot a picture of Bush in front of a graphic of a Texas longhorn in such a way that the animal's horns seemed to be coming out of Bush's head, making him appear like a devil. The administration responded by changing the one-word banners to include slogans printed many times in much smaller type. "If you look at the pictures, it will say 'Jobs and Opportunities' a million times over, like a watermark on any type of website all behind him, all over, so no matter which way you shoot, you're going to get part of that message in there, unless you throw it out of focus with a long lens," Usher said. "So it is a cat and mouse thing, trying to make something different out of what there is."[1]

Such tenacity in controlling the message has been a hallmark of Bush's press relations since he learned about focusing on a simple, consistent theme during his failed race for Congress in West Texas in 1978. After the race, Bush told Kent Hance, the only person ever to defeat Bush in an election, "Hance, you had a message and you stayed with it."[2] Hance was an experienced politician and won for reasons other than just his focus on message, but Bush took the lesson to heart and perfected the technique of "message discipline" to an extent that amazes political scientists and frustrates journalists.

Donald F. Kettl wrote in *Team Bush: Leadership Lessons from the Bush White House* that staying on message is one of the keys of the administration's success in communicating with the public. Kettl wrote that although Ronald Reagan, George H. W. Bush, and Bill Clinton all had media skills, George W. Bush is the best at message discipline. "Despite George W. Bush's limited oratorical gifts, no presidential team has been so effective at framing a message, refining that message to its essence, repeating the message until it got through, and using the media so effectively to talk to the American people—and the world."[3]

Kettl cited as an example that the administration's focus on Iraq and foreign policy kept the press from writing much about economic issues in 2002. "Team Bush has almost always known what it wanted to accomplish," Kettl wrote. "It projected that message firmly and consistently with remarkably little wobbling. There has been little ambiguity that might have given opponents the ammunition it needed to push the administration off message, or that might have allowed reporters room to write a different story than the one the administration intended."[4]

CBS White House correspondent Bill Plante said that "once [Bush] gets a message in his head, he's pretty good at presenting it" and is relaxed and conversational when giving speeches on that message. Plante said that compared to other presidents, Bush is more likely to stick to the topic. "If there is a photo op in the Oval Office, and the issue of the day is Social Security reform, he is not likely to entertain a question of why he dumped Bernard Kerik and who the next Homeland Security director is going to be," Plante said. "He's pretty good at—discipline is a good word—at ignoring questions he doesn't wish to answer."[5]

In fact, when asked to use one word to describe Bush's press relations, CNN White House reporter Dana Bash said, "Discipline." Bash, who was speaking as a panelist at a convention of journalism educators, gave as an example the White House announcement of the nomination of John Roberts to the Supreme Court in July 2005, which was kept secret until the last minute and made with a long-prepared prime-time speech by Bush.[6]

The overlong title of the panel discussion assumed that Bash and her colleagues had been "neutralized" by the White House and asked plaintively "Can the White House Press Corps Rebound during W's Second Term?" The answer, at least in solving Bush's message discipline, is no. Julie Mason from the *Houston Chronicle*, a fellow panelist in that discussion, used two words to describe Bush's press relations: "weirdly impenetrable." She added that it was almost impossible to get Bush off topic. "It's like throwing questions at a wall."[7]

But Bush practiced message discipline long before he became president and the subject of navel gazing at academic conferences. John Blake, director of public relations for the Texas Rangers when Bush was managing general partner, said that the department was able to be more proactive under his leadership, doing things as simple as printing a letter from the ownership in the team program. "Our message became a lot more—I don't know if coherent is the right word—but it certainly became more focused than it was over the past few years of the previous ownership."[8] Bush's consistent discipline in attending games, mingling with fans and always conveying the idea that a Rangers game was a fun, family activity helped turn the franchise around.

Bush put the same focus on message discipline in the governor's office. *Fort Worth Star-Telegram* reporter Jay Root, who covered Bush regularly when he was governor and occasionally as president, said Bush's press organization was "extremely professional. It was very sophisticated—not only the governorship but getting ready for running for the presidency. They did message discipline before message discipline was cool. People have tried to repeat that. It's very maddening and frustrating from a reporter's point of view. You might ask him a question and he would go into a sound bite."[9]

Austin television reporter Neil Spelce agreed that when he covered Bush as governor, Bush tried to control the media message through keeping his employees on the same page. "This business of staying on message is really, really critical to him, all his advisers, whatever. Once they have decided, 'This is what we're going to talk about and this is what it's going to be'—that's it. And that's where they stick and they stay there. You say, 'How is the weather today?' and they'll say, 'Jobs are up.' 'What do you think about the hurricane in Florida?' 'Jobs are up.'—That sort of thing. . . . That is a controlling thing in my mind."[10]

It seems a simple enough concept: Develop a message that you want the press to get and don't let reporters distract you. But few politicians have been able to stick with a message like Bush. Reagan was able to do it quite effectively, and his key media aide, Michael Deaver, is often credited with developing the technique of matching the president's message with good location for background so that the resulting photos and TV coverage would reinforce the message.[11] Deaver is frequently quoted as saying that the words the broadcasters spoke and the print reporters wrote were not as important as the pictures of Reagan looking confident and presidential. But Deaver, the pioneer in message control, considers George W. Bush's White House the most disciplined in history.[12]

Certainly, Bush has had more success emulating the Great Communicator's emphasis on message than either his father or Clinton did. George H. W. Bush, for example, made some effective uses of Reagan's tactics during the 1988 race against Massachusetts governor Michael Dukakis. He won the image battle by, for example, appearing at a flag factory to touch on his theme of patriotism. His hapless opponent, in contrast, appeared goofily wearing a helmet while riding in a tank, symbolizing for voters how uncomfortable he was with defense issues. But the elder Bush failed miserably in developing a message and sticking with it during the 1992 campaign against Clinton. Fitzwater wrote that Bush never gave the voters a reason to reelect him: "We had no message."[13] Perhaps the most egregious example came when Bush misinterpreted an aide's note that reminded him the main point was to let the crowd know he cared about their problems. Bush read the note literally, saying awkwardly, "Message: I care."[14]

Clinton boiled down his message to "It's the economy, stupid," and rode that simple statement about the recession to the White House. But much of his presidency, particularly his first term, was unfocused. Clinton's aides were never able to articulate a clear message for him, and the president himself "seemed unable to leave any question unanswered, even one on MTV about his underwear."[15] Don Baer, an aide who joined the team in 1995, was shocked that "there was no sense of strategy; no coherent effort to sell a message to the press."[16]

Kurtz argued in *Spin Cycle* that Clinton's second-term press aides "imposed some much-needed order." Clinton was ultimately able to connect with voters despite his various scandals and impeachment by developing simple, concentrated messages on things like reducing teenage smoking and improving food safety standards. Pundits ridiculed these initiatives as "downsizing" the presidency, but the Clinton administration found the issues resonated with many Americans.[17] He was able to weather his scandals, but just barely. Kurtz argued that Clinton survived in part because, in times of peace and prosperity, the people were tired of scandal, which had become commonplace news at all levels of society from sports figures to politicians.[18]

Clearly Clinton's lack of discipline in his personal life spilled over to his press relations. He had trouble sticking to a message; it required extraordinary effort from a man who was interested in so many topics and had an energy level that wore out the journalists who covered him. "Clinton would just go 24–7," Usher said. "We'd be exhausted with Clinton, absolutely exhausted. He'd start out here, on the East Coast, fly to some place in the Midwest and then on out to L.A., and then we'd be out until 2 A.M. L.A. time doing something, which could be pretty rough. He used the clock all the way, and Bush likes to get started at the crack of dawn and then be done by 10 o'clock—seldom that we're ever out past 10 o'clock or 11 o'clock."[19]

On airplanes, Clinton would stay up all night talking to reporters. Wayne Slater recalled that during a Texas campaign trip for the 1992 Democratic presidential nomination, Clinton demonstrated an energy level that was astounding. "He would talk in the morning; he would talk in the evening," Slater said. "I remember we flew in at about 10:30 at night in this airplane to Laredo, and . . . he tried to engage you in conversation because he seemed to enjoy your company. I think basically he enjoyed being Bill Clinton, and he had this energy level. I finally pretended I was falling asleep because I was tired. Everybody else was asleep. Hillary was asleep. Everybody else on this plane was asleep because it had been a long, long day. But Clinton still wanted to engage because he was a very social kind of person."[20]

Such wandering conversations can get a politician off message and sometimes in trouble. For example, during the 2000 campaign, Clinton was supposed to bolster Al Gore with a call to a *New York Times* reporter but instead got off topic and ended up expressing doubts about the election. The *Washington Post*'s Dana Milbank referred to the episode as Clinton's "flop as a freelance press secretary."[21]

Bush, on the other hand, adheres to a rigid schedule. He goes to bed early, sometimes as early as 9 P.M. He rises early as well and exercises regularly and hard. He even brings his own pillow with him when he travels to reinforce his sense of routine. The morning after he turned 40, he stopped drinking, and he has rigidly stuck to that self-imposed denial. In matters of faith, Bush reads through the entire Bible once a year.[22]

"The very characteristics he has as a person, that he's always had, which is a lot of discipline, a focus, and a toughness . . . those were the characteristics that our country especially needed after September 11 . . . in a leader," First Lady Laura Bush told *U.S. News & World Report*. The *U.S. News* story emphasized that goal-oriented determination permeates everything Bush does, from lifting weights to refusing to let protesters deter him from giving a scheduled speech in the Philippines.[23]

Some Bush observers believe his battle with alcohol has lead to his tight control in other aspects of his life. David Frum, a Bush speechwriter, wrote that when he met the president for the first time in February 2001 he was surprised how commanding and self-assured Bush seemed compared to his public appearances. "Bush relaxed in his chair as he talked. Yet there was something taut about him even when he slumped. Bush's fiercest critics paid tribute to his likeability, but in private, Bush was not the easy, genial man he was in public. Close up, one saw a man keeping a tight grip on himself."[24]

Frum compared Bush to George H. W. Bush, who had no *id*, no unruly side, and with Bill Clinton, who gave his id the run of the White House. George W. Bush, Frum wrote, had an id as powerful as Clinton's. "But sometime in Bush's middle years, his id was captured, shackled and manacled, and locked away. By the time he entered politics, he was the disciplined, guarded man I saw in the Oval Office in February."[25]

All of these personal habits are those of a man who is extraordinarily suited to the concept of message discipline. Comparing Bush to Clinton, one can see how a president's character impacts his press relations. Clinton, who was gregarious but lacked personal self-control, had difficulty staying on one message that he wanted to convey to the public through the press. Bush, the reformed drinker and obsessed athlete, was a natural at staying on message because control is part of his nature.

Bush did not have that discipline in the 1978 campaign, but he has used it consistently, some might say fanatically, ever since. The basis of his 1994 gubernatorial campaign was sticking to four simple themes: tort reform, juvenile justice reform, education reform, and welfare reform. He entered the campaign a decided underdog to the popular Ann Richards but was determined to stick to his plan. Karen Hughes, who started working for Bush during this campaign, recalled that she got an early lesson in the candidate's stress on focus. Bush saw her carrying a number of phone messages from reporters. To the press secretary's horror, Bush ordered her not to return the calls because it would distract the campaign from developing a focused message. Hughes told him they would have to then develop that message and, she wrote in her memoir: "Figuring out what to say, how to respond to press questions, how to make news and stay on message is what we have been doing ever since."[26]

Hughes may have helped Bush develop the message, but the fact that he innately understood its importance is illustrated by a memo he sent to his campaign staff with the introduction that it was "a rare ranting by the candidate." Bush typed the memo himself and faxed it from his home. The memo cautioned the staff to refrain from debating the other camp on its terms but to always "hammer" Bush's issues and ensure that "the message is always confirming the fact that I want to help everyday Texans have a better life."[27]

Although Hughes gave Bush the credit for realizing the importance of message discipline, a lot of Texas reporters give her the credit for fine-tuning Bush's philosophy. Slater said that Hughes herself was never off message with reporters. Early in Bush's first term as governor, Slater went to dinner with Hughes during the National Governor's Association convention in Washington. "It's the first time I had ever gotten to talk to her outside Austin in some detail. I was *appalled*, amazed about how the entire conversation was absolutely on message. I'd talk about her son, talk about Jerry, her husband; I'd talk a little bit about something going on in Austin, immediately it was back to the four issues. Immediately it was back to Bush was the greatest guy in the world. She might have been on a platform somewhere making a speech to a thousand people rather than sitting in a restaurant."[28]

R. G. Ratcliffe of the *Houston Chronicle* said Hughes "was very much a believer in focused messages, and no matter what the question is, you keep answering with the message answer, and part of that is built on the idea that reporters are lazy and they take the answer and just go away and use it. And that is particularly true I think of TV, and of course TV is what they really want–is how they really want to communicate, and so they give them a sound bite and they put it on the air. The print reporters found it frustrating at times with Karen but Karen–Bush really came to trust Karen."[29]

Karl Rove was of course a strong influence as well, and he shared Hughes's philosophy. "Message was everything with Rove," according to Lou DuBose, Jan Reid, and Carl Cannon, who noted in their Rove biography that the consultant had Bush so focused on message that at one point in the 1994 campaign Ann Richards called Bush a "windup doll."[30]

Slater said Rove, Bush, and Hughes together developed the formula that has worked so well for Bush: "You do a few things and you do them well." Bush picked out four issues and ran on them relentlessly. Rove figured out the political dynamic that the public does not want to hear about too many issues. If the candidate tries to force discussion on a myriad of issues, the candidate's overall message will be muddled. "It played to Bush's strength," Slater said. "He's not a stupid guy, but on the other hand he's able to manage four or five things in great detail and he was very, very successful. He figured out the four or five things that are important to him, and he basically defined the political personality based on that."[31]

The *Austin American-Statesman*'s Dave McNeely said that Rove had conditioned Bush so well that "he sort of never strays off message, and that can be frustrating." McNeely recalled an instance during a debate with Richards when he was asked a question about something and answered by talking about his own issues. "[It's] a time-honored political ploy for avoiding to answer the question that jerks like us want you to answer," McNeely said.[32]

Hughes constantly reminded Bush not to let the media pull him in other directions. "What Hughes did in keeping with that was really reinforced with him in private conversations: Stay on message," Slater said. "If they ask you about health care, go back to juvenile crime, if they ask you about some agency head across town who was involved in something else, go back to tort reform. That's basically what it's all about. And I think she was really instrumental in understanding what's going on."[33]

Slater believes that Bush's success with the media is about half his own ability and half input from Rove and Hughes. He said Bush was not ready to deal with the political press when he first ran for governor. Slater and some other reporters questioned Bush about state issues at an appearance in San Antonio, and his answers were not convincing. "If very quickly it is determined by reporters that you don't know what you're talking about, you're dead. And that was what was going to happen to George Bush. He may have been the friendliest guy in the world, but . . . it was very clear [that if] he didn't know the size of the budget and he didn't understand really how health and education spending were allocated then he was quickly going to come across as a rube, and we were going to do it." Slater said Rove solved the problem by taking Bush on a tour of rural Texas, where he could hone his skills with less aggressive small town media.[34]

Richards accused Bush of being a "phantom candidate" because he had so little contact with the press. Angered by a Bush press release that criticized her appointment of a felon to head the state's drug and alcohol agency, she told reporters that Bush was not a serious candidate. "He's not someone you see in public very much, not someone you see answering questions of the media, not someone holding press conferences and being responsive, but someone who makes it easy to do stories from a written release." Rove replied that Bush had held more than 150 press events and three press conferences since the campaign began.[35]

Bush himself wrote that it was part of a strategy to campaign in rural areas early in the campaign before fall, when he "would have to make news in major media markets."[36] Rove admitted in a *Texas Monthly* interview that the small-town tour helped the candidate polish his speaking skills but argued that it also was a good way to get press attention early in the campaign. "If it's January and you are running for governor and you go to Dallas, as we used to say, you gotta run naked down Main Street in order to get good coverage. But if you go to Palestine, they'll write you up in the paper: They'll have you on the radio."[37]

Even Ann Richards's press aides admitted that Bush was outstanding at sticking to his message. Chuck McDonald, Richards's campaign press secretary, told *Texas Monthly* that their campaign hired an operative to follow Bush and tape his small-town remarks to try to catch him in a gaffe. "It was a gigantic wasted effort," McDonald recalled. "He had his note cards, and he would show up and make his speech. There was no deviation. There wasn't a new sentence. . . . It was a good strategy."[38]

Mary Beth Rogers, Richards's campaign chair, said Bush's strategy of "bridging"—making a bridge from whatever question was asked by the press to his four issues worked particularly effectively against Richards because she was trying to explain the details of policy while Bush was repeating "sound bites" about his four chosen issues. "And so you could ask him about leadership in Texas and he would go right to putting juveniles in jail. It didn't matter what was asked by the press or by others, he would bridge to the four messages he had."[39]

Bush made an impression on at least one editor in those smaller markets. David House, now the ombudsmen for the *Fort Worth Star-Telegram*, was the managing editor of the *Corpus Christi Caller-Times* during Bush's first campaign. House recalled being impressed by Bush's manner and his knowledge when he visited the paper's editorial board.[40]

House had expected Bush to be a flashy, wealthy businessman. "But he had a tremendous amount of charisma in a very calm way," House said. "He seemed very centered and balanced and at ease and clearly wanted to talk with us about a lot of things." Bush struck House as a man who was "extremely intelligent."[41]

Arnold Garcia was impressed by Bush's first editorial board meeting with the *American-Statesman*, which had a solid reputation as a Democratic newspaper. According to Garcia, all the candidates know the ritual of the editorial board meeting; they are expected to show up even if they don't have a chance of an endorsement. Still, some will try to pretend they don't have any differences with the newspaper. Not Bush.

"He was very self-assured," Garcia recalled. "He sat down and he said—I think I'm remembering this because it made quite an impression—he said, 'I do not expect to receive the endorsement of your newspaper. But let me tell you what I'm going to do as your governor.' And then he proceeded to outline his platform." Garcia was impressed because Bush was so confident he would beat Richards, who was still a heavy favorite. He was also impressed by Bush's honesty about their differences. "He was just telling the truth from his perspective, and I respected that, even admired it a little bit, but certainly respected it," Garcia said.[42]

Although Texas journalists disagree on when Bush became a polished candidate for governor, there is no doubt that he excelled at handling the political press by the time he took office. The *Star-Telegram*'s Root found Governor Bush to be well practiced at giving interviews: "In some ways Bush knew how to give reporters a quote without giving up too much."[43]

Ratcliffe recalled that during Bush's 1998 reelection campaign he gave a speech on ending "social promotion" in the schools. Ratcliffe researched the issue and found that if the standardized tests were put into place in Texas, about 150,000 students would be held back a grade. He asked Bush about that at a subsequent speech and got brushed off with a "political answer" that the administration would phase it in. After the speech, Bush grabbed Ratcliffe by the arm and asked him, "Off the record, is it really that high?" Ratcliffe's statistics had obviously surprised Bush but not thrown him off the message. Ratcliffe observed, "Bush, you know . . . they get him on message, and he fully understands what it means to be on message. And he just will not let you drag him off message."[44]

Bush took the message discipline he had practiced as governor on the presidential campaign trail in 2000 and would not let the national reporters drag him off message, either. Bush built his presidential campaign around two main issues—taxes and education—and the theme of returning civility to political discourse in Washington.[45] Frank Bruni, who covered the 2000 campaign for the *New York Times*, wrote that one could argue that Bush benefited from the "rigorous sameness" of his remarks—Bruni considered "message discipline" a euphemism—because the press feels obligated to first report what a candidate says before parsing it. Bruni's description sounded very much like Spelce's when Bruni wrote that Bush "made journalists feast on a main course of his most carefully considered sentences and most carefully constructed themes by not putting anything else on their plates. If you asked a Bush aide what he had for breakfast, the reply would be 'the country must have tort reform.'"[46]

News events sometimes threw Bush off message by leading reporters to ask him questions that he could not avoid answering. Bush would appear frustrated by the change and try to move back to his message. For example, during the height of the 2000 campaign, a story broke that accused Bush's campaign of sneaking the word "rats" as a subliminal message in a commercial attacking Gore's health care plan. At about the same time, another article suggested Bush had dyslexia, which could be a possible cause of Bushisms. The *Houston Chronicle*'s Clay Robison noted Bush "tried mightily to stick to the message he wanted to emphasize," which was health care, but instead found himself dealing with rats and reading.[47]

On the trail in 2000, access was tightly controlled, especially in comparison with John McCain, Bush's main rival for the Republican nomination. Reporters noted the professionalism of the operation. Robison wrote that before the first campaign swing, the Bush organization had recruited "scores" of experienced workers who ensured travel and events were well managed.[48] Bush's "different approach," reporters noted, was to stay on message and avoid mistakes. Bush spokeswoman Mindy Tucker inadvertently revealed the campaign's mind-set when she told a group of reporters: "We're not going to have one big, fat news conference on our schedule where everyone can come and ask about what you think the news is. It's not in our best interest. We have a message of the day, and we want to stick with it."[49]

Bush even maintained his discipline during the weird interregnum between the election and the U.S. Supreme Court decision that effectively ended the recounts and the campaign. Bush assumed the demeanor of the winner and acted as if he knew that the recount would merely confirm it. He went to his Crawford ranch, where he could better control media access and the message, which symbolically was that he was the president-elect and was getting ready for the transition by interviewing potential cabinet nominees. Hughes explained to the press that Bush's home was a "tranquil place, where it's easy to do some thinking and reflecting."[50] His campaign even set up transition offices in Washington.

Bush did emerge to rush to Austin to deliver his own speech when Gore said on national TV that he would open the entire state of Florida to a recount if Bush wanted. Bush instinctively understood the situation and said: "So long as the Florida Supreme Court was rewriting the law and people were divining intent, we had a battle on our hands. And if he wasn't willing to address that, then all the rest of it was PR. That's why I rushed back: PR."[51]

Once Bush was elected, he inculcated his message discipline philosophy in the new members of his administration. Bush advised Linda Chavez, his first choice for secretary of the Department of Labor, to not get distracted by arguments during her confirmation hearings. Bush warned her not to "take their bait" when political opponents tried to get her off message.[52]

Ari Fleischer, Bush's first White House press secretary, recalled in his memoir that Bush was disciplined and usually remained on message during the two or three days a week that he would take questions from reporters. "He would often repeat the same statement to the press, no matter how many different ways they asked their questions," Fleischer wrote. "He seldom made mistakes or inadvertently created a controversy through what he said, and for many reporters, who are always looking for the next big story, the White House's message discipline came to be frustrating."[53]

Fleischer strove to be as disciplined as his boss, and in the beginning of his tenure took "a big three-ring binder containing 'talking points' arranged in alphabetical order" to the podium for his press briefings.[54] As he got accustomed to his job, he abandoned the binder in favor of a sheet with a few handwritten notes, but he maintained regular contact with Hughes, National Security Advisor Condoleeza Rice, other administration sources, and his own aides, who kept him abreast of what other departments were doing. His staff would role-play questions and answers with Fleischer before the briefings. "Getting along with each other and talking to each other isn't complicated, and it sure helped us sound like we were one White House that spoke with one voice."[55]

Speechwriter Frum noticed Bush's relentless focus on message when the president edited Frum's copy, marking boldly with his black Sharpie where he thought the speech was soft on the main message the administration was trying to convey. Bush, Frum wrote, "was an exacting editor" who "insisted on strict linear logic." Once when Frum had included the phrase "I've seen with my own eyes . . . ," Bush circled "my own eyes" and wrote "DUH" next to it. Although Bush didn't usually cite statistics while he talked, he wanted the writer to include them in his speech. If the speech stated that the Bush administration was going to take action, he would write on the draft that he wanted more detail.[56]

Perhaps Bush's emphasis on detail harked back to his experience as governor, like the time Ratcliffe called him to account over education statistics. At any rate, Bush clearly knows as much about the media as his high-powered aides and cabinet officers, if not more. A good example is Paul O'Neill, Bush's first treasury secretary, who cooperated with Ron Suskind in an extremely critical portrait of the administration called *The Price of Loyalty.* The book is perhaps best known for O'Neill's scathing description of Bush at cabinet meetings as being "like a blind man in a roomful of deaf people."[57] O'Neill himself was blind to the way the media works, an astonishing shortfall for a man who had been CEO of Alcoa, the largest aluminum producer in the world. Suskind's book portrayed O'Neill as a no-nonsense, nonpartisan official who even wrote his own speeches. Yet O'Neill shot off his mouth to a German reporter that the United States was not pursuing the policy of a strong dollar, adding that a strong dollar is the result of a strong economy. O'Neill's offhand remark caused the dollar's value to drop, and the treasury secretary had to do some serious backtracking. O'Neill complained to his press aide, Michelle Davis, that the reporter had been irresponsible, and Davis had to explain to O'Neill that reporters will run with quotes that make news. "This is the way the world works," Davis told him.[58]

The White House eventually instructed Davis to control O'Neill, and she wrote him a detailed memo before Bush unveiled his budget. The memo clearly stated that O'Neill's role was to repeat the administration points and "be monotonously on-message."[59] O'Neill, however, continued to be noted for his extemporaneous comments, something that made him popular with reporters but unpopular with Bush, who greeted him at one meeting with the comment: "You're getting quite a reputation as a truth-teller. You've got yourself quite a cult following, don't ya?" It was evident to everyone in the room that Bush wasn't joking, and the president fired O'Neill later that year.[60]

O'Neill, however, was the exception to the rule of Bush employees staying on message. Most of Bush's aides and cabinet officials are so in sync that it's almost spooky for White House reporters. "It's sometimes a little eerie when it happens, but I know I would call the White House on something on some matter and get a particular set of answers and rhetoric, and then I would call one of the agencies and talk to a person there and that person basically would give me the same thing, often using the same words and phrases," said Edwin Chen, *Los Angeles Times* White House correspondent. "Of course, it's no accident. They plan these things. They have morning conference calls to talk about . . . what to talk about."[61]

Chen said that Bush himself is almost always on message. "You can see that he goes back to his talking points," Chen said. "You can see that he goes back to almost the same words from his different speeches." At one press conference, Chen asked Bush if it bothered him that his administration was perceived by some to favor the wealthy and big business. Chen said Bush ducked the question about the perception of his administration by falling back on some talking points about tax cuts for small business. "It's very hard to get him to say something in an ad lib sort of way or extemporaneous," Chen said.[62]

Dan Froomkin, a *Washington Post* columnist, agreed that Bush is very good at using a reporter's question as a launching pad for his own message. "He knows how to handle them, he really does," Froomkin said. "But I think he has gotten better at that. But he was pretty good in the beginning; he'd take a curveball and manage to hit a wobbly double."[63]

To continue the baseball analogy, all the president has to do is make contact to get a hit. CBS's Bill Plante said that the proliferation of media makes getting the message out for Bush easier than it was only 20 years or so ago during Reagan's time in office. But that increase in message channels makes message discipline crucial. "You have many, many avenues," Plante said. "The broadcast networks, the cable networks, and you have a web of television operations that exist to serve local stations, so it's very easy to get the message out in a very broad way. I think they do a pretty good job of getting his message out, but I don't think it's that hard anymore. The thing that works well for them is that they tend to stay on message. And they don't lose any time going back over worrying about whether they were wrong about weapons of mass destruction. They don't allow debates on their mistakes. They don't play. Not that they don't allow [debates]—they don't engage in them; they don't do anything to get them off message is what I'm saying. They just go merrily forward."[64]

Bush's team went merrily forward with message discipline in the 2004 campaign. *Newsweek*'s analysis of the campaign, which was written based on extensive access to the candidates, summed up Bush as a "zealot for order" who "demanded a tightly wound, top-down, on-time-to-the-minute operation."[65] Bush's ultimate message was that he was a strong leader in the war on terror, and this message was planned even during the Democratic primaries when many thought former Vermont governor Howard Dean would be the nominee and the strategy would be Bush as steady and Dean as reckless.[66] When Kerry won the nomination, the Bush campaign still naturally portrayed the president as a strong wartime leader; Kerry was portrayed as an indecisive "flip-flopper."

The race was a tight one, and Bush had many disadvantages, not the least of which was a war that appeared to be going badly with a steady drumbeat of terror bombings and American casualties. But even opponents like Mike McCurry, Clinton's former press secretary who had signed on with the Kerry campaign, gave Bush grudging respect for his press tactics. McCurry, himself no stranger to trying to keep everyone on message in the wildly chaotic Clinton White House, said the Bush camp was "effective and disciplined at managing a message and getting through," although he cautioned that Bush might pay a price by not getting practice by regular contact with reporters.[67]

But it was the other candidate who paid a price for lack of discipline, both among his staff and in his own personality. John Kerry was in love with his own nuanced style of speaking. The former debating champion gave speeches and press conferences as if he were back on the debate team and could vanquish an opponent by the length of his answer.

Media writer Ken Auletta in a *New Yorker* article described a Kerry campaign that was so disorganized that reporters said dealing with the Kerry press office was like dealing with the Department of Motor Vehicles. Unlike the disciplined Bush campaign, which kept internal fights internal and had only a few trusted advisers for Bush, Kerry's camp had so many advisers that one former aide told Auletta it threatened to turn the camp "into post-war Berlin with four zones."[68]

Until August 2004, Kerry did not have the same kind of rapid response team that Bush had. While Bush had a team that monitored every Kerry appearance, recorded every national news broadcast, digitized every Kerry vote, and clipped every newspaper article, the Kerry campaign had one volunteer monitoring three TVs. The Bush camp by August had collected six million web addresses and a million volunteers, three times and two times, respectively, the number Kerry had. A Bush strategist told Auletta that the campaign could instantly communicate with 10 percent of the voters Bush needed to win the election.[69]

In addition to his undisciplined staff, Kerry himself frequently went off message by trying to answer questions in too much detail. Kerry famously said in response to questions about an appropriation bill for equipment for troops in Iraq, "I voted for the $87 billion before I voted against it."

Bush is not as easily distracted, said Ron Hutcheson, Knight-Ridder's White House correspondent. "Most of Bush's press conferences are not very illuminating because . . . he doesn't get sucked in," Hutcheson said. "He's not like John Kerry. You know, it was said about John Kerry that he would start giving out a pretty good answer from a political standpoint and then keep going until he went too far and said something stupid. Bush doesn't have that problem."[70]

Bush had solved the problem of how to deal with reporters years before. He had been practicing message discipline since Kent Hance took him to school on it in 1978. The lesson served him well in his final campaign.

4

PLUGGING LEAKS

When asked if Bush was secretive when he was governor, Arnold Garcia said, "Oh, good lord, yes." One time, Garcia learned from sources that Bush was going to appoint someone to a post in the Texas government. Garcia called the man, who was a friend, to congratulate him and tell him he would write an editorial about the appointment in the *Austin American-Statesman*. "He said, 'For God's sake, do you want to kill me?'" Garcia recalled. "He says, 'With this governor, if he reads it in the newspaper, the guy is dead. It won't happen.'"

Garcia said it reminded him of the oft-repeated tale of Lyndon Johnson calling a press conference to appoint J. Edgar Hoover FBI director for life in response to press leaks that Hoover would be fired. LBJ supposedly told an aide to call Ben Bradlee, whose publication had reported the leaks, and say, "Fuck you."[1]

All modern presidents have been bedeviled by leaks—stories slipped to friendly reporters to advance an agenda that is usually detrimental to the administration, although politicians also use "controlled leaks," releasing information they want published but not attributed to them because of its controversial nature. LBJ, for example, was enormously secretive. He hated news of appointments to administration jobs to appear in the press before he had announced them and would sometimes cancel them if they were publicized prematurely. Leonard Marks, who was his appointee to be head of the U.S. Information Agency, said LBJ called him out of the blue to tell him of his appointment and refused to accept a no from the hesitant Marks. Johnson finally relented and said he would give Marks the day to explain it to his wife. Johnson announced the appointment himself two hours later.[2]

Bush no doubt developed his hatred of the practice through observing how leaks had affected not only his father but also his vice president, Dick Cheney. Both the senior Bush and Cheney had worked in the Gerald Ford administration, George H. W. Bush as director of the CIA and Cheney as chief of staff. The Ford administration was particularly damaged by leaks in the post-Watergate era, when the press was at its highest point in the seesaw battle between reporters and presidents. The elder Bush told Ford he would try to curtail bad stories about the agency by limiting access to the press.[3]

Cheney had been personally damaged by leaks while he was Ford's chief of staff. (Cheney had been Donald Rumsfeld's aide under Richard Nixon and Rumsfeld's deputy chief of staff under Ford before both men were promoted—Rumsfeld to secretary of defense.) Leaks from other White House sources had described Cheney's supervision as too lax, leading to sloppy work by the staff. John Dean noted that Cheney "had been burned badly by leaks when he first became Ford's chief of staff. His scars were deep."[4] Cheney's wounds were reopened when he served in Congress and as defense secretary during the elder Bush's presidency. As a congressman, Cheney was "appalled" by leaks during the Iran-Contra investigations, and he disciplined military personnel for leaking information when he became defense secretary.[5]

As president, George H. W. Bush told reporters flat out at a March 11, 1992, press conference that commenting on stories that had been leaked to the press was one of the things he hated the most about his job. "I read about ideas that I'm considering that I haven't even heard of yet. I don't know. What I'd say to the American people is, please ask for a name to be placed next to the source so I can get mad at the guy who's doing this."[6] At a press conference a month later, Bush responded to a question about a story reporting that he wanted George W. Bush to shake up the campaign by telling NBC reporter John Cochran that it was "ridiculous" that people made their living by writing "inside" stories.[7] Later in the year at another press conference, Bush lamented how "extraordinarily difficult" it was to find leakers. He acknowledged that it was considered good journalism but said it was bad government because the leaker was able to influence policy by releasing a document before internal debate on the policy had taken place. When Cochran, again the questioner on a leaked story, reminded Bush that the leak in this case—over a story about a controversy involving

Environmental Protection Agency (EPA) administrator Bill Reilly—was supposedly friendly to the administration, Bush replied, "Well, help me find [the leaker], John. Help me find him. He'd be gainfully unemployed."[8]

Although George W. Bush observed his father's struggles, he didn't blindly try to control leaks to the media. An observer of Bush's lifelong interaction with journalists can easily see how his relations with the press have varied depending upon his job. For example, most sportswriters described his administration of the Texas Rangers as an extraordinarily open one. Chuck Cooperstein, who covered the Rangers as a radio reporter at KRLD, recalled that the organization was not secretive. "We were dealing with [General Manager] Tom Grieve, who was a very open guy. You could always get hold of him. And [Manager] Bobby Valentine, who loved to talk to the media. With Bush, he was around, and everybody knew he was around, but it was not like he was dictating policy."[9]

Newspaper columnist and radio host Randy Galloway said he and other sportswriters could get quotes from Rangers executives and owners besides Bush, and Bush did not try to control that. "I never heard he put the fear of God in them. . . . I never heard anyone say, 'Boy, George is real touchy about that.'"[10] Another columnist, Gerry Fraley, said he was familiar with news reports that the Bush presidential administration is secretive. "That disappoints me, because he wasn't that way at all. He thought it was important that the ticket-buying public was versed in what the club was doing. He wasn't paranoid at all back then. Now, obviously from a distance, it seems like his administration is. But he was not that way at all here. It was a very open administration in terms of baseball."[11]

Phil Rogers, who covered the Rangers as a beat writer, also said he was disappointed in the secretiveness of the Bush presidential administration compared to the baseball administration, although he acknowledged that running government is more serious than running a sports team and that, in general, sports teams want coverage for publicity, even if it's negative. "His access was tremendous," Rogers said. "I would never have thought of him as secretive or restrictive in what he did. I never heard about any midnight shredding at the Rangers' offices."[12]

As a baseball executive, Bush did not place restrictions on his employees talking with the press, whether they were club front office personnel or players. As governor, Bush continued to make himself available, but he limited access to his staff. Reporters' calls to his senior staff were always rerouted to his press office.[13]

The *Star-Telegram*'s Jay Root said it is like comparing apples and oranges to compare President Bush to Governor Bush. Root noted that the perception now is that Bush is secretive and inaccessible, so "it seems ludicrous" to say how accessible Bush was as governor. Nevertheless, Bush made an effort to be available to reporters, he said. "They took [press relations] very seriously," Root recalled. "You always got a return phone call. I can't remember ever not getting a call back—ever. I didn't always get what I wanted, but they got back to me. I think they treated reporters well, if you define that as they did their part, a lot of which is calling back. In day-to-day things they were very professional."[14]

The callbacks were not anonymous leaks, however. "Those people [in the Bush governor's office] were very, very well disciplined. They did not [leak], which I always viewed as a journalist as a professional challenge," Garcia said. "You can always find someone to talk."[15]

Still, it was difficult to find those sources. The *Houston Chronicle*'s Clay Robison observed that Bush had a "strong preference" for doing business in private as governor, and that much of the bipartisan work he did with Democrats, especially Lieutenant Governor Bob Bullock and House Speaker Pete Laney, was done in closed meetings. Bush summed up his philosophy his first year as governor by saying: "The way to forge good public policy amongst the leadership of the legislative branch and executive branch is to air our differences in private meetings that happen all the time. The way to ruin a relationship is to leak things [to the media] and to be disrespectful of meeting in private." Robison suggested the secret meetings of Bush's presidential energy task force, which was sued in 2002 by the General Accounting Office for access to information from the meetings, was part of a Bush habit that was "hard to break."[16]

Bush became more cautious as he seriously contemplated running for president. Wayne Slater noticed that Bush started to clean up his speech and swear less often in front of reporters.[17] Bush let his aides and the press know when they had given out stories he didn't want published yet. Bush was furious in February 1999 when Rove let slip to a *New York Times* reporter that he would file papers to start an exploratory committee for president. Bush publicly chastised Rove at a press conference: "Maybe Karl Rove should have spoken to me before he talked to the press. It's best that people not put words in my mouth."[18] Bush also told the author of a *National Journal* cover story on Rove "that he didn't like his aides getting star treatment."[19]

Once the 2000 presidential campaign began in earnest, reporters were allowed access only to designated spokesmen, and some employees had to sign agreements that they would not talk to the press. At least one press secretary, David Beckwith, "was fired for being too glib with the media," and an anonymous source claimed press secretary Ari Fleischer's job was similarly in jeopardy early in the campaign.[20] The policy certainly seemed to work. Ratcliffe claimed that "almost no" leaks came from the campaign for more than a year.[21]

The fear of retribution for leaks continued into the administration. Michael Getler, the *Washington Post*'s ombudsman, told *American Journalism Review* that journalists had difficulty reporting on the run-up to war because of lack of sources. "This is a very, very buttoned down administration, a very closed-up and on-message administration, and you have subjects that are very hard [for the press] to get at with any sense of authority. You have an environment in which leakers are in some professional danger."[22]

Experts predicted such a policy would serve only to alienate the White House press corps, which would find other sources for news—sources unfavorable to the administration.[23] Bush, with his knowledge of the press, understood that reporters would be angry. But he and his staff decided that an effective communication strategy was worth the tradeoff.[24] Bush was right. The policy undoubtedly alienated some reporters, but they have been largely powerless to do anything about it.

By most accounts, Bush has been the most successful president ever at controlling information coming out of the White House, carrying over the extraordinary discipline in his Texas administration to Washington, D.C. Leaks were so few that speechwriter David Frum noted in his memoir that the date the first one occurred in the administration, June 14, 2001, deserved a footnote to history. The resulting story, a Robert Novak column about administration infighting over environmental policy, was hardly the stuff to bring down a president. Frum noted the episode produced a few reprisal leaks from the other faction, but he never mentioned any more in his book.[25] At any rate, Bush has been able to keep that sort of thing to a minimum through his unusual ability to get tremendous loyalty out of the majority of his employees.

Austin television reporter Neal Spelce said Bush is able to generate that loyalty because it is a two-way responsibility between Bush and his staff. "I'm not going to hang you out to dry if you don't hang me out to dry," was how Spelce described the philosophy. "I think Bush places a lot of priority on that quality—loyalty—and as a result of that, that translates into 'Don't you go spreading information that is kept in the confines of this room.'"[26]

Frum wrote that Bush created loyalty by revealing a little of himself to his staff and also by showing that he cared about them. Bush revealed himself by doing things like dropping brutally frank, behind-the-scene comments about foreign leaders or public policy. These comments, Frum argued, were a gift of confidentiality that bound the staffer to him like a direct marketer obligates a survey respondent by giving him a dollar. Even when Bush criticized people, he was able to get them on his side by showing a human touch. Frum said one of his friends was among a group chewed out by Bush in the Oval Office over a slow project. Bush asked Frum's friend to stay and told him that he didn't blame him personally and concluded the conversation by asking after his children by name. "When he emerged from the Oval Office, my friend would have charged a machine gun for George W. Bush," Frum concluded.[27]

Karen Hughes, who is perhaps as close to Bush as any of his aides, wrote in her memoir that Bush fostered loyalty by sharing credit for success. Her description of the inner workings of the Bush administration emphasized a sense of collegiality among the workers—that they were all on the same team. She recalled that at Bush's first staff meeting as governor, he told his employees, "Always return each other's phone calls first."[28]

Fleischer also recalled the feeling of being on the same team, which Bush fostered with get-togethers at Camp David. Fleischer described one such gathering early in the first term as a relaxing trip with no formal agenda—just appreciating the tranquility of the surroundings, dining together, and doing fun activities like watching movies and bowling. "Our unity and desire to serve the President's agenda was formed, in part, by how well the President treated us, by the little things he did. Just like a CEO who quietly but effectively pays attention to personnel issues, Bush was building a strong team that worked well together," Fleischer wrote.[29]

At the start of his second term, Bush sought to further strengthen that sense of teamwork. In early 2005, the administration started a new policy requiring cabinet secretaries to spend several hours a week working in an office set up for them adjacent to the White House. The policy required the secretaries to "meet with presidential policy and communications aides in an effort to better coordinate the administration's initiatives and messages."[30] Paul Light, a professor of public service at New York University, said he found "it absolutely shocking" that the White House would require the secretaries to keep office hours and that the move was done to control the secretaries and their agencies. Labor Secretary Elaine Chao, however, said the policy was "a great way to build an effective and cohesive team."[31]

Knight-Ridder White House correspondent Ron Hutcheson said Bush is so good at controlling his team and plugging leaks that future presidents are going to want to emulate his style. But they won't be able to do so, Hutcheson said, because Bush has a unique talent for getting loyalty from his people. "I think everyone's going to try to mimic it, and I think just about everybody is going to fail," he said. "I think they're better at it than most, partly because they put more effort into it, but largely because it is a well-disciplined, highly loyal group of people unlike, certainly unlike you saw during the Clinton years, and unlike you saw during the Reagan years. I think it's . . . Bush in some ways is unique in his ability to get loyalty from his staff, which is the key to the whole thing."[32]

But in addition to personal loyalty to Bush, many of the members of his administration simply don't want to talk to the press even if he gives them the freedom to do so. According to Fleischer, administration officials such as Chief of Staff Andrew Card, Deputy Chief of Staff for Policy Josh Bolten, and Karl Rove preferred to focus on governing rather than talking to the press. "To much of the press, it appeared as if we were trying to manage the news and deny reporters sources," Fleischer wrote. "In reality, it was more the nature of the people who worked in the White House that decided whether reporters got their calls returned. If the top staff had wanted to talk to the press, they would have and they could have. No press secretary can control who picks up the phone either to make or to receive phone calls."[33]

Certainly in comparison to the sieve-like Clinton administration, the Bush White House has been a watertight ship of state. Edwin Chen, White House reporter for the *Los Angeles Times*, said one "very top" Clinton official, who he declined to name, told him he was amazed at the success of Bush in controlling leaks. "This person told me that when President Clinton would have a meeting on some subject and there would be some discussion and some back and forth, at the end of these sessions it was almost always said by somebody, a chief of staff or senior person, 'Let's please leave this discussion in this room'—that is, not leak it, you know, not talk to the press about it. But almost always, more often than not, this person told me they would read about it the next day in the paper. That's almost unheard of in the Bush administration. It's a real big difference."[34]

U.S. News & World Report writer Michael Barone said the White House was so effective at controlling the message that "you only need to make one phone call, and you've heard everyone's story." When debating Ron Suskind at a forum at the University of Southern California's Annenberg School for Communication, Barone said that the Clinton administration had the same policy but was less centralized. But Suskind said he could get information from 30 different sources in the Clinton administration so that he could get closer to the truth.[35]

Suskind was one of the few journalists able to pierce the veil surrounding the Bush White House with his book *The Price of Loyalty*, which was written with the cooperation of former Treasury Secretary Paul O'Neill.[36] Suskind's unflattering portrait of Bush generated some publicity, but the story quickly died because there were no other cabinet members leaking supporting details, and the White House largely ignored the story. The public yawned as well at the disgruntled account of the White House. A cartoon by Matt Davies illustrated the conundrum, showing O'Neill waving his arms and saying, "Unless we were talking about Saddam or tax cuts, the president was strangely disengaged," while a man in a "Joe Voter" shirt looks bored and thinks, "Whatever."[37]

In fact, most of the unfavorable accounts of the inner workings of the administration have come from people—like O'Neill—who published them after they left the administration. Another official often cited as an inside source critical of Bush—Richard Clarke—was not really a part of the Bush team but was rather a longtime bureaucrat who had worked for Democrats as well as Republicans. Clarke, the counterterrorism czar in both the Clinton and Bush administrations, wrote in *Against All Enemies* that Bush ignored the threat from al-Qaeda.[38] Clarke and his book earned a lot of media attention, and Clarke testified prominently before the 9/11 investigation commission. But most current and former Bush administration members supported Bush's position, and Clarke's book did not seriously damage the reelection campaign.

Shortly after Bush's second inauguration, Christine Todd Whitman, a former New Jersey governor and Bush's first secretary of the EPA, published a book that was critical of not only Bush's environmental policies but also his foreign policy and political strategy. She attacked the architect of Bush's success, Karl Rove, as well, for appealing to the conservative Republican base while alienating moderate Republicans like herself.[39] But it is notable that she voiced those criticisms after the election and did not damage Bush while she was in office. She praised some of

Bush's environmental policies but said that they were not publicized, much to her frustration, because the administration did not want to upset a conservative base that would be unenthusiastic about environmental regulations.[40] In effect, Bush's message discipline was so focused that even good news was controlled when it was thought to interfere with the main point the administration wanted to make. In the 2004 election, the administration message was that Bush was an effective war leader in dangerous times rather than a tree-hugger who would protect the environment, and that was the message that the public got. Whitman, like most Bush cabinet officers, loyally served the president.

Reporters are so desperate for someone to break ranks that they sometimes fall for leaks that are just plain wrong but are too tempting to pass up. Frum gave a particularly interesting example in his memoir. Other administration officials had warned Frum about syndicated columnist Robert Novak, who, although a conservative, was not averse to publishing damaging information about Republicans and was famous for saying that there were only two types of people in Washington: "sources and targets." Novak reported on CNN, which later issued a retraction, that Bush had fired Frum because an e-mail written by his wife disclosed he had written the "axis of evil" line in one of Bush's more famous speeches. Novak reported that Bush fired Frum because he didn't want aides leaking information like the details of speechwriting. The White House issued a statement that Frum had resigned in writing a month before the e-mail fiasco, but the story did not die immediately. Frum asked a friendly reporter why the story, which he believed was a simple one, had such legs. She told him that Bush had been so effective in controlling information, that "we go kind of crazy" when a chance comes to look inside the administration. "The idea that this administration is so paranoid that it would fire somebody for an e-mail fits all our prejudices," the reporter told Frum. "And the possibility that there might be a disgruntled former employee eager to dish the dirt . . . well, we've been waiting for that for more than a year."[41]

In truth, the press has been thwarted in attempts to access even the most lowly of White House sources. Freelance photographer Chris Usher, who has covered both the Clinton and Bush administrations, was working in 2005 on a longtime project of a book of photographs of ordinary people who work behind the scenes at presidential events. Usher said he was always struck by the number of people it takes to get an appearance ready and how different the scene looks up close compared to the version presented on television. When walking through the White House, Usher frequently tries to take pictures of seemingly innocuous details like the Marine band rehearsing or even a cleaning man buffing the floor. Unfailingly, a press aide will chastise him, saying, "C'mon Chris, you know that's not allowed."[42] The message is clear: The press is only supposed to photograph or talk to people approved by the administration press office.

Usher was one of a select few journalists in the press pool that accompanied Bush on his famous Thanksgiving 2003 visit to Baghdad. Usher took some casual snapshots aboard Air Force One of reporters and Bush staffers chatting in the airplane, although he was not supposed to be taking photographs at that point. Some Bush staffers later asked him for copies of the photographs, which Usher thought indicated they could not take their own pictures—only officially sanctioned ones allowed. The aides kept the journalists away from the president, who never went back to the press section during the trip.[43]

When asked what his favorite picture was, Usher replied that the trip was so tightly controlled that he didn't get any he wanted to include in his portfolio. Of course, much secrecy was required to protect the president from terrorist attack, but the event allowed no photos beyond what the White House wanted to show. Usher eventually took some standard photos of Bush posing with a turkey. But from Usher's viewpoint as a photojournalist, the shots were unsatisfactory because they showed no context—there was nothing to indicate that Bush was on a historic frontline visit.[44]

"We flew in the dark, we landed in the dark, and we arrived at a room full of soldiers, but it could have been anywhere," Usher said. "We joked that maybe they didn't really take us to Baghdad but some other military base in the States."[45] Still, Usher thought it was a masterful display of public relations. The message was that Bush cared about the troops enough to risk a visit to them, and it stole the thunder from a political rival, Senator Hillary Clinton, who was also visiting troops overseas.[46]

Bush knew from watching press coverage of his father's invasion of Panama that a president can be hurt by not controlling wartime photos. One reason the Pentagon may have barred photos of war dead arriving at Dover Air Force Base in 1991 is that they wanted to avoid the embarrassment that occurred when the media in 1989 showed a split screen of George H. W. Bush joking with reporters on one side and coffins of Panama invasion casualties on the other.[47] The George W. Bush Defense Department banned the release of coffin photos during the first year of the Iraq War, citing concerns for privacy for soldiers' families.[48] But what happened to George H. W. Bush could not have been lost on his son.

Privacy and security issues raise the question of how much of the administration's concern for secrecy is warranted. The public, and even some journalists, agree that Bush's change from being an open and accessible governor to an inaccessible and secretive president is explained largely by the restrictions of the office and the demands of fighting the war on terrorism.

Tracy Ringolsby, who covered the Rangers as a beat writer for the *Dallas Morning News*, said Bush's baseball administration was very open, but he understood why the presidential administration was secretive. "I think with 9/11 and the things that have gone on, I don't know that we're in an open time," Ringolsby said. "I think at times we get carried away with the public's right to know—not that we should have secrets or whatever, but there are only so many things they can be open about. It's one thing to talk about a potential trade, and it's another thing to talk about a potential attack. . . . Is that being secretive or is that being intelligent? There is a discreteness now that didn't have to be there before."[49]

Research has shown a significant part of the population agrees with Ringolsby's assessment. A study done by *American Journalism Review* and the First Amendment Center about a year after the September 11, 2001, attacks showed public support for governmental restrictions on the press during the war on terror. For the first time in the history of the annual survey, almost half of those surveyed said the First Amendment goes too far in guaranteeing rights. According to a story based on the study, "More than 40 percent of those polled said newspapers should not be allowed to freely criticize the U.S. military strategy and performance." Similar or greater numbers said they would limit professors from criticizing the military and that the press has been "too aggressive" in asking the government for information on the war.[50]

In 2003, two years after 9/11, the percentage of the population who believed that the First Amendment "goes too far" was down to 34 percent—which was still more than a third of respondents. When asked whether there was too much freedom to publish or too much censorship, 43 percent responded there was too much freedom to publish compared to 38 percent saying there was too much government censorship. The figures were up from 42 percent and 32 percent, respectively, from the 2002 survey.[51]

Bush, according to longtime press adviser Hughes, considered leaks especially inexcusable in wartime. Bush, referring to a newspaper story reporting that the military would attack 13 camps in Afghanistan, told Hughes, "There's an act of treason in the newspaper this morning. . . .

Whoever did this is a traitor; they're putting lives at risk." Hughes concluded, "We had never liked leaks, but now they could have deadly consequences."[52]

Fleischer captured the administration's mood by describing Bush flying into Washington on 9/11. Air Force One passed over the Pentagon, and Bush, looking out the window, said, "The mightiest building in the world is on fire. That's the twenty-first-century war you just witnessed."[53] At a senior staff meeting the next day, Card told Fleischer and the other staffers that Bush said to act as if the nation was at war, and "there were to be no loose lips."[54] Bush personally repeated the "loose lips" remark to Fleischer, Hughes, and others when the press began inquiring about military plans against the Taliban in Afghanistan. According to Fleischer, Bush "laid down the law" to his staff. "I wasn't to confirm, deny, or acknowledge any of the press's questions on military matters," Fleischer recalled. "He made clear he knew his job was to keep the public informed, and he would do so, not the staff."[55]

The old saying is that "loose lips sink ships," but for journalists they help launch good news copy. Journalists started complaining early in the administration that it was more secretive than Clinton's White House. Investigative reporters noticed an immediate change when Bush took office. One anonymous source told *American Journalism Review* that while Clinton staffers might be reluctant to release information, they would obey the law, but Bush appointees would actively seek ways to avoid following the law. The magazine quoted William Powers of *National Journal* as claiming that the Bush administration might be the most secretive ever, and John Dean called the administration "Nixonian." The *Review* article asserted that an October 2001 memo from Attorney General John Ashcroft that said agencies could refuse Freedom of Information Act (FOIA) requests whenever they could find a reason to do so was the most famous Bush decision on secrecy matters. The article noted other similar but less well-known moves, including an effort to exempt the Homeland Security Department from FOIA and an executive order declaring presidents don't have to obey the Presidential Records Act. The article stated that White House reporters believe the administration does not respect them, tries to keep them from doing their jobs, and encourages public sentiment that the press has a knee-jerk reaction to demand access to material. The White House refused interviews for the article.[56]

Ashcroft, speaking for the administration, went on the offensive against critics of the Patriot Act. Ashcroft, in responding to criticism of the government policies while testifying to the Senate Judiciary Committee in December 2001, said, "To those who scare peace-loving people with phantoms of lost liberty, my message is this: Your tactics only aid terrorists, for they erode our national unity and resolve."[57] Early in 2005, when he was about to leave office, Ashcroft took some of the blame for not explaining the Patriot Act better and said that it was misunderstood. But he refused to go back on his 2001 statements: "Everybody ought to raise real questions about lost liberty but if they are just fabrications of lost liberty . . . I stand by my statement, people who do that divert us."[58]

There was at least some evidence to bolster Ashcroft's claim. Much was made of Ashcroft's tightening of FOIA guidelines in the October 2001 memo. He had urged agencies to carefully consider national security, privacy, and law enforcement worries before releasing information, while the Clinton administration had emphasized openness. But a survey of U.S. FOIA officials showed 48 percent said it had little effect on how much information was released.[59]

The administration's refusal to bow to pressure from journalists and their trade publications seemed to drive the scribes to madness. The *Review* article was just one of many in journalism trade publications that used hysterical language to describe the Bush administration. *Editor & Publisher*, for example, used "apparatchiks"—the old term to describe Communist party hacks in Soviet Russia—to refer to Bush officials who had issued an executive order delaying the automatic release of millions of documents that would have been declassified in 2003. "The White House warriors who since Inauguration Day have been blasting away at the people's right to know are at it as furiously as ever, but now they are using the cover of the shooting war to advance their campaign of government secrecy on little cat's feet." The order was described as being as "loaded with nasty surprises as a Volcano M87/M87A1 landmine. For the first time, the vice president is invested with the power to classify government documents, a task Dick Cheney surely will undertake with an unnerving enthusiasm." A study of the National Security Agency showed that organization's FOIA system was "in extreme disarray." "Just the way, in other words, that Ashcroft and his commander in chief in the fog of war want it to be."[60]

Robert Leger, president of the Society of Professional Journalists, compared the Bush White House to the Chinese Communists. In a column in the society's magazine *Quill*, he wrote that Bush's policies were similar to the Chinese government's cover-up of the SARS epidemic, referring to the fact that the administration had removed some information from government websites. "While the Bush administration may not go to the extremes of the Chinese, it shows the same tendency to believe that secrecy is best. It was on that path before Sept. 11, 2001, and the attacks on the World Trade Center and the Pentagon only accelerated the trend," Leger wrote.[61]

Another *Editor & Publisher* article compared the Patriot Act to Frankenstein's monster and mocked Ashcroft's religious beliefs.[62] Whether it was designed bias or not, the magazine's editors hammered home their disdain for the administration in the same issue by using only negative editorial cartoons about Bush to illustrate a story about the syndication of cartoons and other copy.[63]

Jane Kirtley, a law professor at the University of Minnesota, suggested that the Bush administration might try to suspend certain First Amendment rights. Her basis for that assertion was that the administration has tried to keep the press out of deportation hearings. A judge said that such closure would mean the government could operate in virtual secrecy resulting in wholesale suspension of First Amendment rights. "The Bush administration has demonstrated that, left to its own devices, it might do just that," she concluded.[64]

John Dean, the former Nixon aide who was quoted comparing Bush to Nixon, published a polemic during the 2004 campaign arguing that the Bush administration's secrecy was worse than the Watergate scandal. "Never before have we had a pair of rulers—it is difficult to call them leaders—like Bush and Cheney, men whose obsession with control of information, and spin, is so strong that they are willing to subvert the democratic process for their short-term political gain. Not since Nixon left the White House have we had such greed over presidential power, and never before have we had such political paranoia."[65]

Dean claimed one of Bush's main tactics for preserving Nixonian secrecy was "shrink-wrapping the White House." He wrote that Card had "leakproofed" the White House by organizing it in a compartmentalized fashion so that the various groups only shared information on a need-to-know basis. For example, speechwriters were isolated from scheduling and decision-making meetings.[66] Dean, a lawyer, wrote that the Bush administration has "cobbled together the equivalent of a new unofficial secrets act more awesome than anything Congress might give them," citing as an example the administration's 20-count indictment of former intelligence analyst Jonathan C. Randel for leaking unclassified information to a British journalist. "Clearly this was a warning aimed at potential whistleblowers in the federal bureaucracy, advising them to keep quiet or risk jail."[67] Dean claimed that Bush's refusal of interviews and berating reporters who asked challenging questions were tactics "strikingly familiar to anyone who witnessed Richard Nixon's precedent-setting moves in controlling such information."[68]

One journalist who appeared to have torn a hole in the shrink wrap was famed investigative reporter Seymour M. Hersh, who wrote an article in the *New Yorker* based largely on anonymous sources about Bush administration plans in the Middle East, especially in dealing with the development of nuclear weapons by Iran. Hersh attributed his information to such sources as a "retired senior C.I.A. official," a "former high-level intelligence official," and a "Western diplomat."[69] The article showed how reporters can develop inside information by going to former officials who may have a grudge against their employers and have less to fear because they no longer work for the administration. Of course, the protection also calls into question the legitimacy of the comments. The sources, because they are protected, are free to make up stories without being called to account, and the reader is never quite sure how authoritative the sources are, or even if they exist.

Hersh's article on the Iranian nuclear situation reported details such as American commando units infiltrating Iran from Afghanistan to search for underground weapons sites so they could be successfully targeted in air strikes. Some observers wrote that Hersh had gone too far by revealing American plans to a potential enemy. Tony Blankley, a conservative columnist for the *Washington Times*, even suggested the article was treasonous.[70] But others pointed out that the information in the Hersh article was likely leaked by the administration on purpose to put pressure on the Iranians. News about U.S. Special Forces in the country would undoubtedly lead the mullahs to panic and make their government even more restrictive at a time when the population was already getting restless with its repressive government.[71]

It may never be known whether the Hersh piece was a coup by an investigative journalist or a plant by the Bush administration. A likely scenario is that it was a little of both. Certainly it fits a previous pattern of the administration feeding information to high-powered reporters and then using their stories to advantage. For example, the administration, including Bush himself, gave great access to Bob Woodward, who made his reputation by bringing down Nixon and built on that triumph with exposés of every succeeding administration, including that of George H. W. Bush. Woodward wrote two books about George W. Bush's administration, *Bush at War* and *Plan of Attack*. The books showed some infighting among the upper levels of the administration, and readers could conclude that Bush was ill informed and made ill-considered decisions.[72]

Conservative columnist Wesley Pruden wrote that Bush had foolishly cooperated with Woodward in the vain hope that he'd get fair coverage in exchange for access. Woodward had instead portrayed "the president and his men as rowdy schoolboys, eager to lob bombs at Iraqi innocents and throwing biscuits and stink bombs at each other for the honor of pushing the buttons to start a reckless and unnecessary war to assuage cowboy egos."[73] But readers could equally conclude that Bush was a decisive wartime commander waging a battle against an elusive, deadly enemy abroad and critics at home. In fact, historian Stephen Graubard argued that the books were "eulogies" to Bush because they showed him as being decisive, unwavering, and in control of his subordinates. "Woodward, delighted to have been given so much time with the president, never considered the possibility that he had been taken in, sold a bill of goods, and used for White House propaganda purposes, or that his portrayal of all the president's seconds-in-command, his loyal courtiers—Cheney, Rumsfeld, Powell, and Rice—were partial, incomplete, and self-serving in the best sense of the word."[74]

The Bush team, as it did with many media stories, turned a potential disaster into a success. *Plan of Attack* was put on the Republican website as a flattering portrait of the president. Conservative commentator Fred Barnes reviewed *Bush at War* favorably, concluding Bush emerged a "winner."[75] The books remained on the best-seller lists for weeks. Whether the portraits of Bush were good or bad was up to the readers, but there is no question the titles of the books emphasized the president's main 2004 campaign strategy: The United States was at war.

Woodward was certainly the most threatening reporter in Washington because of his record of exposing scandal. The *Washington Post*'s Howard Kurtz wrote in his portrait of Clinton's media relations how the mere mention that Woodward was sniffing around was enough to send press aides scrambling to deal with the potential story.[76] Because of Woodward's reputation, the White House may well have decided to cooperate with him and spin the story once it came out. But the administration will also use leaks proactively to start stories of their own.

Vice President Richard Cheney, like Bush and many others in the administration, is experienced with handling the press and has proven to be a master of the designed leak, as well as controlling leaks as chief of staff during the Ford administration. Ford hired Cheney for his hard work and loyalty, and, as was mentioned earlier, he was needed in a leak-prone administration like Ford's.[77] As vice president, Cheney has demonstrated a talent for feeding stories to the press. *American Journalism Review*, in an article outlining the reporting on Iraq's possession of weapons of mass destruction before the war started, indicated Cheney may have been quoting his own leak as a way of bolstering the case for invading Iraq. A September 8, 2002, *New York Times* story attributed information about Saddam Hussein trying to get aluminum tubes for nuclear weapons to anonymous administration sources. That same morning, Cheney referred to the *Times* story when asked about the aluminum tubes on *Meet the Press*. Bob Simon, a CBS reporter who reported on the aluminum tubes issue on *60 Minutes*, told the *Review* that he was surprised at the audacity of quoting your own leak. "You've got to hand it to them. That takes, as we say here in New York, chutzpah."[78]

When Defense Secretary Donald Rumsfeld was under fire for the Abu Ghraib prison torture scandal, Bush took what *Time* magazine called the unusual step of attending his senior White House staff members' meeting, where he warned them not to leak anything: "If I hear any speculation coming out of the White House about the Secretary," he said, "you'll hear from me."[79]

But who leaked Bush's threat on leaks? The magazine did not provide a source. Did Bush threaten the staff not to leak and then authorize the leaking of the threat as a way of showing his support for Rumsfeld while maintaining his ability to deny it if he wanted to? The quote as printed in *Time* definitely bolstered Rumsfeld's position. As with so much news about the Bush White House, what appears to be an inside account may actually be a plant.

The administration may also have leaked to punish leakers. Someone revealed to Novak that Ambassador Joseph Wilson's wife was a CIA employee. Bush critics said the administration was trying to punish Wilson for his outspoken criticism of Bush's Iraq policy. Hughes wrote in her memoir that the outing of a CIA employee was wrong and would not have come from the White House because Novak's column identified the leakers as "senior administration officials" rather than "White House officials."[80] In the summer of 2005 the affair was still under a criminal investigation by the government. Although various press reports suggested Karl Rove may have been the source, it remained unclear whether any laws had been broken and doubtful whether Rove or anyone else would be thrown to the wolves by the intensely loyal Bush. Like its reaction to O'Neill's criticisms, the public yawned. Terror bombings in London and war protests at home pushed the leak story from the news agenda. Columnist Mark Steyn summed up public reaction by writing that he "couldn't care less" about the scandal, which he dismissed as political fighting. "The police have found the suicide bomber's head in the rubble of the London bus, and Iran is enriching uranium," Steyn wrote. "The only distraction here is the pitiful parochialism of our political culture."[81]

Another short-lived embarrassment for Bush was the revelation in the winter of 2005 that several conservative columnists had been paid to support administration policy in their writings—a sort of pay for publishing pro-administration leaks. The administration denied any direct responsibility, arguing that the pay-for-print idea was generated within various departments, not the White House. The scandal was encapsulated neatly by a Chip Bok cartoon in the *Akron* (Ohio) *Beacon Journal* that showed Laura Bush bringing the president a snack while he is busy writing in an easy chair. She asks Bush if he is editing his State of the Union speech. "Nah," the cartoon Bush replies, "Armstrong Williams' next column."[82] Democrats called for an investigation; Republicans said the situation looked bad but was not illegal. Bush called the practice a "mistake" and said, "Our agenda ought to be able to stand on its own two feet."[83]

Like the Novak affair, it is unlikely a smoking gun will emerge connecting Bush to the policy even if he did order it. Such an action seems absurd. Payments would be in the public record and extremely hard to conceal. They would give Bush's enemies a sword while offering little, if any, benefit—the conservative columnists would have written favorably about administration policy without being paid for it. Still, presidents, like all human beings, sometimes do strange, counterproductive things. Nixon, for example, did not need to bug the Democratic headquarters because he was going to beat George McGovern in a landslide based on policy differences. If Bush did order the payments, Dean has more proof of the president's Nixonian character. However, the administration explanation that the practice was initiated within federal departments rather than emanating from Bush makes more sense, given his knowledge of the press.

What seems more in line with Bush's press experience is the extraordinary increase in spending on public relations during the president's first term. The administration spent more than $88 million on public relations contracts in 2004, an election year, compared to about $37 million in 2001. Bush's first-term total was about $250 million, almost twice as much spent by Clinton during the previous four years. Democratic congressmen said the expense was excessive and proposed legislation to control the spending. However, White House spokesman Trent Duffy said the expense was warranted because public health scares like anthrax and major policy changes like the No Child Left Behind Act required that the government communicate information to the public.[84] At any rate, the budget shows Bush's belief in the efficacy of public relations.

Bush's knowledge of public relations and how to handle the press, combined with a natural charisma that has generated an unprecedented loyalty among White House staff has enabled him to both control and use leaks to an extent that no president has been able to do before. Will future presidents try to do the same?

"That's what we're afraid of," said White House correspondent Chen. "That's what we're all afraid of."[85]

5

THE DARK SIDE

Bush usually keeps his displeasure with reporters private, but during the 2000 campaign he inadvertently let the *New York Times*'s Adam Clymer—and everyone else at a Naperville, Illinois, political rally—know what he thought of him. Bush, who was standing on a stage next to Dick Cheney, pointed at the reporter and said, "There's Adam Clymer, major-league asshole from the *New York Times*." Cheney replied, "Oh, yeah, he is, big-time." Unbeknownst to Bush, his comments were picked up by the on-stage microphone. Bush press aide Karen Hughes later told reporters that Bush thought a number of Clymer's articles were "very unfair." Bush himself did not apologize, but said "I did not obviously realize the mikes were going to pick it up. I regret everybody heard what I said."[1]

Earlier in the campaign, Clymer had written a story about Texas's historical lack of attention to public health care. He asked Bush's press office for copies of speeches Bush had made about the subject, and a low-level aide told Clymer that Bush had not made any, which Clymer reported in his story to the chagrin of the Bush camp. The day the story was published, Bush spotted a television reporter reading it on the campaign plane. "He laughed, and sort of tapped the paper and said, 'Welcome to the NFL, Governor Bush,'" Clymer recalled. "His manner was, well, you know, this happens."[2]

Later in the campaign, Clymer wrote a story giving a Bush campaign ad a zero for accuracy because it referred to Bush's Medicare plan when Bush had not released any formal plan. Then, right before Labor Day, Clymer wrote a story based on an examination of Cheney's tax returns that showed he had made millions since leaving the government in the first Bush administration but had given only a minuscule amount of money to charity. "Cheney was very angry about that story," Clymer said. "He thought it made him look like a cheapskate."[3]

The Bush campaign cited the health care and Medicare stories as examples of unfair stories, but Clymer thinks the Labor Day comment was sparked by the Cheney piece because Bush referred to a "mean story about my buddy Dick Cheney" when he talked about the incident on the David Letterman late-night comedy show.[4]

For Clymer, who had been punched by a segregationist while covering the civil rights movement in Selma, Alabama, and thrown out of Moscow by Russian officials, the incident was just part of the news business—people sometimes get angry about stories. Clymer said he wasn't mad at Bush for the remark. "All he did was call me a name," Clymer said.[5]

Others didn't take the story so lightly. The incident had occurred on Labor Day, the traditional kickoff of the fall campaign, and it dominated coverage for a few days. Clymer was inundated by interview requests, including some persistent invitations to appear on Letterman's show. He turned most of them down, including Letterman, because he didn't think campaign coverage should focus on a reporter.[6]

"I got so many e-mails, my computer kept crashing—largely from right-wingers saying, 'Yes, he was right. You are a terrible person.' Those were the more quotable versions," Clymer recalled. "I felt I couldn't go back on the campaign plane that year because if I did, then I'd be the story. It would be the kind of stuff television would love. So I stayed away."[7]

Clymer, however, continued to cover the race from a distance. The Bush campaign didn't hold a grudge, as far as he could tell. "There was never a blink in the professionalism of their press office," Clymer said. "I mean nobody ever thinks a press office is perfect and informative, but they were as helpful or as unhelpful as they had been before. Now when they came to Washington—this is easily the most secretive and least forthcoming-to-the-press presidency of my experience, which goes back to the Kennedy administration—but I never felt it was harder on me than on other people."[8]

After the election, Clymer, as president of the Washington Press Club Foundation, invited Bush and Cheney to address the group. They didn't address the foundation directly but instead made a humorous videotape poking fun of themselves and Clymer over the Labor Day incident. Later in 2001 when Clymer's mother died, Bush sent him a personal condolence letter. "It was a very nice gesture," Clymer said.[9]

Nevertheless, the Labor Day remark has entered Bush lore as an example of his sometimes prickly relationship with the press. Bush, like everyone, has a temper. And some observers believe he uses it to intimidate the press. In comparing Bush to his father, one *Washington Post* story noted George H. W. Bush fought the "wimp factor" label in the media, but that his son is facing the "bully factor"—being labeled a bully for using the power of his office to intimidate those who come out against his policies.[10]

Edwin Chen, *Los Angeles Times* White House correspondent, said he thinks Bush's famous bestowing of nicknames is an intimidation tactic. "It's a reflection of his belief that he is a really good reader and a quick reader of people and so he assigns them nicknames as sort of a manifestation of that, but I think it's also . . . there is a quality of Bush being a bully," Chen said. "He thinks of himself as the president and he can assign nicknames to people whether they like them or not."[11]

Is Bush a bully toward journalists? If he is, he is only following a long presidential tradition. Richard Nixon, of course, is usually cited as the premier example of a president who tried to intimidate the press. Indeed, longtime White House correspondent Helen Thomas wrote that Nixon usually "displayed downright hostility" to reporters.[12] Harry S. Truman also had a cantankerous reputation. Truman, who once said 90 percent of the press was against him, told John Hersey that he was "saving up four or five good, hard punches on the nose" to deliver personally after he left office to reporters who had insulted him.[13] Even John F. Kennedy, who is generally considered to have enjoyed excellent press relations, had some problems with his family dealing with the media. Thomas wrote that the First Lady, Jackie, did not like press coverage at all. When her father-in-law gave her a German shepherd puppy, some reporters sent her a note asking what she would feed the dog. She replied, "Reporters."[14]

Bush's immediate predecessor, Bill Clinton, also battled the press and on occasion displayed a ferocious temper. Howard Kurtz detailed in *Spin Cycle*, an account of Clinton's press relations, how administration press aides used intimidation tactics every bit as intense as those reportedly used by the Bush team. During the 1992 campaign, Clinton was angry about a *New York Times* story that implied he had weakened ethics legislation in Arkansas. According to Kurtz, Clinton "raged out of control" in front of his aides and Associated Press reporter John King. "Look at this piece of shit," Clinton roared, throwing down a copy of the *Times*. "This story is a fucking piece of shit!" King asked if he should step outside, but Hillary Clinton pulled the then governor into another room to calm him down.[15] Although he didn't curse ABC's Peter Jennings during an interview upon the opening of his presidential library, Clinton's hatred of the media was still evident four years after he left office when he angrily told Jennings that the media had devoted too much time to scandal during his administration.[16]

Hillary Clinton, according to Kurtz, viewed "the media as the enemy" from her first days in the White House, creating a plan—never carried out—to move the media from the West Wing to the Old Executive Office Building. When she was angry over a gossip item in *Newsweek* that claimed she threw a lamp at her husband, she granted interviews to *Time* and *U.S. News & World Report* but "pointedly refused to talk to *Newsweek*."[17]

Clinton regularly used aides such as George Stephanopoulos and Mike McCurry to "lean on reporters."[18] Stephanopoulos once persuaded CNN not to run a story about Clinton sex harassment accuser Paula Jones. McCurry publicly criticized *Newsweek* columnist Howard Fineman for ridiculing Clinton, and he "summoned Paul West, the Washington bureau chief of the *Baltimore Sun*, for a chat," after *Sun* reporter Carl Cannon wrote a piece in the *Weekly Standard* about Clinton's lies.[19]

When persuasion was not enough, the Clinton White House made overt threats. When a *Washington Post* financial reporter wrote a front-page story in 1993 that claimed the economy would have recovered no matter who had won the 1992 election, Clinton economics adviser Gene Sperling warned the reporter, Clay Chandler, that the White House might cut off his access for that type of story, spelling out what Kurtz noted "is usually an implied threat."[20]

It's telling that Kurtz indicated such threats are not unusual; what's unusual is to speak them plainly. All politicians are going to fight with the press, and sometimes they will fight dirty. Bush's attitude has been formed through both his long personal experience with the media and also seeing what the press has done to the people he loves, beginning with how his grandfather Prescott lost his first U.S. Senate race in large part because of an erroneous Walter Winchell radio report linking him to the Birth Control League—a fatal charge at that time because of Connecticut's heavy Catholic population.[21]

Bush was only about five years old during that race, but it is a well-remembered episode within a family that has an attitude that is suspicious if not contemptuous of the press. Peter and Rochelle Schweizer, who interviewed a number of Bush family members, including Jeb Bush and George H. W. Bush (but not George W. Bush) for their Bush family biography, asserted that the clan has a strictly enforced understanding about protecting the family from the media. If you say something bad to the media, you can get frozen out. "I think you could burn down the house in Kennebunkport and you'd be in less trouble than if you gave a bad quote to the *New York Times*," John Ellis, a Bush cousin said.[22] Jeb Bush, who has had plenty of contact with the press through his own Florida gubernatorial campaigns, seemed contemptuous of the political reporters who try to write about the family, saying the coverage can be "mean and distorted" because they don't know what they're doing. "You have the political press writing about nonpolitical issues," he said. "Most of these people are not the most brilliant people in the world, and when you get them out of their area, writing about the family, it can be a little bit scary."[23]

As was shown in an earlier chapter, George H. W. Bush had rocky relations with the press when he was president. United Press International reporter Helen Thomas recalled that when a reporter would irritate him, he would dismiss the reporter with, "You're history," and that he called photographers "photo-dogs,"[24] although some thought it was a term of endearment. The elder Bush said that as president he believed in freedom of the press, but after the presidency he believed in "freedom from the press."[25]

Thomas wrote that one time one of the family dogs bounded out of the limousine when the elder Bush pulled up and headed straight for Thomas, who was standing at the rope line. She shrieked, and Bush asked someone what happened. When the aide explained, Bush muttered, "Sic 'errrrr."[26]

Bush almost called his son "my boy" at the Republican National Convention in 2000, but cut himself short when he remembered what had happened when he made a similar comment in New Hampshire earlier that year, a comment that was reported as showing his son was a diminutive political figure. "The national press went ballistic," he said. It was "the nastiest, meanest kind of reporting I've seen. So I've got to be very, very careful." Barbara Bush later apologized for her husband's honest but unpolitical comment, saying: "I don't like to criticize, but several years ago he joined Press Bashers Anonymous. And he had a little slippage today. I promise you he's going back on the wagon right now."[27]

Barbara Bush usually tried to be more circumspect when commenting on the media. When son Neil was being investigated in 1989–1990 in conjunction with the failure of Silverado Savings & Loan, she and her husband blamed themselves because they thought Neil was being persecuted just because he was the son of the president. She would not be combative with reporters but when pressed for a comment, she would look at them with "sad eyes" and say, "You don't want to see a grown woman cry, do you?"[28] When asked during the 2000 primaries what she thought of press coverage of her son, including references to drug use allegations, she said she had no complaints about the coverage.[29]

But those were comments made in campaign mode. Between campaigns—specifically in her memoirs written after her husband left office and six years before her son ran for president—she let her real feelings out. She wrote that "one of the first lessons someone in public life must learn is: THE PRESS HAS THE LAST WORD."[30] She wrote that she believed one of the main reasons her husband lost the 1992 election was biased press coverage. She acknowledged that many reporters were fair, but concluded that "the overall experience has left a bad taste in my mouth about the media, and makes me question what I read. I hate that. I respect and like many members of the press. I just wish I could respect more of what they do."[31]

Her presidential son appears to have the wary attitude of his mother and also, like her but unlike his father, is usually cautious about complaining about reporters or coverage. In fact, George W. Bush's view of the press appears to be that reporters are not worth losing your temper over. In the immediate aftermath of 9/11, a number of journalists criticized Bush for not returning straight to the White House and looking shaky on some of his first public appearances. Bush told the *Washington Times*'s Bill Sammon that such criticism was only "a momentary bother." The critics were "elites, these kind of professor types that love to read their names in the newspapers. I can't remember the exact quotes or who they were now—it's just faded. They're obscure people."[32]

Bush hasn't always been so indifferent to criticism. He has been known to curse reporters, both publicly and privately. But these instances are relatively few in number compared to the towel-snapping repartee that he is more famous for. When considering Bush's lifelong press relations, the striking thing is how the most famous of these press confrontations occurred during Bush's drinking days or before he became a serious politician. Bush's use of temper, like his control of press access and his emphasis on secrecy, have varied depending upon his situation. Outright displays of temper have gradually been replaced by a sarcastic remark, or a word from an aide, as Bush's relationship with the press has evolved from representing other organizations and politicians to representing his own businesses and administrations.

This evolution has not been from a towel-snapping governor to a White House bully but rather from a joking governor/presidential candidate to a president-in-the-bubble. Ron Hutcheson covered both the 2000 campaign and the subsequent Bush presidency. When he saw Alexandra Pelosi's humorous documentary of Bush's 2000 campaign, *Journeys with George*, Hutcheson was reminded of the time spent talking and laughing with Bush on the campaign trail. "It reminded me of why I used to like the guy," Hutcheson said.[33]

Does that mean Bush is no longer likeable as president? "Don't read too much into it," Hutcheson said. "Mainly it means I don't have a real relationship. You know how people will say, 'What's George Bush like?' And when I say, 'Oh, he's a nice guy on a personal level,' I'm really talking about going back to the [2000] campaign because you know what I see now is a professional relationship, really—and a limited professional relationship at that. We observe him, but we don't interact with him, other than the, you know, highly staged professional interactions: We ask him a question and he decides whether he wants to answer it or not."[34]

But throughout his long dance with the press, Bush has had some decidedly unprofessional moments. Perhaps the most famous was an incident in 1986 in which he cursed at *Wall Street Journal* reporter Al Hunt while the journalist was eating dinner with his family at a Mexican restaurant in Dallas. Hunt's prediction that Jack Kemp and Richard Lugar would be on the Republican ballot in 1988 had just been published in *Washingtonian* magazine. He didn't mention George H. W. Bush as a candidate. Hunt told Bush biographer Bill Minutaglio that George W. Bush "was quite clearly lubricated" that night when he walked up to his table and said to him, "You no good fucking sonofabitch, I will never fucking forget what you wrote!"[35] Bush apologized to Hunt—but not until 13 years after the confrontation, when it became a topic of some stories during the 2000 campaign. The incident has been retold many times in Bush profiles as an example of his temper and vindictiveness. For example, Paul Waldman, a Bush critic, wrote in *Fraud* that the Hunt episode shows Bush "has a serious mean streak."[36]

A similar episode, although one apparently not fueled by alcohol, occurred when Bush was running for Congress in West Texas in 1978. Mel Turner, a local radio host, moderated a debate between Bush and his opponent, Kent Hance. Turner asked Bush whether he was involved or knew anyone involved in the Trilateral Commission, which some conservative West Texans perceived to be a force for world government and a threat to the United States. George H. W. Bush had been a member of the commission. The younger Bush answered angrily, "I won't be persuaded by anyone, including my father." After the debate, Bush called Turner an "asshole" and refused to shake his hand.[37]

Hance said the Turner incident was the only time he saw Bush snap at the press during the campaign. "I think the thing that happened with Mel Turner—Mel was [asking] him questions that had been a distraction and a nuisance—been a nuisance to their campaign," Hance said. "And I think he thought it was an unfair question. You know he was 30 years old at that time, and I can see that happening. You're going to get some questions that you think are unfair questions but you can't let them know it bothers you, and you got to answer them. It may not be fun, but you got to do it."[38]

Bush lost Turner's support[39] and the election, although it was a respectable race for a first-time candidate who was running against a seasoned politician. But Bush's press relations were not refined at that point. When a story appeared he didn't like, he would immediately call the reporter without first discussing the prudence of such action with a campaign aide.[40]

On the other hand, he impressed Hance, the only man ever to beat Bush in an election, with his "people skills." Hance said the race attracted national and regional media because the race was very competitive and because of Bush's famous family. The area TV stations covered the race aggressively. "I had had a long-term relationship with the [press] in Lubbock because I'd represented them for four years and had been the state senator, and that was pretty easy," Hance said. "Bush, the first time he announced to run for Congress, he went around when the press conference was over [and] he helped the TV guys put up their equipment. He was really friendly and was working them just like they were voters, and that was not lost on us." Hance didn't start copying Bush's helpful moves because he thought the reporters would see it as pandering, but he took note that Bush was a serious opponent.[41]

At any rate, Bush's early confrontations with the press may be attributed to immaturity, alcohol, or the fact that, as in the Hunt episode, he was protecting his father rather than representing himself. According to Minutaglio, Bush was still learning how to deal with the national media during his father's 1988 campaign but was picking it up by working closely with Lee Atwater, considered a master of media seduction and the art of holding friends close and enemies closer.[42] *Washington Post* reporter David Hoffman told Minutaglio that Bush "disliked journalists, and I felt he was suspicious. I never felt that he wanted to talk or give an interview."[43]

The *Dallas Morning News*'s Wayne Slater also said that Bush's handling of the media when his father was president was not good. "He was seen as the enforcer for the father—I've talked to Bush about this—and basically his explanation is, look, in those days you really love your dad and you're there as the enforcer and the protector of the father, and it's really harder to do that than to defend yourself—it's easier to act on your own."[44]

But when Bush became managing general partner of the Texas Rangers baseball team, his role with the press changed, and his demeanor did as well. Bush was clearly the public face of the ownership, and he worked assiduously to cultivate the press, and through them, the fans of the struggling franchise. The Rangers were a losing team on the field and in the box office, where attendance was so low that if Bush's group had not bought the team, it might well have been moved out of the metroplex. In such an atmosphere, it would have been foolhardy to fight with the local sportswriters. Furthermore, as managing general partner of the Rangers, Bush was not the protector of his father. Any bad press about the team was not bad press about his family but rather his own business and, of course, sometimes himself. But Bush has said many times it is easier for him to handle criticism of himself than criticism of his family.

Randy Galloway, a Dallas–Fort Worth sportswriter who had several self-described "shit storms" with Bush over columns about the Rangers, said Bush "tolerated" him as a journalist because he didn't write about his family. "He told me one time that 'the reason I get along with you is because you never bring my family up.' And I never did. I never mentioned the *Fortunate Son* aspect or took a shot at foreign policy or mixed in Mom or Dad or brother Jeb. It was strictly about baseball and strictly about George—good or bad. I didn't figure that was my role and I never said anything. Man, did he appreciate that—shockingly so. Very, very protective of family. He was protective of his father to the point where you would have thought he would have been used to it."[45]

Galloway did see Bush's temper when he castigated the Rangers' ownership for a variety of faults, including being too greedy and not getting the players necessary to win a championship. "He was a red ass," Galloway said. "George was a huge red ass. . . . George likes to snap at you. He is too adversarial to be the so-called quote-unquote 'good with the media.'"[46]

Galloway would call Bush up for a comment on an issue such as ticket prices and would include the information in his column, but then would write his own opinion, sometimes negative, about the Rangers' policy. Bush would think he had explained his position and then would be angry when he saw the opposite in the paper. "Galloway, you son of a bitch, we talked about this," Galloway recalled Bush saying after one column. Galloway joked that he felt honored to have been cussed out by the man who would become president of the United States.[47]

"Oh, God, he used to get mad when I'd ripped him for jacking up ticket prices," Galloway said.

"Do you realize what we've paid for this player?" Bush yelled at him on one such occasion. "You're the same guy bitching about us not spending enough on this player. Now you're mad at us for jacking up the ticket prices?"[48]

Nevertheless, Galloway, who described himself as "as big a Democrat as you can find," said he ended up "liking Bush a lot." Galloway appreciated Bush's honesty and explained that Bush, unlike a lot of sources, never held a grudge over a bad story. "If he was mad that morning about a column, by that afternoon or next morning it was hey, new world, new subject, what's going on today?"[49]

But Galloway's report of shit storms was a minority among sportswriters and, later, news reporters who covered Bush as governor. In fact, most reporters said Bush rarely complained about articles. None interviewed for this book could recall him ever claiming he was misquoted. "He never once said he was misquoted. He never tried that trick, which I respected him for," said Gerry Fraley, another Dallas–Fort Worth sportswriter. "He always stood by what he said and was willing to talk about things, so that was a big thing for me."[50]

Fraley, however, did not get along with Rangers Manager Bobby Valentine. "[Bush] would defend Valentine, and that's what he should do," Fraley recalled. "I respect him for that. But he would just say, 'You're too hard on the guy.' But he would move on."[51]

When Bush fired team president Mike Stone, who was a holdover from the previous ownership, *Fort Worth Star-Telegram* columnist Jim Reeves wrote that the new ownership was "Bush League" and should sell the team. Bush's reaction to digs like that was low-key, if he reacted at all. "I wouldn't say he criticized me," Reeves said. "He and I differed on that story. I actually don't remember George saying anything in particular about that column. There were times I would write something and he would make a little aside about it while we were talking. But mostly, it was done in a joking, not caustic manner. It let me know, 'Hey, I saw that. You were wrong, but that's okay.'"[52]

By most accounts, Bush carried this easy-going press style into the governor's mansion. He rarely showed anger to journalists. The *Austin American-Statesman*'s Arnold Garcia could recall only one display of temper, and it was not directed at him personally. Garcia was at the governor's mansion for a cocktail party during Laura Bush's Texas book festival. It was also, however, the time of the drawn-out recount of the 2000 election. George W. Bush walked by, and Garcia—feeling, as he described it, "a little smartass"—said, "Hello governor. What's new?"[53]

Bush wheeled around, gave Garcia an angry look and "just went off" about the recount. Garcia, in reflecting on the episode years later, said he had greeted Bush insensitively and didn't blame Bush for his reaction. "He was just venting—'They're trying to steal the election; you guys have got to tell the story'—stuff like that," Garcia said. "He didn't use profanity. I never heard him swear."[54]

Slater, who as a reporter instead of a columnist saw Bush more often and in different situations than Garcia did, recalled that Bush used a lot of profanity, but *with* the reporters, not at them. "He talked like your basic guy," Slater said. "He talked like what you would expect coming out of the baseball tradition: Tough guy in the locker room . . . seeing the press as the old paradigm—drinking, smoking guys."[55]

Slater laughed when told about Galloway's anecdotes of Bush's cursing at him. Slater suggested it was done in a locker-room fashion rather than out of meanness. "I virtually never saw him do a real mean [thing] or a real temper in Bush," Slater said. "I heard from aides over the years he could be very demanding and very difficult, as any highly accomplished chief executive can be with a big temper. But I got to tell you, with me—and I was with him for years, daily—I never saw any serious show of temper."[56]

R. G. Ratcliffe, who covered Bush as governor and during the 2000 campaign for the *Houston Chronicle*, said Bush called his editor to try to talk him out of running a story that he didn't like. Ratcliffe declined to provide details because he and Bush had a discussion about the story that was off the record. "There was no effort to intimidate. . . . Let's just suffice to say he wasn't happy," Ratcliffe said with a laugh.[57]

The story detailed how some of Bush's former business associates had made money dealing with the state, although it noted there was no evidence that Bush had intervened on their behalf. Clay Robison, a *Houston Chronicle* columnist, noted Bush's unhappiness with the story and chastised him for not realizing being an elected official means giving up privacy. "As the son of a former president, Bush should know this better than most people," Robison wrote. "But he sometimes displays a touchiness that makes one wonder how much confidence he really has in the voters' ability to decide what information is important about a public figure."[58]

But Ratcliffe said Bush handled negative stories better than some politicians. He cited as an example Phil Gramm, a former U.S. senator from Texas, who did everything he could to cut off his access for about 10 years after Ratcliffe wrote some negative stories about him. Ratcliffe said that Bush as governor tended to think reporters were for him or against him, but he wouldn't punish them by denying them access when they wrote unfavorable stories.

"[The] difference with Bush was you do a negative story on him, and he may come away feeling you are against him, he can't really trust you, whatever–he's not going to freeze you out. You may not get any special treatment or special access, but you're not going to get frozen out because that just wasn't how they operated," Ratcliffe said, although he added that the relatively small number of reporters in the state press corps makes it somewhat impractical to freeze out reporters. Washington officials have more luxury in cutting off reporters because there are always others to talk to.[59]

Instead of using personal intimidation, Bush sometimes applied pressure through aides criticizing stories or implying that the journalists who wrote them might lose access. "You know Bush never bullied the press that I saw," Slater recalled. "Karen [Hughes] would. Bush would tell her–and that's what a politician should always do with his press secretary–'Call that reporter and tell him I'm not happy' with that reporter. Karen would call and say, 'This is wrong. That's wrong.' Or, 'We didn't like the tone of this' or whatever."[60]

Slater wrote a story after Bush's first legislative session as governor that Bush didn't like because he thought it implied Bush was taking credit for the success of the session. Taking all the credit is no way to get along with the lieutenant governor and speaker of the House, both of whom were crucial to Bush because of Texas's weak-governor structure. "Bush was very upset about that, although he never told me," Slater said. "But he told Karen, who called me."[61]

Hughes's correspondence files in the governor's records in the state archives illustrate her gentle but firm attempts at correcting the press. Many letters are rapid responses to articles that were unfavorable to Bush. In most cases, they were a simple recitation of how she thought facts had been misinterpreted or corrections of factual errors. Others were more forceful. For example, she wrote a letter of two pages to an *Austin American-Statesman* reporter charging that a story was unfair.[62]

Still, Hughes's tactics were mild compared to those attributed to long-time Bush political adviser Karl Rove. Slater is an expert on Rove and his relationship with Bush. He interviewed Rove extensively for the book *Bush's Brain*, which he cowrote with Jim Moore.[63] Slater described Rove as "tough" in his relationship with reporters. "He calls you; he threatens—I don't mean physically threatens you. But even if there are no words there, the implication—reading between the lines—'My gosh, my access is shut off, I'm going to be in somewhat big trouble here.' This guy Rove is a formidable character."[64]

Slater said Rove would also feed negative stories to reporters about the opposition. He said that for the first two years or so of Bush's governorship, Rove would call with information—most of which Slater did not consider newsworthy or that didn't check out—that would damage holdovers from the Ann Richards administration. "Bush would never do that," Slater said. "But the result of those stories—and I wrote a few things that were legitimate—but the result of that was that Rove was the dark side, dealing with us and peddling information, and he did that to help Bush. But at the same time, Bush himself never got his hands dirty, and I think that's the key of the relationship."[65]

Slater has talked to Rove since the book was published and thinks Rove privately likes the book, despite the fact that it illustrates some of his "dark side" tactics, because it reinforces the idea he is formidable. "Hey, what's not to like?" Slater said. "Now, he would prefer the book to be a hagiography—that he's the most wonderful guy in the world—and it's not. It basically is a pretty truthful account of the way this guy operates in politics. But that's not all bad for Karl because it creates this kind of image that he is a man to be reckoned with at the right hand of power in a city that really respects power, and really respects people who are serious about using it."[66]

Other reporters have noted Rove's use of power tactics. A trio of Texas journalists who profiled Rove in *Boy Genius* wrote that Rove told Anne Marie Kilday of the *Dallas Morning News* that she needed to be careful of her reputation because he was looking at the phone records of a state official who was a reputed lesbian, and she had called her a number of times at her home.[67]

Rove, in that sense, may be Bush's Spiro Agnew. Nixon's vice president will always be famous for attacking the media as elite, "impudent snobs."

Bush learned a lot about politics from Lee Atwater, a longtime Republican operative who was one of his father's chief campaign advisers. Atwater had learned a lot from Nixon, who at one meeting counseled going after the media with "a nut-cutting spokesman" like Agnew.[68] In addition to Rove, Bush has had a legion of surgeons in the form of right-wing bloggers, who numbered Dan Rather among their patients during the 2004 campaign.

On the other hand, Bush has sometimes told his aides to treat reporters better. Bush publicly chastised Hughes for insulting Frank Bruni of the *New York Times*. Bruni had written a story about Bush during the 2000 campaign that Hughes thought unfairly portrayed Bush as not working hard during the campaign. Shortly afterward, Bruni took a few days off because he was tired. Hughes couldn't resist pointing out the irony and told a group of reporters: "He's tired, after covering the campaign that's not working hard enough? How could he be tired?" According to Hughes, the other reporters didn't appreciate her attacking one of their group behind his back and complained. She apologized, but Bush still teased her about it in front of the press corps to the point she said, "I've already apologized, do I have to grovel?" Hughes wrote that she learned the lesson that you could make fun of other politicians and yourself, but not the press.[69]

Hughes's side of the story was published in her memoir about two years after Bruni's account, which took several pages of *Ambling into History*, his recollection of the 2000 campaign. Bruni wrote that he had temporarily left the campaign so he could return to Washington to do some work that he couldn't do on the road, but when Hughes noticed he wasn't on the airplane, "she took off: Was the campaign's supposedly sluggish pace too much for me? Was the fire in my own belly a mere ember? Had I not, during the final week in New Hampshire, spent a day and a half in my hotel room while a *Times* colleague took my place at events?" Bruni admitted in his book that he had taken the days off, but argued that, unlike Bush, he wasn't running for president.

Numerous other reporters called Bruni about Hughes's comments, so he e-mailed her that he would appreciate her talking to him in person before criticizing him publicly. He considered her subsequent e-mailed apology to end the matter. But he later heard that Bush had asked her whether she had apologized, and when Bruni next saw Bush, he wrapped his arms around the reporter's shoulders and said, "You know we love you!" At the next campaign event at a high school, a student asked Bush about his press coverage. Bush gave his standard response that he would like to change some of the stories "but respected the independence and commitment of the press and even liked some of its representatives." Then he looked in Bruni's direction and said, "I love you, man!"[70]

Bruni called Bush's reaction to the episode "civilized and at least superficially amiable." Bush "saw no percentage in any enduring rift. He understood that the past could not be changed but the future was always up for grabs. He also liked the environment around him to be as happy and festive as possible, and reporters like me were part of the climate."[71]

The climate was one with more intense competition and less of a sense of humor than anything Bush and his aides had experienced in Texas. Hughes thought it was joke; Bruni and his national press comrades did not. Bush, of course, had dealt with the national press on behalf of his father and was certainly aware of the difference between the two groups.

On the national campaign trail, Bush needed good press relations, especially given the attention Republican rival John McCain, a prominent U.S. senator from Arizona, got from his extraordinarily open policy with the press during the primaries. Bush didn't want to unnecessarily anger the reporter for the influential *Times*, so he made sure Hughes apologized to Bruni.

He also muzzled family members who got in the way of good press relations. His brother Marvin told reporters at one point in the campaign, "That giant sucking sound you hear is the media's lips coming off John McCain's [bottom]," referring to his belief that the press had been fawning over McCain. The reporter who wrote the anecdote suggested Marvin was apparently revealing something his older brother did not want on display because Bush "hustled" his little brother back to the family section of the campaign airplane.[72]

Regardless of how Bush and his family felt about the press, Bush was reluctant to get into arguments over coverage. His strategy was to ignore stories when possible, and say as little as possible when reporters insisted on a quote. For example, during the 2000 New Hampshire primary, the *Manchester Union Leader* endorsed Steve Forbes in a front-page editorial that called Bush "Gov. Smirk" and accused him of insulting New Hampshire voters by talking down to them. Bush's only response was a terse sentence that he disagreed with the *Leader*'s decision.[73]

But the tactic of aides complaining about stories on Bush's behalf has continued at the White House. Ari Fleischer, Bush's first presidential press secretary, was responsible for two of the most famous incidents. When a story was written about one of Bush's daughters that the Bush family believed was an unnecessary invasion of privacy, Fleischer told a briefing rather ominously that the story "had been noted in the building." When a story on the war on terror was published that the White House believed was unpatriotic, Fleischer said reporters needed to think about what they were doing. Fleischer wrote in his memoir that the quote had been taken out of context, but it has served as an example for those who argue Bush's White House tries to intimidate the press.[74]

Ron Suskind is one journalist who says the White House uses intimidation as a press tactic. "If you write something the White House doesn't like, they take you in and say, 'If you ever write something like you did today, nobody from the White House will ever talk to you again,'" he said, describing the administration's attitude toward the press as "pissed."[75]

Freelance photographer Chris Usher said Bush at times will smile and ask photographers how they are doing, but at other times he appears annoyed with the press. One of the latter episodes that Usher witnessed occurred during a routine event in the Roosevelt Room. The press was jammed into the room with a narrow aisle down the middle. Some of the photographers were kneeling in the aisle while they were shooting. Bush decided to walk down the aisle to shake hands with someone he recognized in the back of the room but one of the kneeling photographers was in his way.[76]

"He just took his hand to his forehead and pushed him back as he walked through . . . in, it seemed to me, a not very friendly way," Usher recalled. "Like, you know, you're just trash, get out of my way—very quickly—just get out of my way."[77]

White House photographers who get in the way of the presidential message can quickly find themselves unwelcome. During one photo opportunity, the White House allowed photographers to shoot from outside the Oval Office looking at Bush through a window. They were told to wait until they were given a signal they could shoot. One photographer, who Usher declined to identify, took a picture before the signal was given. "[Bush] was gesticulating and didn't look quite so in control, I guess, and he shot that picture when he wasn't supposed to and then moved it, and he really didn't shoot there again," Usher said. "A lot of feathers were ruffled by that."[78]

Some Bush critics claim that the White House gets vicious when its feathers are ruffled. John Dean wrote that the outing of Valerie Plame as a CIA agent through news leaks was the "dirtiest of dirty tricks" by the Bush White House because it threatened national security, hurt her career, and potentially endangered the lives of her and others.[79] Plame was the wife of former ambassador Joseph C. Wilson IV, who had written a newspaper column criticizing Bush's 2003 State of the Union address in which the president suggested Iraq had sought uranium from Africa. Wilson embarrassed the administration by asserting that he had not found any evidence Iraq had purchased uranium from Niger when he was sent to the country to research the issue by the CIA. Wilson, who had been recommended for the CIA mission by his wife, asserted in his column that the administration had manipulated intelligence to "exaggerate the Iraqi threat."[80] Columnist Robert Novak subsequently reported Plame's identity based on two anonymous "senior Bush administration officials." Dean wrote that the episode showed Bush's White House was worse than Nixon's. "Nixon never went after his enemies' wives, and he never employed a dirty trick that was literally life-threatening."[81]

A federal special prosecutor, Patrick Fitzgerald was assigned to investigate the affair to determine if a crime had been committed. It is illegal to intentionally leak the identity of an undercover officer. The White House's repeated statement during the investigation was that Bush wanted the matter investigated and that "anyone with information on the case should come forward."[82] Although Karl Rove appeared on the covers of *Time* and *Newsweek* during the summer of 2005 as a potential source of the Plame leak, Fitzgerald indicted only I. Lewis "Scooter" Libby, a top aide to Cheney, when the grand jury expired. Fitzgerald indicted Libby for perjury, making false statements, and obstruction of justice, not for outing an undercover agent.

However the complicated case is ultimately resolved, it has contributed to the Bush administration's reputation for intimidation. Dean included an anecdote in his book that he admitted sounded like a prank because it fit what he saw as a pattern of behavior. According to a story by *Los Angeles Times* reporter Elizabeth Shogren, National Park Service workers were so fearful of retaliation by the administration that they wore disguises and even used a voice modulator to hide their identities when they met with her to criticize Bush's environmental policies.[83]

Bush himself rarely appears angry at federal employees or reporters. Some celebrated incidents between the president and journalists may in fact be more sarcastic humor than an attempt to use intimidating presidential power. At a joint press conference with Bush and French president Jacques Chirac, NBC reporter David Gregory asked Chirac a question in

French. Bush mocked Gregory, saying, "Very good, the guy memorizes four words, and he plays like he's intercontinental. I'm impressed. Que bueno. Now I'm literate in two languages."

Paul Waldman surmised Bush "sneered" at Gregory because he despised intellectuals and thought Gregory was trying to make him look dumb.[84] Bill Sammon, White House correspondent for the *Washington Times*, noted that Bush told Gregory after he left the podium, "As soon as you get in front of a camera, you start showing off." Sammon wrote that the episode illustrated Bush's disdain for the press and placed it in the context of Bush dealing with headlines claiming he knew about the 9/11 attacks in advance. Bush was suspicious of reporters' political leanings and had carried Bernard Goldberg's book entitled *Bias* in such a way that he would be photographed with it. "Sometimes, when a president holds a book, it promotes sales," Bush said.[85]

But was Bush being mean to Gregory, or was he teasing him and the other reporters for taking themselves too seriously? Bush does like to tease reporters publicly. The *Fort Worth Star-Telegram*'s Jay Root covered Bush regularly as governor and once covered a presidential event when Bush made one of his frequent trips to the Western White House in Crawford. Bush noticed Root in the front row and pointed to him, saying here was a Texas reporter who used to cover him as governor. Bush joked that Root had lost a lot of hair in the interim and made several comments about it during the press conference. "He was trying that banter with the press," Root said. "He just would not let it go. It was in the White House transcript. Someone later wrote a story about it, that Bush made fun of a bald guy, but I didn't feel he was making fun of me."[86]

The motivation and appropriateness of such teasing is open to interpretation. Does Bush tease reporters because he hates the press? Rove said Bush respects the press but also views it as an "elitist" group of people who are trying to get a story that will grab attention.[87] Bush's standard answer to questions about how he feels about the press and politics is that he respects freedom of the press although he sometimes disagrees with what is written about him. He has also often said he doesn't follow the media closely.

"I have great respect for the media," Bush said in a lengthy interview with Fox News's Brit Hume. "I mean, our society is a good, solid democracy because of a good, solid media. But I also understand that a lot of times there's opinions mixed in with news. And I . . . I appreciate people's opinions, but I'm more interested in news. And the best way to get the news is from objective sources. And the most objective sources I have are people on my staff who tell me what's happening in the world."[88]

Bush also has often joked about the relationship. He once told a group of reporters at a Washington Press Club dinner that he thought of them as dentists. "Drill away; do what you have to do," Bush said.[89]

Joking with reporters can make politicians look good. Americans appreciate a good sense of humor in their leaders as well as their fellow citizens. But a well-timed fight with reporters can be helpful as well, particularly for conservatives, who argue passionately that the media are biased against them. Bush's father benefited from his well-publicized tussle with Dan Rather during the 1988 campaign, when Rather badgered the elder Bush about the Iran-Contra affair in an interview that was supposed to be a standard campaign profile. However, Bush was prepared to hit back with a preplanned critique of Rather. When Rather got confrontational, Bush got testy right back and asked the newsman how he'd liked to be judged for walking off the set in a huff earlier in his TV career. Political observers credit the episode for helping Bush shed his wimp image.[90]

Some political observers believe Bush's son used a similar tactic in the 2000 campaign. A couple of sources have insisted to Clymer that George W. Bush's campaign orchestrated the Labor Day episode as a Machiavellian plot to bolster support from the right-wing by fighting with the liberal media. Clymer said he never bothered to find out, but that he doubts the conspiracy theory because Bush's campaign had planned at that time to announce a Medicare proposal, and the Labor Day incident drowned out their message.[91]

At any rate, Bush usually keeps his angry moments with reporters private. Disagreements seem to be more spur-of-the-moment incidents between two people, part of the everyday friction that occurs whenever people with different goals encounter each other during the workday.

Paul Burka, the editor of *Texas Monthly*, thought Bush was an excellent governor and wrote a number of positive articles about him. Burka said he never had a bad interview with Bush. Nevertheless, Bush got so angry at one of Burka's stories that he refused to shake his hand when he saw him in the capitol the day the story appeared.

To Burka, the story was no big deal because it just reported what everybody knew: that Bush's tax-cut plan was dead in the Texas legislature. The story, however, included a joke along the lines that some legislators said that they could get in to see Bush if they were from Iowa, implying Bush was more interested in the presidential caucus than his gubernatorial duties. Bush thought it crossed the line and told Burka that a friend had told him it was the cheapest shot he'd seen in 20 years.[92]

Later that day, Burka called Karen Hughes on another matter, and she told him not to worry about his relationship with Bush. A *New York Times* reporter had called and rudely demanded to speak with Bush. Hughes denied the interview request because Bush had already met with another *Times* reporter that day. The second reporter didn't take the rejection well. "Don't worry," Hughes told Burka. "You're not first on the list anymore."[93]

After Bush was elected president, Burka saw him briefly when he returned to Austin for the ceremonial hanging of his portrait in the capitol. Only a limited number of dignitaries were admitted, but Burka wangled a press pass that allowed him to watch from the rotunda balcony. Bush looked up and spotting Burka, saluted. Burka touched his notebook to his forehead, returning the commander-in-chief's gesture with a reporter's salute.[94]

"I thought we got along pretty well," Burka said when it was suggested to him that he and Bush appeared to have a good working relationship. "I mean there was . . . I'm trying to think of what to say, because I don't feel . . . I mean, I thought that given the limitations of what public officials are, and given what journalists are—within those limitations, I thought we were friends. And I would use that term. But I wasn't a friend if I sat down to write, if I thought he'd done the wrong thing."[95]

This duty to write the tough story and ask the tough questions is often hard for a source to accept, even if, like Bush, the source has enough experience to know how reporters work. Robert Shogan, a longtime political reporter for the *Los Angeles Times*, covered Bush's 1998 reelection campaign for governor, where Bush often spoke of a group called True Love Waits that advocated abstinence before marriage. Shogan, of course, knew of Bush's own reputed wild days as a young man and asked Bush on his campaign plane if he thought a candidate needed to practice what he preached.

Bush, Shogan recalled, gave him "a look that would curdle ice-cold milk in a bottle." Bush snapped that he had never committed adultery, if that was what Shogan was aiming at. Bush then asked Shogan if he could turn the tables and ask him a question. When Shogan assented, Bush said, "How does it feel to belong to a profession where you have to ask people questions like that?" Shogan gave the standard it's-my-job reply but admitted in his book that the question made him ponder the nature of his profession and that the question had no simple answer.[96]

Knight-Ridder's Ron Hutcheson said the personal relationship between presidents and reporters is complicated because they have different perspectives. "Journalists, we have this feeling that we can smack you upside the head with a two-by-four and then tomorrow you are supposed to be nice to us because we're only doing our jobs," Hutcheson said. Most politicians, especially one like Bush who places such an emphasis on loyalty, find the relationship "mystifying," Hutcheson said. "They don't understand how somebody can be real pleasant chatting with you one day and then write a story just ripping you the next day. At some level, it's a betrayal in their minds, I think. It's a funny aspect of the relationship."[97]

During the 2000 campaign, Bush said he tried to keep the relationship friendly by not reading critical pieces about himself. Slater said Bush actually did read at least some of what the reporters wrote, but that he recalled Bush saying during the 2000 campaign he did not want to watch the Chris Matthews television show before he appeared on it because he wanted to be friendly with him during the show.

"I was reading this column, and Bush came down the aisle and stuck his head down below mine with a goofy face . . . and said 'Watcha' doin'?' I said, 'Hey, this is something you ought to know. Look at what Anthony Lewis is saying about you,'" Slater recalled. "And he shot up as if he were hit by a lightning bolt. And he moved down the aisle. He did not want to know, more importantly, he did not want us to think that he was paying any attention. He wanted to build a collegial relationship with these colleagues, these alleged colleagues on the plane."[98]

Once Bush became president, the easy access on the plane changed to the more limited access of the White House bubble, but he still maintained he didn't read the news closely. When Fox News's Hume asked Bush how he got his news, Bush said he was briefed by his aides, implying he didn't watch TV news. "In all due respect, you've got a beautiful face and everything," Bush teased Hume. "I glance at the headlines just to kind of [get] a flavor for what's moving. I rarely read the stories, and get briefed by people who are probably read[ing] the news themselves. But like Condoleezza [Rice], in her case, the national security advisor is getting her news directly from the participants on the world stage."[99]

Fleischer wrote that Bush, in fact, is well read. When Bush flew over Baghdad, Fleischer noticed that Bush was so well versed with the maps that he could point out places of interest from the plane.[100]

But the fact that even his reading habits are subject to press scrutiny and misinterpretation tends to make anyone cautious. Hutcheson noted that Michael Moore took Bush jokes at a Gridiron Dinner about how nice it was to be among the haves instead of the have-nots to show him in a negative light. "You know, at the point where even a joke is used against you, it tends to make you a little stiffer when you are around people," Hutcheson said.[101]

Bush, because of his background in dealing with the press, certainly understands coverage better than most politicians. The *Washington Times*'s Sammon wrote that Bush said he was bothered by a Hillary Clinton speech questioning whether he knew about 9/11 in advance. "I also understand how the news cycles work," Bush said. "Bits of news kind of churn through our system quite quickly. It wasn't the truth. The truth is what really matters, and I think the American people understand that."[102]

Bush, the Yale history major, also could put the presidential press relationship in historical context. He told Hume that Abraham Lincoln inspired him and provided a lesson on how difficult it is to unite the country to achieve objectives. "When you read the other presidents' writings, they always complain about the press and the fact that Washington is too political; it's not very civil," Bush said.[103]

This philosophical attitude seems to allow Bush to be able to run the White House without worrying too much about what reporters think. "He's also a real student of organization theory, management theory, and particularly in the White House," Hutcheson said. "I mean he came into this job with really clear ideas about how he wanted to organize the White House—the chief of staff—but on the media part it is the exact same way."[104]

Bush's father consciously tried to win reporters over by schmoozing with them at barbecues. He was rewarded with biased coverage that he and his family believe contributed to his 1992 defeat. The younger Bush likes to towel snap reporters because that is who he is; he likes to joke and have fun. Sometimes he gets angry at reporters just like any source will get mad about an unfavorable story. But he doesn't need towel snapping or yelling to get his message out. Tactics such as plugging leaks and message discipline do just fine.

Reporters who think Bush has a vendetta against the press may be taking themselves too seriously. Clymer, for one, didn't really care why Bush called him a name at the Labor Day rally and didn't let it bother him. "My theory was always, if we wanted the people we did business with to love us, we'd be Good Humor salesmen instead of reporters," Clymer said.[105]

Bush may not love the press, but he doesn't hate it either. Perhaps Dan Froomkin, who doesn't personally cover Bush but writes a column on the White House press for the *Washington Post*, summed up Bush's attitude best: "He doesn't fear the press."[106]

6

THE PLAIN TALK OF BUSHISMS

In 1989, when Bush met the Dallas–Fort Worth sports press for the first time to formally announce the agreement of his group to buy the Texas Rangers, he certainly did not appear to the sportswriters to fear the press. In fact, the sportswriters were impressed with his public relations skills. He adroitly handled the most pressing question: would he move the Rangers out of the metroplex?

On the one hand, Bush kept his options open by refusing to promise to keep the team in the suburb of Arlington, but he did give a hearty pledge to keep it in the Dallas–Fort Worth area. "To us, this is not a takeover," Bush said. "To us, this is the transfusion of new blood into a very stable franchise. So long as Rusty and I are managing general partners of the Rangers, the team is not to move from the metroplex, period."[1]

Sportswriters immediately noted the contrast between Eddie Chiles, 78, who "sometimes fumbled for words" at the press conference, and Bush, who was 42 and well spoken. "In Bush, the Rangers have a new owner who is articulate, a veteran of the presidential campaign trail, young and robust," the *Dallas Morning News* reported.[2] Columnist Blackie Sherrod wrote that Bush showed the "early earmarks" of a politician, being able to talk at length without revealing his plans. "Young Bush's presence, his poise, his public exposure, certainly stands him in good stead as Ranger spokesman."[3]

Such a quote seems odd, to say the least, when Bush's intelligence and speaking style have been satirized in countless books, calendars, websites, and comedy routines.[4] Andrews McMeel Publishing, which issued one of two Bushism-a-day calendars and a series of Bushisms books, even produced a "Bush in a Box" cardboard figure to which the Bush-obsessed customer could affix word balloons of Bush's misstatements. The box also included a booklet that promised "his best (or worst) misstatements" that would make the reader "laugh out loud!" The speech balloons include some of the most widely quoted Bushisms, such as "I know how hard it is for you to put food on your family" and "Rarely is the question asked, 'Is our children learning?'" The last statement, which opponents used as a way of commenting on whether Bush could lead education reform, was used as the title of an anti-Bush polemic written during the 2000 campaign by former Clinton aide Paul Begala.[5]

The metamorphosis of Bush from an articulate, poised young executive to a cartoonish (literally, in the case of the Bush in a Box) boob has puzzled many of the journalists who covered him as a baseball owner and governor. "Nobody here thought he was dumb or dyslexic or any of those things," said Paul Burka, editor of *Texas Monthly*, although he granted that Bush was not a gifted speaker.[6]

It's not that Bush didn't misspeak occasionally as baseball executive and governor. It's just that the Texas press didn't use them to represent the essence of his personality.

The truth is that all presidents, indeed, everyone who speaks in public, makes verbal mistakes. Helen Thomas published a number of such gaffes in her memoir of humorous presidential anecdotes. For example, she wrote that Lyndon Johnson repeatedly mispronounced *tarpaulin* as "tarpaulians" when referring to how the Russians wrapped their missiles for shipment after the Cuban Missile Crisis ended. Thomas noted that even the Great Communicator, Ronald Reagan, had bloopers, like the time he referred to Liberian head of state Samuel K. Doe as "Chairman Moe." Reagan toasted the country of Bolivia at a 1982 state dinner in Brazil but explained the geography error by saying that Bolivia was his next stop. He was actually going next to Colombia.[7]

Bush's father was known for his malapropisms at the same time the younger Bush was being praised as the new, articulate spokesman for the Texas Rangers. In fact, the first book of Bushisms was actually an attack on George H. W. Bush, mocking his speech but also claiming it was significant because Bush showed through his misstatements that he had no core beliefs and nothing important to say.[8]

Thomas wrote that George H. W. Bush "was the founder of a dynasty of disjointed communication." The senior Bush joked about the press's coverage of his misstatements in one speech to reporters, saying, "And thanks to my best efforts—and your indelicacy in pointing out my best efforts—the English language may never by the same again, either."[9]

The press has not always devoted its best efforts to reporting presidential misspeak. In the earlier, more friendly era of presidential press relations described in chapter 2, reporters would sometimes give politicians a chance to rephrase a statement rather than hang them by their dangling participles. Longtime Associated Press reporter Walter Mears wrote in his memoir that reporters were friendly with Barry Goldwater during the 1964 campaign and treated him fairly, even though most disagreed with his policies. Mears wrote that some reporters would ask Goldwater to stop and slow down when he said something questionable, so he got a chance to make himself clear. That wouldn't happen today, Mears concluded, because every statement is recorded and the scandals and the lies of subsequent presidents have led to new ground rules.[10]

Still, some politicians get a break. Bush's opponent in the 2004 race, John Kerry, had his own misstatements, but few seemed to notice. For example, at a campaign stop in Ohio, Kerry spied a young man wearing a "Titanic Swim Team" shirt. When Kerry asked the kid what events he swam in, the kid said he was actually on his school's track team. Kerry remained clueless: "So you stole the shirt? I thought you were on the swim team. You faked me out there."[11]

Kerryisms, however, did not become a staple of campaign coverage, and no one published a joke book of Kerry bloopers. Perhaps Kerry made fewer gaffes than Bush. After all, even Bush and his supporters readily acknowledge that the president is prone to mangled syntax. A more important question is whether the national media went overboard in covering Bush's misstatements and did so for less-than-honorable reasons.

When Bush was a baseball owner, most sportswriters either didn't notice anything strange about his language or else thought emphasizing mangled syntax was inappropriate. Phil Rogers, who covered the Rangers for the *Dallas Times Herald* and then the *Morning News*, said that since he has watched Bush on the national stage, he has pondered why Bushisms have become a phenomenon. Rogers said it is easy to "trap" sources to make them look stupid in print if a reporter has constant access to the source. "I think anybody who had their words tape-recorded and played back on a daily basis would look stupid a number of times," Rogers said. "Maybe a Mensa member could avoid that, but I don't think any of us could. I think, by and large—obviously it's different now when you're talking about subtleties of language that may affect how leaders of other countries see your viewpoint, and there is a need to be precise in language—but by and large, those of us who cover sports don't hold a guy to each dangling participle."[12]

Gerry Fraley, who covered Bush as the baseball beat writer for the *Morning News* and now writes a column, said he did not notice misstatements like those reported by the national media. "I don't really remember it being that big a deal," he said.[13] Jim Reeves, *Fort Worth Star-Telegram* columnist, said Bush was not "the most polished speaker in the world," but agreed that mangled sentences are not something people noticed in the casual one-on-one interviews Bush usually had with sportswriters.[14]

Randy Galloway, the sports columnist and radio host who had self-described "shit storms" with Bush, said sportswriters would not emphasize minor speech errors in stories. "The totally politically incorrect comments come back to hit them over the head, but the misspeaking that George is accused of—most of the time we weren't in front of TV cameras and playing it back. It was just media guys sitting around interviewing George. . . . If he would misspeak, so what? We were probably doing the same. It wasn't that big a deal."[15]

Galloway compared reporting the misstatements to catching a public figure in an embarrassing moment on television. It might be funny, but wouldn't necessarily be newsworthy. He offered as an example that Bush was once caught picking his nose during a televised game. Galloway said he and other sportswriters unmercifully teased Bush, who was mortified. But they never wrote about it because it wasn't important.[16]

Although major league sports attracts major league publicity, Bush's job still did not require the number of public speaking engagements and interviews that he would face as a politician. Bush would occasionally misspeak as governor, and the reporters sometimes noticed, but it wasn't written about to the point that it became his signature. Wayne Slater covered Bush as governor and presidential candidate in 2000 and said he noticed a "quick evolution" in the way the media began to cover the misstatements when Bush began to run for president. "One of the things about the media is that we as a little group decide fairly quickly what the conventional wisdom is, and it's hard to shake us," Slater said. "In those months in 1998 and 1999 he would begin to misspeak, and if he did it three times even over minor things, the conventional wisdom was he was susceptible to these Bushisms."[17]

R. G. Ratcliffe, who, like Slater, covered Bush as both governor and 2000 presidential candidate, said Bushisms weren't as noticeable when Bush was governor because he didn't have as many opportunities to misspeak. "There just weren't that many forums for that kind of stuff to come out. For the most part, most of these Bushisms came from him trying to deliver memorized portions of speeches—or memorized spin. And most of our contact with him here [in Texas] involved conversation."[18]

Ratcliffe said interviews and conversations are not the type of settings where people make such dreadful verbal gaffes. "All his verbal mistakes [that] have gotten wide publicity have been sitting in front of a crowd of people or talking to a crowd of people trying to deliver this 30-minute-long memorized speech and mangling part of it or having set answers to issues and messing them up in how he answered them."[19]

Many reporters who interviewed Bush in informal settings confirmed Ratcliffe's assessment. Arnold Garcia, as editorial page editor of the *Austin American-Statesman*, often talked with Bush on the phone or in the office but did not follow him on the campaign trail. "He didn't talk like Yogi Berra when I talked to him," Garcia said, adding that he would be ashamed to see what his own speech looked like in the transcript for this interview. "You can make anybody look like an ass if you want to. And there are some people who have a natural facility for the sound bite, and he's not one of them. But he was never much of an orator."[20]

The *Fort Worth Star-Telegram*'s Jay Root said that you have to consider the context of Texas politics when you try to understand why Bushisms did not become a phenomenon until Bush ran for president. "We have had a lot of colorful politicians who were not particularly talented at public speaking. We've had racial slurs," Root explained. "I do think there is a combo factor. A Bushism is a Texasism. It's not outside the range of accepted political discourse. It's not bad considering what we've heard in Texas. We've had a string of small town figures that have brought their vocabulary with them. Or oil men who've brought their lingo with them. The second factor is when you go from the oil patch to Kazakhstan you put a lot of stress to carry the bar higher. Third, seen through the national lens, they are not so funny or even appropriate."[21]

White House reporters do tend to make the argument that the president and presidential candidates must be held to a higher standard than other politicians. After all, the reasoning goes, a national leader who is careless with speech can sometimes be merely humorous but at other times can convey dangerous messages. Columnist Robert Novak, for example, wrote that Bush seemed tired and bored when he told NBC's Matt Lauer on the *Today* show during the 2004 Republican National

Convention that he "doubted" the war on terror could be won. Bush meant that the war would not have a formal ending with a surrender ceremony, and he explained that immediately in speeches and on the Rush Limbaugh radio show. Novak wrote that Bush aides wouldn't speculate on why the president misspoke, but Novak concluded that Bush looked like he was bored.[22]

Bush critics argue that the misstatements demonstrate ignorance or intellectual laziness. Mark Crispin Miller, in *The Bush Dyslexicon*, wrote that the Bushisms illustrate a number of character flaws, including the fact that he wasted his expensive private education like "a feckless prince" might waste food in front of beggars. "To snicker at this president for his stupidity is not productive, for his unfitness isn't really funny—and in any case he isn't stupid. True, he is the most ignorant president in U.S. history, probably the most illiterate, and easily among the least concerned about the contents of his mind. Moreover, his off-the-cuff remarks betray what is apparently an inability to reason."[23]

Justin A. Frank, a psychoanalyst and professor of psychiatry at George Washington University Medical Center, concluded that Bushisms "were no laughing matter."[24] Frank, who purported to analyze Bush's mental state, including his use of words, in *Bush on the Couch*, claimed Bush's speech patterns are a way for Bush to control communication by deflecting questions and distracting interviewers. Frank's study of Bush's speeches and interviews led him to assert that Bush's "perversion of language reflects his disregard for other people's words—and what are laws, after all, but formations of words? In Bush's troubled perception, law is as easily perverted as any other language."[25]

Former Clinton adviser Begala, on the other hand, suggested that Bushisms show Bush is lazy. Begala wrote that the fact that people ask whether Bush is dumb presupposes that it is a legitimate question. Begala answered the question by concluding: "Bush is worse than dumb. He's lazy, arrogant, and defiantly ignorant. He clearly has an adequate God-given intellect, but because everything's been handed to him on a silver platter (usually by a butler) he's never developed it."[26]

But others, particularly some who covered Bush in Texas, argue that the emphasis on misstatements might indicate more about the writer than Bush and might be motivated by other forces, such as bias and boredom. Slater acknowledged that because as a presidential candidate Bush was dealing with such issues as nuclear war and the economy, every word was scrutinized and often reported verbatim. But some of that verbatim reporting was done as shorthand to convey the impression Bush was stupid, Slater said. "There was this predisposition with the national press that he was stupid, and so one way to frame 'He's stupid' was to seize on these goofy statements he made—which he did—as evidence of that larger intellectual deficiency," Slater said. "So that's really what Bushisms are about in the national press."[27]

Slater said Bushisms are unfair if they are used to convey the idea that Bush is stupid. "That's a substantial segment; there are a lot of people who feel that way—Democrats and those who don't know him well. I am here to tell you he is actually a very smart and very astute guy," Slater said. "Here's the deal: How many times has Mario Cuomo, or Bill Bradley, or some other people who we are predisposed to think are really smart—how many times have they said things that are slips of the tongue, that are mistakes that collectively could become Cuomoisms or Bradleyisms, but they aren't? My guess is that is not because they've never, ever misspoken—even three times to make a trend—it's because any time they would say something that was kind of silly or was a misstatement, it doesn't resonate as reflecting the larger sense that Cuomo is stupid, because the press thinks Cuomo is smart, which he is."[28]

In fact, both of the main Democratic contenders for the 2000 presidential nomination made a number of flubs. Dana Milbank wrote that Bradley was a poor speaker and compared him to a "foreign student of English" when Bradley said "Let us come with me" when he was supposed to say "Come with me—let us walk toward that dream together." Al Gore once confused Michael Jackson with Michael Jordan and in another instance referred to Missouri when he was speaking in Minnesota.[29]

Ratcliffe conceded that there may have been some bias in the emphasis on misstatements. "I'll say this: Most of the time when Bush did these Bushisms—the majority of them were at night at the last event of the day, and he was tired. I remember one speech where he got lost in the speech and delivered the same part of the speech three times before he found his way out. But you know everybody makes verbal mistakes. I actually think most of his verbal mistakes are to do with some sort of undiagnosed dyslexia, but they were sort of seized on by a lot of people who wanted to portray Bush as stupid. And you know that's always been one of the problems Democrats have with Bush. They want to portray him as stupid, and I think the people that know him know that he may not be well informed, and he may not necessarily be well educated on a lot of issues, but he is not stupid."[30]

Some Texas journalists believe that the bias about Bush's intelligence might be rooted in a regional stereotype. "I do think that there is a great deal of prejudice about Texas and Texans in the Eastern press," said Garcia, who during the 2000 campaign wrote a column taking issue with national press coverage that suggested Bush would appoint right-wing ideologues to the federal courts if he were elected. Garcia added that he is not sure if he would write the same column after seeing Bush's federal judicial nominees, but he wrote at the time that there was nothing in Bush's gubernatorial record to suggest the criticism. Bushisms, Garcia said, are a way to make Bush look bad. "They're more prone to do that to Texans. They're looking for the rube. They desperately want to play that stereotype."[31]

Slater said reporters in the elite Eastern press at first had the same bias against Clinton because he was from Arkansas, but Clinton won them over because he demonstrated early on in conversations that he was intellectually gifted. "Bush never did that," Slater said. "I think what he demonstrated was he's a nice guy. But I don't think in any conversations he had did he demonstrate he was a brilliant guy. He started self-consciously carrying books around toward the end of the campaign. He never did before because I don't think he read any of these books except the DiMaggio biography, and I think, his early conversations were such that he played instinctively to the idea he is a regular guy, which was interpreted by these guys as he is a rube from Texas."[32]

Slater cited an example from the 2000 campaign when Bush and only a handful of reporters were flying back to Austin after most had been dropped off in Washington. "We were chatting," Slater recalled. "Bush has his ball cap on, doing the basic I'm-a-Texas-rube act; I'm just a regular guy. In a way, it's quite charming." A couple of women reporters asked Bush a question about his feelings. When Bush gave his standard response of not wanting to be "put on the couch," one of the reporters said they just wanted to explore Bush's feminine side. "He just jumped—he straightened up and moved the bill of his cap and said, 'I'm from Midland,'" Slater recalled. "And it was his way of saying, 'I'm a man. I'm a man's man.' In a funny way, he then reinforced this idea [that he's a rube]. 'I'm a man, I'm a regular guy, I'm from Texas,' which can be misconstrued, I think, by some media that he doesn't really have a subtle, nuanced sense—a feminine side, sophisticated. That's not really politics but about who you are, but it's interpreted by Washington–New York press that you are just not very sophisticated, you are not very smart. And if you don't disabuse them of that, as Clinton did, then I think that's how it goes."[33]

Los Angeles Times White House correspondent Edwin Chen, however, said that there was no bias in reporting Bushisms. "A president, for better or worse—every word he says in public is monitored and analyzed and scrutinized—taken apart," Chen said. "I'm sure he was not subjected to this kind of scrutiny to this extent as governor or baseball club owner, but he is as president, and everything he says does become magnified, including when he makes verbal gaffes and mistakes. I don't think there's any regional bias at all. It's not regional. Anybody, any president who would speak in this manner would get the same press."[34]

At least one Texas reporter, the *Austin American-Statesman*'s Dave McNeely, agreed, saying Bushisms were "not unfair" because Bush is president, and everything he does is a big deal. "I mean you live in a bubble up there, and you've got 3,000 [reporters] living in the same gerbil cage," McNeely said. "They got to write about something."[35]

The *New York Times*'s Frank Bruni indicated that during the 2000 campaign some reporters were writing about Bushisms out of boredom, trying to relieve the monotony of hearing the candidate repeat his stump speech over and over. The tedium is one reason—not a noble one, he admitted—that the press corps focused on Bush's gaffes. "It caught the ear and quelled the boredom." But he insisted that "not since Yogi Berra—or maybe Dan Quayle—had a public figure produced such a bumper crop of bloopers." The online magazine *Slate* began running a tote board later compiled into a book, and John Berman, an ABC producer, wrote a daily written report to his network that included a regular feature called "The English Patient."[36] Yet Bruni admitted that Bush sometimes did so well that he shocked and impressed reporters, like the time he gave a thoughtful answer to a question about the mapping of the human genome, which Bruni had thought Bush might think was a car.[37]

In such an atmosphere, it seems easy for reporters to go overboard in looking for gaffes, and indeed it appears that is just what happened. The *Houston Chronicle*'s Clay Robison wrote during the 2000 campaign that Bushisms were nitpicking. He cited as an example that at one rally Bush had said Gore's tax plan would require hiring more "IRA agents" instead of "IRS agents." Robison wrote that most people probably didn't notice the mistake, and "certainly no one doubted" what Bush meant, but almost immediately after the rally the Gore camp was e-mailing the mistake to reporters. Robison wrote that among one group of reporters, none had thought the anecdote worthy of coverage. But the four scribes were interrupted that night at dinner by a call from an editor. Someone in the press corps had written about the IRA gaffe, and the editor demanded to know why his reporter didn't have the story. Robison concluded both sides were guilty of "questionable finger-pointing," like the Democrats playing up Bushisms or the Republicans' emphasis on Gore's "exaggerations." The characterizations had little to do with the candidates' fitness for office and turned the campaign into a game of "gotcha."[38]

Unfortunately, the general public is the loser in such a game because the press was focusing on jokes rather than issues. "Look, those guys disagreed on a lot of important things," the *New York Times*'s Adam Clymer said of Bush and Gore. "But at times we had a burlesque of a campaign between the exaggerator and the verbal illiterate."[39]

Such coverage was wrong, said Mark Halperin, political director of ABC News, in analyzing the campaign three years later. The press, he said, had viewed Bush through the prism of misspeaking and Gore through exaggeration, although both candidates had both of those faults. "It's not fair to those candidates when we hold them to different standards based on those stereotypes."[40]

The stereotype has held through Bush's second term and likely will dog him to his presidential library. Of course, the stereotype has some truth. As Ratcliffe said, it was sometimes hard not to write about the Bushisms because they were simply funny. "One night when Bush got all mangled up on the 'us versus them' part of his speech about four of the print reporters who were listening to the speech, me included, broke up laughing so hard—we actually had to leave the speech because we were laughing hysterically because he had so badly mangled the speech. He gets ones like—I can't remember the exact quote—but he said, 'I look forward to the day when man and fish can live together in harmony.'"[41]

The problem with enjoying the occasional Bushism is that, like enjoying an occasional drink, it can lead to an addiction. The gaffes become the story rather than the issues the politician is addressing. The fact that Bushisms are overdone is evident from the reporting of ones that are noticeable or funny only to the addict. In one 2004 speech, Bush said that terrorists "never stop trying to hurt our country, and neither will we." Bush's meaning was plain—that the United States would never stop trying to catch terrorists—and the reporter noted that no one reacted to the misstatement. Yet the reporter devoted a sidebar to the quote—an episode that, according to the reporter's own story, he alone of the people in the crowd noticed.

Such emphasis raises questions about fairness and bias. News reporters are supposed to be objective. Unless the gaffe is newsworthy because it attracted the attention of the crowd or comment from other sources or for some other factor, it is not fair to devote coverage to it without scrutinizing the gaffes of the opponent in the same manner. Most basic journalism textbooks stress that reporters should be consistent in the way they quote people. *News Reporting and Writing*, for example, which was written by a group of professors at the University of Missouri School of Journalism, warns budding reporters that the *Washington Post* was criticized for quoting the grammatical errors of an ordinary citizen but cleaning up the quotes of a politician.[42]

The *Associated Press Stylebook*, the main reference source for most print and many broadcast journalists, states plainly that reporters should "never alter quotations even to correct minor grammatical errors or word usage"—indicating that reporters should not clean up Bushisms. But it continues: "Casual minor tongue slips may be removed by using ellipses but even that should be done with extreme caution. If there is a question about a quote, either don't use it or ask the speaker to clarify." The manual states that abnormal spellings like "gonna" are permitted "when relevant or help to convey a desired touch in a feature."[43]

It is significant that the AP recommends asking a speaker to clarify remarks that are confusing; it doesn't say to repeat them verbatim. A reporter could defend writing about a Bushism by saying it is necessary to convey an effect in a feature story, but how many feature stories are needed about Bush's mangled syntax? The self-described image of Bruni fumbling with eagerness to get his tape recorder ready to catch Bush misunderstanding the word *genome* is a troubling example of journalists injecting their own bias into the campaign. It was unfair to comb Bush's speeches for misstatements without subjecting other candidates to the same standards.

The authors of the joke calendars and books are not held to the same standard of objectivity as the mainstream news press, of course. Yet the authors worked so hard to fill their pages with gaffes that a close reading shows they, too, are stretching their material. For example, a reporter in the summer of 2001 asked Bush if he thought about Al Gore and the 2000 election, to which Bush replied, "Not really." That exchange was listed as a joke, although it appears to be a natural response—Bush wasn't dwelling on what was unimportant.[44] Another entry was a Bush quote that was obviously intended as a joke: "You've heard Al Gore say he invented the Internet. Well, if he was so smart, why do all the addresses begin with 'W'?"[45]

One calendar included a series of four entries in a row, all drawn from a famous incident in which a reporter gave Bush a pop quiz on the names of foreign leaders. Spreading that episode over four days suggests a dearth of entries for the calendar. Bush tried to turn the quiz back on the reporter. When he was asked whether he could name the president of Chechnya, Bush said, "No, can you?"[46] When he was asked to name the foreign minister of Mexico, Bush also asked the reporter whether he could name the person. The reporter admitted he couldn't, but said he was not running for president. Bush said that not knowing the name did not mean that a person was incompetent as a reporter or a president, but his syntax was garbled, obscuring the valid point that such knowledge is not a pure test of competence.[47] Instead, the calendar and Bush critics focus on Bush's speaking ability, not his ideas.

Another calendar entry that obviously misconstrued Bush quoted him in a presidential debate as saying, "My opponent seems to think that Social Security is a federal program. I believe that money is yours and you should be able to invest it yourself." The calendar entry noted archly that Social Security is, in fact, a federal program.[48] Obviously, Bush's point was that Social Security funds belong to the taxpayers. In another entry, Bush referred to the executive branch as the administrative branch.[49] But doesn't the executive branch conduct the administrative functions of the federal government?

The *Presidential (Mis)Speak* calendar for 2005, which billed itself hopefully as a "Farewell Edition," may in fact have been indicative of the end result of a campaign in which some Bush opponents mocked the president's religious beliefs with a clueless insensitivity toward Christian voters—one of the decisive blocs in the election. The February 4, 2005, entry quoted Bush as saying, "The true strength of America is the fact that we've got millions of fellow citizens who are willing to love a neighbor just like they would like to be loved themselves. That's the real strength of this country, because we're a deep and compassionate nation." The editor's commentary noted that he felt "like a noncontributory to 'our deep and compassionate nation'—I admit it, I just don't always 'love my neighbors.' There was this one time, in fact, when . . . ."[50] Is quoting the Bible a Bushism? The entry seemed to indicate a move from what could be considered good-natured laughing at malapropisms to poking fun of religion, and that's a style of humor that can backfire.

The problem with Bushisms, at least for those who intend to use them to denigrate Bush, is that they are a one-joke attack that gets dull over time. A Hollywood television producer wrote, tongue in cheek, that he was rooting for Kerry to win because the Massachusetts senator was a pompous blowhard of the kind that makes for a great straight man and great comedy material, while Bush's misstatements are about as funny as the shtick of Norm Crosby, a moderately successful comedian whose act is based on malapropisms.[51]

Slater said he doubted the Bushisms had much effect on the public. "The Bushisms, as mild as they were, did reflect badly in some quarters, although I wonder how much they really did. I wonder if, in fact, they only reinforced the attitude among Bush's real supporters: 'Yeah, he's a regular guy, not a phony-baloney politician.'"[52]

Bush himself told Ron Hutcheson that he understood why the press wrote about his misstatements and that they were legitimate stories. But he told Hutcheson that he wished reporters would put them into context by mentioning that he usually made gaffes when he was tired.[53]

Certainly Bush learned to embrace the misstatements. In fact, he turned them from a negative stereotype to a positive symbol. Bush reinforced his regular-guy persona by using self-deprecating humor to let the audience know that he was aware of his own faults. This lowered public and press expectations for his performances in speeches and in debates so that when he made a mistake it was no big deal, and his opponent had to significantly outperform him in order to be perceived as a winner. Bush ultimately used his misstatements as an example of plain speech. Such an emphasis was particularly useful to contrast himself with Kerry, who had a reputation for lawyerly language and nuanced positions on issues.

The Bush camp played the expectations game successfully against both Al Gore in 2000 and John Kerry in 2004, but Bush had actually been doing it almost his entire life in a variety of circumstances. One Bush family biography noted that George W. Bush became the family clown as a way of dealing with not being able to live up to his father's and grandfather's academic and athletic success at Andover and later at Yale. He wanted to lower expectations of himself so he wouldn't disappoint family members, and "W. found he could lower expectations by quietly mocking the system."[54]

Long after he graduated from Yale, Bush used lowered expectations to help him defeat Ann Richards in the 1994 gubernatorial campaign. To be sure, *Bushism* was not a household term at that time, but Bush was a political newcomer in terms of experience and appeared like a kid next to the popular incumbent. Liberal columnist Molly Ivins popularized the nickname "Shrub" to convey the impression that Bush was not mature and was trading on his father's name. Political observers, including his own mother, Barbara, expected him to do poorly against Richards, but Richards was the one who ended up making a costly "Richardsism." She gave a speech to a rally of teachers in which she told them: "You know how it is. You are working your tail off and doing a good job and then some jerk comes along and tells you it's not good enough."[55] An aide claimed Richards did not directly call Bush a jerk, but it was reported that way, giving the impression she was mean and desperate. Bush reacted by saying he wanted to stick to the issues and made a joke about organizing "jerks for George."[56]

Before the candidates held their debate, Richards tried some trash talking to unnerve the young candidate. She told Bush, "Are you ready for this? This is going to be rough on you."[57] But Richards, as the incumbent facing a neophyte, had to deliver a clear knockout. One of her campaign aides, sounding bitter in an interview on the 10-year anniversary of the debate, said Richards was "superb" but that wasn't enough because Bush had met his expectations. "He had a couple of answers that were kind of stupid, but that's not how it played. Immediately afterward, everybody was spinning, and I realized that the press was in awe of Bush because he didn't make a major mistake. He didn't do what his dad did and look at his watch. So people thought, 'This guy's not so bad. There's nothing scary about him.' After the debate, he came off looking like a knight in shining armor."[58]

On the other hand, Bushisms sometimes make the president seem more like a court jester than King George. But Bush makes fun of his own shortcomings, and judging by his electoral success, the self-deprecating humor is more endearing than ridiculous. In any case, he regularly poked fun at his gaffes during the 2000 campaign and later. For example, Bush joked in the second 2000 presidential debate, "Well, we all make mistakes. I've been known to mangle a syl-LAB-ble or two myself, you know."[59]

In a speech to the Radio-Television Correspondents dinner, he made fun of a number of his misstatements, reading "Rarely is the question asked: Is our children learning?" from a book of Bushisms. "Let's analyze that sentence for a moment," Bush said. "If you're a stickler, you probably think the singular verb *is* should have been the plural *are*. But if you read it closely, you'll see that I'm using the intransitive plural subjunctive tense and so the word *is* are correct." He finished by saying, "I don't think it's too healthy to take yourself too seriously. But what I do take seriously is my responsibility as president of all of the American people and to the office that I hold. And that is what I came tonight to tell you. Thank you for inviting me and thank you for your kind horse-pitality."[60]

When he gave the commencement address at his alma mater on May 21, 2001, he mentioned an English class he took and said he wanted to give credit to the school that taught him everything he learned about the spoken word.[61] He said in a June 12, 2001, interview with Spanish TV after mispronouncing the Spanish prime minister's name, "If I don't practice, I am going to destroy this language."[62] Bush joked about his use of the word *misunderestimate* at a March 29, 2001, press conference, laughing and saying he was just checking to see if reporters were listening.[63] The fact that "misunderestimate" became a badge of honor rather than embarrassment was evident in the fact that Bill Sammon, the White House correspondent for the conservative *Washington Times*, used it as the title of a pro-Bush book published during the 2004 campaign.[64]

The Bush campaign team made Bush's speech patterns part of its campaign strategy. Mark McKinnon said that Bush garbled a line during a commercial for the 2000 campaign. It was a story about being in the delivery room when his daughters were born. Bush blew the line and laughed. They decided to leave it in rather than fix it because "it was a human moment. It was so characteristic of him to garble a line the way he did. So rather than cover it up, we decided to make it an asset. The conventional wisdom is that you have to make your candidate perfect. But today, unlike years ago, humanity is more important than perfection."[65]

Karen Hughes told the media, after a particularly embarrassing moment when Bush mispronounced *subliminal* four times at a press conference, that his misstatements were the way Texans talk when they are tired. For later Bushisms, she joked with reporters that his mind worked faster than his mouth. A doctor later told her that there is some truth to her joke—that intelligent people sometimes stumble over words when they are thinking too fast.[66]

But by the time he was president, the staff quit trying to explain Bushisms. A *New York Times* story reported that a White House official merely said, "That's how the president speaks," when referring to the fact that Bush had used the present tense when he meant to use the future tense in reference to U.S. agreements with North Korea.[67]

New York mayor Rudy Giuliani, no stranger to the elite Eastern media, thought that the Bushisms were a help to the president. Giuliani wrote that the Eastern media underestimated Bush just as they had Reagan, because Bush didn't "speak in a way that suits their biases. The Eastern media mistakes pretense for substance and polish for smarts. Their habit of dismissing those who don't press those buttons usually works to such a candidate's advantage."[68]

Giuliani noted in his book on leadership the importance of the use of casual speech. Because Giuliani was a lawyer by training, he was eager at the beginning of his political career to use speeches to present a logical case with a lot of detail. But he found his speeches were never outstanding until he started being more conversational. He quit using formal scripts at the urging of media advisers like Roger Ailes—also an adviser to the Bush family. Giuliani noted that John F. Kennedy did not overrehearse but instead swam or relaxed before an important speech.[69]

Kennedy was not known for JFKisms, but in his relaxed speaking style, he was following a long line of presidents who have sought the common touch through commonsense language. Mark Crispin Miller, writing in *The Bush Dyslexicon*, claimed that Bushisms "seem to represent a culmination of the long strange history of anti-intellectualism in America." He claimed that the first presidential campaign to use this tactic successfully was Andrew Jackson's 1828 battle against John Quincy Adams, which was styled as a contest "between 'the plowman and the professor,' casting Adams as a European sort of fancy-pants, book-smart and effete, while praising General Jackson as a man of mighty deeds and lightning intuitions."[70]

The pattern has been repeated often throughout American history, with candidates emphasizing their humble origins whether the origins are real, like those of Abraham Lincoln, or more imagined, like the stories of William Henry Harrison's faux log cabin. Sometimes presidents have really worked as cowboys, as Theodore Roosevelt had, and sometimes they just dress the part, like Calvin Coolidge, who wore both cowboy *and* Indian costumes for photo ops. The fact is, Americans don't want royalty in the White House; they typically prefer the common man, or at least a wealthy, educated man who can speak naturally at the common man's level.

Even such an intellectual as Franklin Roosevelt realized the use of casual speech and applied it to masterly effect in his "Fireside Chat" radio addresses. One scholar noted that Roosevelt painstakingly edited the chats, which were really speeches, so that they would sound informal. Roosevelt made careful use of the personal pronouns *I*, *you*, and *we* in such a way that they blurred the boundaries between himself, the government, and the people. Sometimes "we" meant government, sometimes the American people. The affectation was so noticeable that John Dos Passos mocked it as FDR speaking to "youandme."[71]

Given the past success of this technique, it is no wonder that history major George W. Bush embraced Bushisms. Bush himself was the victim of the city-slicker-versus-cowboy strategy when Kent Hance cast him as a Yankee interloper in the only election he ever lost—to represent a West Texas congressional district. Bush out-Texaned Ann Richards in 1994 and had solidified his image so well that the 1998 campaign against Gary Mauro was a landslide: Bush had come to be the personification of Texas.

Both of Bush's national elections cast him as the anti-intellectual plain-spoken Texan versus first the wooden, nerdy Gore and later the nuanced Francophile Kerry. The Massachusetts senator tried to counter Bush's virile cowboy persona with a windsurfing, biking, war-hero image, but it couldn't overcome his background and his own deeply ingrained Eastern elite style, and the Eastern style is a loser. As one columnist wrote, there is a reason why Hollywood makes Westerns instead of Easterns.[72]

A reporter for the liberal *New Republic* followed Bush on the 2004 campaign trail and concluded that Bush emphasized his simple style in his stump speech. The speech contrasted Bush's plain speech with Kerry's "nuanced" verbiage. Bush would connect plain speech to whatever town he was in by saying something like, "Now, I know Holland, Michigan, well enough to know not many people talk like that around here." The reporter noted that Bush would correct himself if he used a word that he thought sounded too fancy—even a word like "litigious," which on at least one occasion Bush defined for his audience as a fancy way of saying too many lawsuits.[73]

Knight-Ridder's Ron Hutcheson agreed that Bush turned Bushisms and his reputation for plain speaking to his advantage in the campaign. "I think one of his most effective speech lines was 'I always say what I mean and I mean what I say,'" Hutcheson said, explaining that Bush contrasted his plain speech with the "pin-striped crowd" that spoke in nuances to foreign leaders. Hutcheson said Bush would say, "I go over there and I tell foreign leaders like it is and sometimes that rubs them the wrong way, but I'm a straight shooter, fellow Americans, isn't that what you want?" Hutcheson concluded that Bush is a sophisticated politician who understands what "resonates" with people in the heartland of the country. "He's a great politician; he's got a great feel for the average American because he enjoys mixing it up with them."[74]

How much of an effect did Bushisms have on the president's image? A strong case can be made that they were more positive than negative. For one thing, mocking someone for misspeaking can make the critic look mean, especially in a country where most people fear public speaking.[75] Arnold Garcia recalled that during the 1994 governor's race he thought Bush might upset the popular Richards in part because of a backlash against the mean humor. "The governor [Richards] and her crowd—Molly Ivins calling him 'Shrub'—not everyone is enamored of that kind of humor," Garcia said.[76]

The meanness makes the critic look bad, but the malaprop-prone person is often seen as lovable. Peggy Noonan, who has written speeches for a number of presidents, including Reagan and George H. W. Bush, wrote in a book on speechwriting that Americans are not impressed by smoothness in speeches but instead find an "ingenuous lack of perfection" endearing. If she saw a candidate who was perfect, she would recommend the person "be less perfect."[77] In an interesting coincidence, Jerry Coleman, the longtime San Diego Padres play-by-play announcer known for such malapropisms as "Rich Folkers is throwing up in the bullpen" won the Ford C. Frick award, placing him in the broadcaster's wing of the baseball Hall of Fame, only about a month after Bush's second inauguration. Other hall-of-fame broadcasters include such serious figures as Curt Gowdy and Vin Scully. Upon learning of the award, Coleman said he sometimes made mistakes by saying things too quickly, but that he knows his own shortcomings.[78] In the same way that baseball fans accepted and were amused by Coleman, a majority of voters accepted Bushisms as a humorous quirk that didn't really detract from the president's ability to govern.

The fact that Bush was able to turn Bushisms into a positive is remarkable. American history is replete with politicians who have been destroyed by a careless slip of the tongue. Republican James G. Blaine likely would have defeated Grover Cleveland in 1884 had he not failed to "repudiate" an intemperate comment made by a clergyman who, in remarks introducing Blaine, offended Catholic voters in New York by declaring the Democratic Party the party of "rum, Romanism and rebellion."[79] In the modern era, the presidential debates have become an exercise in caution as candidates try to avoid gaffes like Gerald Ford's 1976 remark that the Soviet Union did not dominate Eastern European countries. Bush had to survive not just one gaffe, but a whole catalog of them eagerly compiled by bored journalists.

The politician who commits too many gaffes runs the risk of being "Quayled"—stereotyped as an idiot with no way to recover. The gaffes of George H. W. Bush's vice president, Dan Quayle, were not compiled in a series of popular humor books, but they nevertheless ruined his career. Quayle, after considering several strategies for fighting his negative image as a clown who couldn't spell *potato*, decided to just do his job and try to prove himself to Washington reporters by growing "an inch a day," but it proved hopeless.[80]

George W. Bush, on the other hand embraced misspeaking as part of his character, used it to show he was a regular guy with a self-deprecatory sense of humor, and rode that image to two terms in the White House.

Austin television reporter Neal Spelce said Bush's handling of his misstatements shows an appealing sense of self-confidence. "I think Bush realizes that's who he is. That's what he does. That's what he says. And it doesn't bother him. It's just, 'Hey, here's who I am.' It's not like some politician trying to put an affectation on and saying, 'Well, I misspoke, well, I didn't really mean it, well, I'm sorry.' He just says, 'Hey, it's me, I mangle the language, sometimes it's kind of fun,' and then he goes about his business. And I think there is a certain amount of self-assurance and self-confidence in an individual who recognizes their own flaws."[81]

CBS anchor Bob Schieffer compared Bush to Reagan in his ability to overcome what for other politicians would be fatal misstatements. "The understatement of the year is to say that Reagan was not really a detail man," said Schieffer, who has covered both Reagan and Bush. "He really looked at it in broad terms. But in the end, when people were wondering if he got a little dotty, and he'd say things, he had such credibility with people that they'd say, 'Well, I know what the old fellow meant to say because I've known him for a long time.' And I think in a funny way they've given George Bush the same kind of pass. They're saying, 'Well, he got it a little mixed up this time, but I think I know what he's trying to say,' and that's a great trick if a politician can pull that off, and thus far I think Bush has been able to do it."[82]

Of course, that doesn't mean that everyone saw Bushisms in a positive light. The *Star-Telegram*'s Jay Root speculated that they were taken more seriously once he ran for president because the national audience was different from the Texas audience. "The audience is the Texas electorate," Root said of Bush's time as governor. "It's okay to offend France in Lubbock."[83] But as the 2004 election showed, it's okay to offend France in a number of other "red states" as well.

Dan Froomkin, who writes a *Washington Post* column on media coverage of the White House, said that in the end Bushisms are probably something that you can interpret depending upon your own bias. He pointed out that during the 2004 campaign Bush's rallies were carefully screened to ensure as receptive a crowd as possible.[84] Such Bush fans were likely to see Bushisms as the president hoped they would see them—an example of plain speech. Bush opponents—and there more than 50 million who voted against him—may well have interpreted them as the Bushism collectors suggested: an example of a president who was at best lazy intellectually and at worst, a dangerous idiot.

The split feelings about Bushisms are even evident in presidential memorabilia. Talking action figures of presidents and other historical figures became popular during Bush's first term. Toymakers created talking Bush figures in a variety of costumes ranging from business suits to terrorist-fighting fatigues. The figures usually included Bush's most historical quotes such as telling the American people in the wake of 9/11 that "We will not tire, we will not falter, we will not fail." One figure, which is more a three-dimensional caricature with an oversized head than an action figure, comes dressed in jeans and a brown leather jacket, looking like it's ready for some brush-clearing on a toy Crawford ranch. It has two buttons for quotes; the one on the right is labeled "Inspirational," while the one on the left is labeled "Funny."

7

TOWEL SNAPPING

Kevin Sherrington, who covered Bush as a sports columnist for the *Dallas Morning News*, thinks Bush got along so well with the press when he was with the Texas Rangers because he was just like a sportswriter. Sherrington recalled that Bush's office in the old ballpark was "not very cush" and not what you would expect for the owner of a major league franchise.[1]

"George was always kind of like a guy you went to college with; he just had that air to him," said Sherrington, who explained that Bush appeared more comfortable around journalists than his presidential father was. "I wouldn't say he was overly impressive," Sherrington said of George W. Bush. "He didn't come off to me as someone who was—and I'm not saying this to denigrate him in any way—he was not a guy who was going to impress you with his intelligence or his ability to command any subject. He seemed like a good guy who was a little bit of a smart aleck—not unlike most sportswriters. I think that probably helped him a lot with his relationship with the media, certainly at that level."[2]

The *Houston Chronicle*'s R. G. Ratcliffe, who covered Bush as governor and presidential candidate, said Bush can easily adapt to different situations. "He's a jock and somewhat anti-intellectual. But he got along with those guys [in sports] because he likes sports, keeps up with sports. I . . . used to hear him and [the *Austin American-Statesman*'s Ken] Herman talk baseball, and they knew amazing amounts of statistics. I see a game last weekend and I can hardly tell you what happened, and they'll tell you what happened in some game in 1963. But that's part of it. Bush adapts to whoever it is he's talking to, by and large. And you know if he's talking to some smart-alecky lowbrow sportswriters, he's going to be a smart-alecky lowbrow kind of guy. And you know if he's talking to wealthy Harvard-educated people he's going to be a little bit snooty. And he's sort of a chameleon that way."[3]

The chameleon adapted equally well to the clubhouse or the statehouse. Around the clubhouse, the *Star-Telegram*'s Jim Reeves recalled that Bush was a "guy's guy" who had a good sense of humor. "He would come to spring training and do his running and show up in the clubhouse in his running shorts and tank top and running shoes and hang around and talk to the players and talk to the media and just have a good time. He was just one of the boys sometimes."[4]

Wayne Slater's description of Bush early in his first term as governor sounds like he was describing a fellow reporter. "He would call me on the phone and call others on the phone: 'What are you doing? What's happening?' Plant a story idea, try to find out what we knew," Slater said.[5]

Bush knew that in the weak-governor format of Texas politics he would need to work closely with Lieutenant Governor Bob Bullock, a crusty, old Democratic politician. "[Bush] would talk to me and others: 'What is Bullock thinking? What's Bullock doing?'" Slater said. "Clearly, Bush was trying to be his own news gatherer. He was trying to understand how the process works, so he was using us as press. It wasn't just that we were getting information from him, he was trying to get information from us. He was a very good news source in that way. I think he was like that earlier, even in the baseball years. He really kind of understood how the media operates to some extent."[6]

Even more, Bush understands how reporters operate. He knows more than just the ins and outs of the news cycle and how to spin—he *knows* reporters; how they think, how they work, and how they play. In a telling moment after a grueling day during the 2000 campaign, Bush drank a nonalcoholic beer on the plane with journalists who appeared to be drinking stronger stuff. "My people!" Bush said. "It takes an animal to know an animal." Then he quickly added, "Of course I'm not admitting I'm an animal with 60 days to go in the campaign."[7] The joke beautifully illustrated Bush's understanding of the press. He was poking fun at himself, the journalists, and the whole process of what he and his father called "gotcha" journalism.

Bush's understanding of the press was evident to Slater in the way he handled reporters while he was governor. Bush regularly invited Slater and other scribes to the governor's mansion for meals and to his office to chat. "He is like a reporter in the sense that he is a regular person," Slater said. "He is a regular guy who sees life directly—or at least seems to see life directly. He'd kid around with you, joke around with you, tell you a dirty joke. Curse. Put a cigar in his mouth. Put his boots on his desk. Be a regular guy. And in a small group of reporters in his office, I defy you, if you came in from outer space, to figure out which one was not the reporter because he talked like a reporter; he acted like a reporter."[8]

Slater's portrait of Bush in the Texas governor's office bears a striking similarity to that of Teddy Roosevelt in the New York governor's office. Roosevelt biographer Edmund Morris wrote that the future president held twice-daily meetings with reporters in his office when he was governor.

> Relaxed as a child, he would perch on the edge of his huge desk, often with a leg tucked under him, and pour forth confidences, anecdotes, jokes, and legislative gossip. When required to make formal statement, he spoke with deliberate precision, "punctuating" every phrase with his own dentificial sound-effects; the performance was rather like that of an Edison cylinder played at slow speed and maximum volume. Relaxing again, he would confess the truth behind the statement, with such gleeful frankness that the reporters felt flattered to be included in his conspiracy.[9]

John Tebbel and Sarah Watts argue in their history of presidential press relations that Roosevelt's methods marked the beginning of the imperial presidency in the sense of the president being able "to manipulate and control the media, with the intent of making them as much as possible an arm of government."[10] Roosevelt, like Bush, was savvy about media operations, once interrupting a conference with the secretary of state so photojournalists could take pictures—at a time when "photo ops" were unknown. Roosevelt, an accomplished author himself, seemed to genuinely like reporters and was passionately interested in the practice of journalism.[11]

Teddy Roosevelt was but one of many presidents who have used personal relations to get along with reporters. Abraham Lincoln, also no slouch as a writer, told one reporter that he thought the journalists were like soldiers, going wherever they were needed despite the risk. "The press has no better friend than I am—no one who is more ready to acknowledge . . . its tremendous power for both good and evil," Lincoln said.[12] Lincoln, like Bush, used reporters for information. Tebbel and Watts point out that Lincoln often got news from war correspondents who had hustled back to the capital, bringing firsthand accounts faster than the official military reports. On one such occasion, Lincoln, overcome by emotion on learning that the Union Army would not retreat after the battle of the Wilderness, put his arm around *New York Tribune* correspondent Henry Wing and kissed him on the cheek. "The contentious editors, the imperious generals, the large questions of policy seem less meaningful than the kind of intimacy Lincoln was able to establish because of the humanity for which he is revered today, alone among all the others who have occupied the White House," Tebbel and Watts state.[13]

Modern presidents may pale in comparison to giants like Roosevelt and Lincoln, but the human side of presidential press relations is always there, and presidents always try to use whatever charisma they have on reporters. "All presidents do; that's not unusual," said *Los Angeles Times* White House reporter Edwin Chen. For example, Bush has tried to connect with Chen through conversations about their mutual interest in jogging. "Bush did it. Clinton did it. Don't they all do it? Kennedy did it."[14]

John F. Kennedy's charm and suave appearance on television in his 1960 debates with Richard Nixon have been discussed so much as to almost be clichéd. Helen Thomas, when comparing the numerous presidents she has covered, wrote that Kennedy was "chummier" than any other president because he was one of them—the firstborn in the 20th century and one who understood the press. She believed that Kennedy and Bill Clinton were the best at press conferences, and that Kennedy seemed to relish sparring with the press.[15]

Kennedy's successor, Lyndon Johnson, tried to court the press but could never match the younger man's savoir faire. He would alternately threaten and cajole the press, using sometimes bizarre methods of intimidation and persuasion. He famously conducted one interview with a woman reporter while he was seated on the toilet. When a novice White House reporter asked for some information that LBJ thought should have been asked of an aide, he said, "Son, I am the president of the United States, the leader of the free world, and you stand there and ask me a chickenshit question like that?"[16]

LBJ's relationship with newsman Dan Rather represents how LBJ tried to intimidate and at other times ingratiate himself with reporters. Rather first met LBJ at a press conference held at the Johnson ranch in about 1955. Johnson was then Senate majority leader and Rather was an inexperienced young radio reporter. Johnson had kept the press waiting for several hours, and Rather was afraid he would miss his deadline. He called his boss from Johnson's den and speculated that Johnson was delaying his press conference so it would get maximum play in the morning newspapers. Johnson suddenly appeared and grabbed the phone from Rather. Johnson said into the receiver, "I don't know who this young squirt is, and I don't know who you are, but I'm going to tell you that he has got the worst manners I have ever heard of with anybody, and what he has just told you is a goddamn lie from start to finish." Later, when LBJ was president and Rather was a White House correspondent, LBJ presented one reporter with a pair of pajamas as a birthday gift. Johnson told Rather that he might get pajamas on his next birthday if he behaved himself.[17]

The press relations of Ronald Reagan, like those of Kennedy, have entered mythical status. Thomas said Reagan, whose timing and self-deprecating sense of humor were outstanding, was the best of the presidents she covered at dealing with the press: "Many have tried, but so far no one has been able to take the title The Great Communicator away from Ronald Reagan. He's the winner and still champ."[18] A *Time* reporter recalled upon Reagan's death that as a much younger journalist he had prepared for an interview with a number of combative questions. Reagan, he wrote, "flicked me off his sleeve."[19] Mark Hertsgaard asserted in a history of Reagan's press relations that "perhaps Reagan's strongest communications attribute was his image as a nice guy."[20] CBS correspondent Susan Zirinsky told Hertsgaard: "Jimmy Carter you felt sorry for, but he was aloof and hard to get to know. But Reagan always made you laugh. It was hard not to like him."[21]

Clinton, as described in chapter 5, did not like the press very much. But he could be extremely charming when he wanted to. In fact, Slater said Clinton was the best politician he has ever met at dealing with journalists one on one because he would engage reporters in conversation and seemed to genuinely care what they thought. During the 1992 campaign, Slater traveled with Clinton for a time while the candidate was touring Texas in an effort to secure the Democratic nomination. "When I would interview him or talk to him, he would go out of his way to try to answer the question," Slater said. "I was doing one of these typical stories that asked, 'What's your favorite thing—What's your favorite movie? What's your favorite color? What's the last book you read?' The boxer-or-briefs deal. And I can remember—this was when [press secretary] Dee Dee Myers was with us—I asked him, 'What was the last movie you saw?' And he agonized over the question: 'Dee Dee, what was it? Chelsea and I just saw . . . no . . . wait . . . ,' and finally I just said, 'Give me an answer.' But Clinton, he wanted to please me; he wanted to give the reporter a real answer, not just a kiss-off. He didn't want to just dismiss this stupid exercise we do as something beneath him; moreover, he wanted to answer, or at least give us the impression that he wanted to answer honestly and truly work at these answers and in some sense give the reporter some sense of worth in what he was doing."[22]

Finding common ground based on movies, sports, or hobbies is a universal trick for starting conversations and making friends. In fact, it is a standard trick of reporters as well as presidents. Many journalism textbooks on reporting include tips for getting interview subjects to loosen up. One feature writing textbook quoted ABC's Barbara Walters and the *New York Times*'s Pulitzer Prize–winning Nan Robertson about getting sources to like the journalist. Robertson said she tries to find something in common with the person, like "books or sports."[23]

Both Clinton and Bush rivaled reporters in being able to use these techniques. The difference between the way Clinton and Bush use the trick is that Clinton more often tries to flatter reporters by talking about policy issues, while Bush is more prone to talk about family, pets, and sports.[24] Reporters might be in awe of Clinton's intellect and ability to command issues, but reporters who covered Bush for any length of time often felt he was an ordinary guy just like them.

Gerry Fraley, a *Dallas Morning News* sports columnist who also covered Ted Turner when he worked in Atlanta, said Bush was not like other baseball owners, the majority of whom are a "very stuffy" group. "He didn't fit their profile of being fat cats—no need to talk to the media; give them little shreds [of information]." Bush took the time to talk to fans about everything from concessions to rest rooms to the state of the ball club, and he made a point of greeting the umpires during every home series. "I just thought he was a pretty decent guy—the kind of guy in your neighborhood you could talk to if he was just raking leaves—that's how he came across to me," Fraley said. "Now if I was naïve, and he was just buffaloing me, then that's shame on me, but I thought he was a generally good guy, and I think I can spot a fraud."[25]

Star-Telegram sports columnist Jim Reeves described Bush as "a genuine person. He didn't make you feel like he was talking down to you or that he didn't have time for you, the media is a nuisance. . . . He knew it was part of the job."[26]

Sportswriter Phil Rogers, who covered Bush for the old *Dallas Times Herald* and then the *Morning News*, said Bush was comfortable both schmoozing powerful businessmen at banquets and mingling with the waiters and kitchen help. "You could definitely see he was very good at making people like him and . . . knowing how to act in different situations. Maybe you don't grow up in that family without developing those political skills. But I never saw him as ambitious; I guess that's the thing. He wasn't a guy—and you do see guys in every line of business, mine and yours, I would think—some guys who are just openly ambitious and wear it on their sleeves, and he never really was like that. It's difficult for me to see him running the country now because based on being around him I would picture him as my next-door neighbor rather than the leader of the free world."[27]

Regardless of the topic of conversation, Bush's interpersonal skills are so good that most reporters agree he is charming even if they are generally suspicious of politicians. Ratcliffe first met Bush at the 1988 Republican convention and thought Bush "was sort of a self-confident frat boy type of guy. But he was very easygoing and seemed to be able to instantly connect with anybody and talk with anybody. . . . When you talk to him, you feel like you are the only person in the room with him. He's not one of these politicians who's constantly looking over his shoulder to see who would be better to talk to."[28]

Ratcliffe said Bush was fun to talk to, and some reporters would do social things with him such as jogging. "He was always sort of fun to talk to," Ratcliffe said. "Bush and I would talk about fishing because I fish and he fishes. We do a different kind of fishing even though we were both fishing for bass. But there were a couple of times where Bush would ask me if I would take him fishing because he didn't have a boat here [in Austin], and I would turn him down because I had this rule about socializing with the people I cover."[29]

Some reporters have played golf with Bush. Rogers recalled one of his golf outings with the then Rangers owner as a very pleasant time. Rogers pointed out that the cynical, mistrusting reputation of journalists is overblown. "We are easier people to get along with than people give us credit for, to tell you the truth," Rogers said. "I am always amazed at people who don't get along with the reporters who cover them, or at least don't start off getting along with them, because as long as you're a decent person and will somewhat work with people, it's not that hard."[30]

The *Austin American-Statesman*'s Arnold Garcia agreed. "I think that there is some legitimate tension between the political people and the press, but I've never thought it had to rise to the level of 'I hate you,' or 'I don't want to talk to you,' or 'I'm never going to talk to you,' or 'I don't want to have anything to do with you.' I don't think it rises to that level of incivility or shouldn't stoop to that. We can all sort of get along and respect one another, and I think that's where Bush was."[31]

Although getting along with reporters seems like common sense, many sources either cannot or will not do it. Dave Montgomery, who has had a long career as both a reporter and editor with the *Fort Worth Star-Telegram*, said some politicians try to keep their distance from reporters. "Everybody is different," said Montgomery, who has interviewed both George H. W. and George W. Bush. "The Bushes to me seem comfortable in being around the press. Some politicians, God, they die when they see a reporter coming. All the good ones ought to be used to it by now. Some of them instruct their staff to not talk to the press, and 'We run a tight ship,' and they're guarded in what they say. To me, the best politicians are the people who you know can be engaging, be open, at least give you the pretense of being sincere, and be accessible. But there are definitely politicians, government officials—you know, they are gun-shy around the press, wish they were a thousand miles away whenever they see a reporter coming."[32]

Bush was always accommodating, said Dale Hansen, longtime sports anchor for the ABC affiliate in Dallas–Fort Worth. Hansen has interviewed Bush as both governor and baseball executive. "He never—like some guys would do—just blow you off and be rude or something. He always acted like he enjoyed the interviews, and I think he did, and in that regard compared to even a [current Rangers owner] Tom Hicks, who is for the most part accessible but never really says anything, kind of flat and kind of monotone and likes to set the ground rules for what questions you can and cannot ask. Bush was always, like, 'Hey, what do you need? What do you want? C'mon.'"[33]

In contrast, some news sources are downright hostile, particularly in the rough world of Texas politics. Garcia said that each journalist–politician relationship is different. Garcia compared Bush to Bullock, who he described as "the ultimate in hate-the-press kind of guy" who would sometimes yell and curse at reporters. "Bullock was always in your face. For my birthday he sent a note that said, 'Three editorials a day, seven times a week'—he did the math, that's however many a year it is—he says, 'Surely somebody is going to read one of them.' And again, it wasn't something I took offense at, it was just the asshole he was," Garcia said with a laugh, adding, "and I could be an asshole right back." For payback, Garcia took Bullock up on his dare to hold an editorial page meeting with him on a July 4 weekend.[34]

Bush, in contrast, often invited Garcia to the governor's mansion to chat. On one occasion after Bush made a trip to Mexico, Garcia called the governor's media office expecting to get a press release. "He called me on the phone; he talked to me about it—his assessment of the trip. He didn't really have to do that."[35]

Gestures like the phone call were a common Bush touch. Because of the nature of his beat, Montgomery has never covered George W. Bush on a daily basis. Even so, when Bush learned Montgomery was going to be assigned to the Knight-Ridder Moscow bureau in the early 1990s, he called him to wish him well. Montgomery said it was a thoughtful gesture. "I think he just does those kind of things, and his father did, too," Montgomery said.[36]

The Bush family has always placed an emphasis on personal connections. Peter and Rochelle Schweizer wrote in their Bush family biography that Barbara Bush maintained a file of contacts with personal information that grew so large it was computerized by the time her husband was in the White House. At one point they sent 10,000 Christmas cards based on the list. She and George H. W. Bush would also practice something they called the "eye contact game." While riding in a limousine, they would try to make eye contact with as many people on the motorcade route as possible in the belief that a personal smile would win a voter for life.[37]

Coming from such a family, it is no wonder that George W. Bush values the personal touch in his own political career, including his press relations. Nevertheless, some journalists are skeptical. Ben Sargent, editorial cartoonist for the *Austin American-Statesman*, first met Bush when he was visiting the newspaper during his 1994 campaign. Bush came up behind him and startled him. Sargent said without thinking, "Hello, governor," even though Bush was still just a candidate. "I blame myself for jinxing the campaign," joked Sargent, who describes himself as a "yellow dog Democrat." The political leanings of Sargent and the *Statesman* are well known in Texas. Yet when Sargent won a Pulitzer Prize, then–vice president George H. W. Bush wrote him a congratulatory note. When George W. Bush saw a cartoon he particularly enjoyed, he called Sargent to tell him and ask for a copy. Sargent said he thought the governor was personable, "but I found his bonhomie a little forced."[38]

The *New York Times*'s Frank Bruni similarly described Bush's efforts as a little overeager. Bruni recalled that Bush gave him the nickname "Frankie Boy" at a time when he had just joined the campaign in 1999 and barely knew Bush. He asked Bruni if he was ready for Atlanta, their next stop, "with the exaggerated, mindless fervor of a college freshman bound for a keg party," then called Laura to meet him as if he were someone important she must know.[39]

Bush's penchant for bestowing nicknames dates from his school days and has been noted so often in profiles that it has even been satirized in the political comic strip "Doonesbury." The nicknames became a sort of status symbol among reporters during the 2000 campaign.[40] With the size of the press corps, a nickname implied that the candidate knew the reporter on a personal level and implied deeper access than was available to others who were just faces in the press crowd. Bush has continued this informality into the White House, occasionally, for example, calling Dick Keil of Bloomberg News Service "Stretch," because he is taller than most reporters.[41]

Bill Plante, a CBS News White House correspondent, said he thinks the nicknaming implies Bush is in control, that he has the power to give nicknames. "I think it is a useful tool for him, and I would not want to be on the receiving end of a nickname," Plante said. "But you know, I think partly because of my age and partly because I have been around a long time, I'm . . . I guess that's why I'm not, and that's fine, I would not be comfortable with that."[42]

Bush calls Knight-Ridder's Ron Hutcheson "Hutch," but then, so do a lot of people—it's always been a nickname for him. Hutcheson said calling him "Hutch" is almost like calling him "Ron," so he's not uncomfortable with it. "If I had a different nickname, I wouldn't like it, or if I wasn't used to having a nickname," Hutcheson said. "It's sort of like there is a familiarity and an element of a superior relationship. Like, we wouldn't go up to him and say, 'Hey, Bushie!' you know?"[43]

Hutcheson was struck by the interesting relationship between reporter and source when he talked to Bush briefly at the 2004 White House Christmas party. "We did the receiving line thing, and as I was leaving he said, 'You're a good man,' and I thought, well, that's nice that somebody thinks I'm a good man. But on the other hand, there is an element of, 'Okay, you have my seal of approval.' And you're not really looking for a seal of approval from somebody you cover, so I mean basically I'm ambivalent about it."[44]

In addition to bestowing nicknames, Bush is famous for goofy, at times roughhousing, humor with reporters. Bruni had an excellent description of this facet of Bush's character in his *Ambling into History*, portraying Bush as the comic actor Jim Carrey trying to incorporate some

Jimmy Stewart into his role of candidate. "He pinched our cheeks or gently slapped them, in an almost grandmotherly, aren't you adorable way. At least twice, on the campaign plane, I felt someone's hands closing tight on my throat and turned around to see the outstretched arms of the future president of the United States, a devilish and delighted gleam in his eyes." He once put his fingers in Bruni's ears to show a quote was off the record and another time grabbed Bruni's head with his hands, pressed his own forehead against Bruni's and growled. Bush would put his hand on the head of balding reporters and assume a posture like a preacher and shout, "Heal!"[45]

For other journalists, Bush the chameleon intuitively understood how reporters wanted to be treated and maintained a more formal attitude with some than with others. *Texas Monthly* editor Paul Burka recalled that Bush as governor was a "very physical person" who would squeeze arms, press cheeks, and hook an arm around someone's neck, although that neck was as likely to be a Texas legislator's as a reporter's. "He was not that way with me, and I was just as happy," said Burka, who, as was noted earlier, considered Bush a friend. "The thing is, I think Bush understood there were boundaries with politicians and the press. The thing is, for someone who doesn't like them, he has a great reading of them."[46]

While some reporters saw Bush's joking side, others, like Burka, were impressed with his seriousness. "What I liked about Bush was he was just a . . . he never put on airs, but was *always* the governor," Burka explained.[47]

Because Bush understands journalists and the way they work so well, he was able to tease them by poking fun at the reporter–source relationship and the way news is reported. During the 2000 campaign, Bush typically ended his stump speech with a reference to upholding the honor of the Constitution "so help me God," an effort to contrast himself with the scandals of the Clinton administration. At one point, Bush dropped the line at a couple of appearances. John Berman, the ABC producer, wanted to know why Bush made the change. Bush seemed to think his curiosity over a small detail was funny and said he just did it to "shuffle the deck" because he had delivered the same speech so often. At the conclusion of the next speech, he paused dramatically, looked Berman in the eyes and said "so help me God."[48]

Hutcheson said that during the 2004 campaign, when Bush would appear at arranged forums with preselected questions, he would sometimes mock the process. "Bush being Bush, sometimes those little absurdities of the role get him, like sometimes even at his own forums he'll make fun of the fact [and say,] 'So, Fred, I believe now you're going to ask me about this,' and the guy will say, 'Yes, Mr. President . . . ,' [and Bush will say] 'Okay, good.' And sometimes Bush rips the façade off and says this is how this is really working with a wink and a nod."[49]

Reporters, though a cynical bunch, do appreciate the humor. Humor is important to journalists because, as Helen Thomas wrote in her memoir of covering presidents, "Watching history from a ringside seat is often painful . . . so we cherish and wallow in the times that we come together to enjoy a good laugh."[50] She wrote that Bush demonstrated this touch at an October 11, 2001, press conference where his response to a question of hers got some laughs and helped ease the tension. She asked whether the war on terror would be widened beyond Afghanistan and said she also had a follow-up. Bush said: "I knew you would. Thank you for warning me."[51]

Hansen said Bush was "incredibly accessible and fun," even when he left the Rangers to go to the governor's mansion. "He had that personality and that politician's style about him from the get-go," recalled Hansen, who used to kid Bush that he would run for president. Bush would always laugh and deny interest in anything beyond the Rangers. When Bush was elected governor, Hansen kidded Bush that he had taken the first step to the White House. "I said to him, 'I really want to sleep in the Lincoln Bedroom.' And—I'll never forget it—his answer was, he looked me right in the eye and said, 'Hansen, even you can't afford it.'"[52]

Time and again, reporters who have covered Bush regularly describe him as an ordinary guy. Slater said that Bush's joking, regular-guy persona became part of his "political signature" and was evident more in small rooms rather than at the podium or on television. "Now this doesn't just extend to the press," Slater said. "I've seen him in small rooms of businesspeople and others, and he has a real gift of engaging people and bringing them around. They may not in the end support him, but I think they come away with a feeling that, you know, he is a nice guy; he's a good guy. In the Bush vernacular, he's a 'good man.' I think that's part of it."[53]

Slater continued: "With the press, the media is not—although we are increasingly becoming one in Washington—an elite force. At least economically, we are somewhere between trade and profession. And most reporters are not millionaires. They are regular folks, very often covering cop shops, city hall. And when you deal with someone like Bush, who is really good, comes across—Yale-, Harvard-educated scion of real political royalty—but comes across as just a regular guy, it pays big dividends, I think, in our circle."[54]

In those small circles, or sometimes larger ones at political rallies, Bush was in his element. The *Houston Chronicle*'s Robison wrote that during the 2000 campaign, Bush worked the rope line with a skill that reminded reporters of Bill Clinton, and the crowds responded enthusiastically. Robison noted that while spending more than an hour mixing with supporters after a New Hampshire speech, Bush paused to "thump a Texas reporter on the stomach and exclaim, 'It's wild.' Or something like that."[55]

But Bush was not all stomach thumping, goofy faces, and lame jokes. He also exuded what the *American-Statesman*'s Garcia described as "star quality." Garcia said this was particularly evident when speculation began to mount that Bush would run for president. Foreign dignitaries and journalists wanted to talk to Garcia to find out what Bush was really like. One time a Mexican official, whom Garcia described as "old-line PRI" and very self-confident, dropped by to chat at the newspaper office. "We are just sitting here talking about things–the U.S., Mexico, economy, you know, standard things. So after we do that, we are walking to the elevator, and he looks at me, here's this guy, literally gets a twinkle in his eye, and he says, 'I'm going to the mansion. I'm going to go meet George Bush. I've never met him.'"[56]

Garcia said most people thought Bush was a good guy. "The guy who was the Mexican consul general here just loves him. . . . The guy returned to Mexico but I still get e-mails from him, and he always writes in very glowing terms about his time in Austin and, as he puts it, 'our friend George Bush.'"[57]

Bush has that rare skill of being sensitive to what other people are thinking and how to make them feel important. Hutcheson cited as an example a moment featured in Alexandra Pelosi's documentary of Bush's 2000 campaign, *Journeys with George*. At one point in the campaign, Pelosi reported on an in-house poll of journalists traveling with Bush. The poll showed that reporters thought Al Gore would win. But while journalists, with their strict code of objectivity, may discuss such things in private, they do not want them known publicly, and the reporters started to ostracize Pelosi. In response, Bush put his arm around Pelosi in front of the press corps to show that he was not mad about it and that the other reporters should treat her better.[58]

"He is incredibly observant to nuances," Hutcheson said. "Bush made a point of 'Hey, look, I'm going to throw my arm around you to show them I'm not mad at you. He does symbolic things like that all the time, and if there is an aide who's in trouble, he'll [say,] 'Walk with me to the helicopter because I want people to see.' He's conscious of those kind of gestures that send signals."[59]

Bush, Garcia said, was the kind of guy who made everyone around him feel comfortable. "The first time I was ever at the mansion, I was not the editorial page editor. I was a local columnist, and Ann Richards was the governor. We were having coffee—a bunch of us—and she reached over and poured me a cup, so that night I called my mother and said, 'I thought about you today and you had told me all those stories about discrimination against Latinos growing up and all the things my grandfather had faced, and I wondered what he would have thought if he knew that the governor of Texas poured his grandson a cup of coffee.'"[60]

Later, Bush not only poured Garcia a cup of coffee but also had Garcia seated at his left side during a luncheon. "That's a hell of a deal," Garcia recalled. "And again, that's not something—maybe other people are used to that kind of treatment, but I can tell you that as I was born a minority and became a journalist, so I don't have—even though I've been in this business 30 or 40 years and even though I've got this title and everything—I don't have an innate sense of entitlement. I don't feel like somebody owes me that cup of coffee. Does that make sense? I don't want to come off all starry-eyed, like, 'Oh, I'm having lunch with the governor,' but what I'm saying is that was my impression of the guy. He was always relaxed and made everybody else around him relaxed."[61]

The impression Bush made was not just on the press but also on others he dealt with in a professional capacity. John Blake, who worked with Bush closely as public relations director during his tenure with the Texas Rangers, said Bush was one of the best he ever saw at working with people. "He was very good with the local sports media, very accommodating, extremely candid, but the thing about him was he had great people skills, and not just with the media," Blake recalled. "In terms of being able to make a fan feel good that might have had a complaint or something like that, I don't know if there has ever been a better person we've had who could do that. He had that personality and that charisma and the ability to make that person feel that you care about their problem. And the other thing is that he has a great knack for remembering people's names. You know, that goes a long way. Certainly, it went a long way with the local media here."[62]

But some say the smoothness only goes so far. Ratcliffe said that although Bush is easygoing and easy to talk to, he is still a product of his elite background and could never quite understand middle-class people, including a lot of reporters. "Bush has a self-image that he is a West Texas

Bubba," Ratcliffe said. "And he certainly has spent a lot of time around West Texas Bubbas. But the underlying thing is he is a child of privilege and in some ways he led a sheltered life and he doesn't fully understand what it's like even to grow up very middle class in a place like Midland."[63]

Ratcliffe cited Bush's daily routine as governor as an example. Bush would take three hours out during the day to eat lunch, exercise, and even take a nap. If someone weren't exercising the same way, he'd think they were being lazy. "He just didn't understand that not everyone can just take off three hours in the middle of the day to exercise. And you know, like, when reporters—and this was particularly true in the [2000] presidential campaign—when the reporters weren't physically in front of him covering him, he assumed we were just goofing off, instead of writing stories and filing updates and calling people to talk to sources. And frequently our filing time in the presidential race would be his jogging time, and he just didn't understand why we weren't exercising like he was, and he's just not completely in touch."[64]

It seems equally probable, however, that Bush was towel snapping the reporters by kidding them about exercise. There is no doubt Bush grew up in circumstances that many Americans would consider privileged. But in other ways it was more upper middle class than upper class because the Bushes, while wealthy, were not on the level of, say, the Kennedys. George H. W. Bush, for example, did not have enough personal wealth to buy the family compound at Kennebunkport without taking several years to raise the funds. The family also has a credo that the members of each generation must go out and earn their own fortune.[65] Of course, that fortune is easier to earn when you have a leg up with a private school education and elite contacts, but it doesn't mean that you don't go through a period of living cheaply on your own. When George W. Bush was struggling in the oil business, he lived in a small apartment with little furniture and few new clothes. He came from wealth, but he had experienced middle-class life. He was certainly aware of reporters' deadlines and news cycles if for no other reason than to calculate the best time to release stories.

Was Bush's "bonhomie," as Sargent called it, also a calculated act to get better press coverage? Sportscaster Dale Hansen said there is no doubt Bush's friendliness was done as part of his job, and that he did that part well. "Some reporters are always offended by that, but I've always believed that everybody handles the press," Hansen explained. "Some just do it better than others. Anyone with half a brain, in my opinion, has to handle the press. That offends a lot of reporters when they hear that, but it never bothers me. Everybody does that. . . . My point is that I don't think George Bush liked Dale Hansen—I don't think he cared a damn about Dale Hansen—but he knew that I had a pretty big platform to talk about the Rangers so he glad-handed me when he saw me and said, 'Hey, Dale, how you doing? Hey, Dale, what can we do for you?'"[66]

Hansen said Bush was so enthusiastic and passionate about projects like construction of the new ballpark in Arlington that it was hard not to like him and hard not to agree with his spin on events. "I'm sure there were many days when he didn't care to sit down and do an interview or talk baseball or talk to Dale Hansen, but if it was part of his particular job that day he put on a smiling face and did it," Hansen said. "Is that an act? Yeah, probably. But hell, we all do that. Just like tonight at 6 o'clock, I don't particularly feel well, but I guarantee, I doubt very seriously at 6:30 anybody who watches me will be able to tell that. Now does that make me a phony? No. That's my job. That's what I do. Whether he's president, or whether he's owner of the Rangers, or governor of Texas, that's part of the job of handling the press, and I think he did a hell of a good job of it."[67]

Fraley also noticed Bush's charm and realized he was working the press. He said that Bush used the same kind of physical behavior that Bruni detailed in *Ambling into History* and that was evident in *Journeys with George*. "He was that way," Fraley said. "He would emphasize a point with a shot to the shoulder. Sometimes it was a way of recognizing you, of getting his point across. Again, in the sports world that's not atypical. A lot of people tend to be that way. He could be extremely charming. Believe me, I'm not naïve enough to say, 'He really likes me.' He had a purpose, too, but he was cool about it."[68]

Some journalists see Bush's behavior as just part of his overall character. Tracy Ringolsby, who covered Bush as a baseball writer for the *Dallas Morning News*, said Bush was remarkably unaffected, considering that he was the son of a president. Ringolsby would talk to Bush almost every day during the season because Bush was usually down on the field before games. Ringolsby, who described himself as coming from one of the strongest Democratic labor families in America, grew to admire Bush. "I remember telling him he was such a good guy that he must have been an orphan born to Democrats and adopted by Republicans because he was too good of a guy to have been a Republican—just bullshit with him about things," Ringolsby said. "I talked to him about baseball, and he was interested in learning as much as he could, you know, he knew he was relatively new to it. He was just an enjoyable guy."[69]

Ringolsby ended up voting for Bush in 2000 despite his family heritage. After the election, Bush attended a game at Coors Field in Denver. A Secret Service agent told Ringolsby, who by this time was working for the *Rocky Mountain News*, that the president wanted to talk to him. They chatted about baseball and other things. "I told him, 'You did something nobody in history has been able to do.' He said, 'What's that?' I said, 'You got a member of my family to vote for a fucking Republican.' His reply was, 'It's about time someone in your family has some fucking sense.'"[70]

Ringolsby said Bush was good at personal relations because people are important to him. "He didn't forget people," Ringolsby recalled. "He just made everybody feel like they were—he never made you feel you were below him, he knew more than you. He was interested in different phases [of baseball]. He never had the attitude that he had every answer or had the attitude that he didn't want to know how things worked. 'How could things be better?' What could he do to make things better? He just—I like the guy, like I said, even though he is a Republican."[71]

Neal Spelce, a longtime Austin television reporter, rejected the idea that Bush was nice to reporters as part of a "charm offensive" to get better coverage. Spelce cited as an example an incident from early in the 2000 campaign. "In New Hampshire on the campaign trail, a cold day, the bus pulls up at some school; I can't remember where. He was about to get out, and the hordes of reporters standing there waiting to greet him, etc. And he hadn't seen me . . . at all up to that point in New Hampshire. This is my first day to get up to New Hampshire, and he steps off the bus and starts walking by the row and the first thing he says as he gets off the bus—and I wasn't in the front row—he says, 'Hi Neal, you better stay warm here. It's a lot colder here than in Texas.' And he just kind of kept going. That wasn't any quote 'charm'; that was just the way he was."[72]

Reeves agreed. He thought Bush's joking was part of his personality. "I didn't think about it as a ploy or something he was particularly styling to be buddy-buddy with you. I think George just likes being around guys, and I think he enjoyed baseball and the clubhouse atmosphere, and I think he is a pseudo-athlete himself, or would like to think he is."[73]

It's important to note that Bush's attitude toward reporters did vary depending upon his role at the time. When he was campaigning for his father, he was protective of the older man and resented, often vocally, what he considered unjust criticism. Bush himself was often quoted as explaining that it is harder to take criticism of your family than of yourself. This dichotomy between the charm offensive and the scorched-earth defensive is illustrated in his relationship with *New York Times* columnist Maureen Dowd. Bush disliked Dowd's columns and regularly mocked her at family gatherings during his father's administration.[74] Dowd recounted in the preface to her collection of Bush columns, *Bushworld*, that she had irritated Bush once when his father was president. Dowd was the *Times* White House reporter and as a joke on a visit to the Bush house at Kennebunkport had worn a "Bob Dole for President" shirt and a "Jesse Jackson for President" hat. George W. Bush saw her as he drove by her in a golf cart and gave Dowd "a scary glare" and sent word to her that he wasn't pleased. But when she covered his own races, the younger Bush "was genial, appreciatively noting my green cowboy boots." On the day he announced he would run for president, he and Dowd discussed the golf course incident: "Grinning disarmingly, W. asked, 'Are you still holding that against me?'"[75]

Whether Bush is acting or not is debatable. However, most journalists who have covered him regularly say he can be very charming. But so what? Does it really affect coverage? Critics of Bush and of the press tend to answer with an emphatic yes. In fact, partisan observers claimed Bush co-opted the press with his charm, mesmerizing them into writing feel-good stories and ignoring his faults. Democratic attack dog Paul Begala, who wrote the 2000 campaign polemic *"Is Our Children Learning?,"* said he was astonished at "how compliant" the press was during the campaign. "Far too many people traveling with Bush suffered from Stockholm syndrome," Begala said.[76]

Critics continued to pursue this theme after Bush took office. In a 2002 *Newsday* column from which this book takes its title, Robert Reno wrote that Bush had a towel-snapping relationship with the White House press corps that got him favorable coverage.[77] The criticism reached its zenith following the March 6, 2003, presidential news conference in which Bush made his case for war with Iraq. One critic even suggested the entire White House press corps should be dumped in the Atlantic Ocean.[78] The coverage of the press conference generated such agonizing navel-gazing among journalists—including an *American Journalism Review* cover story asking "Are the media too soft on Bush?"[79]—and shrieks of outrage from left-wing critics that it will be addressed in detail in chapter 9. It's sufficient at this point to say that a substantial number of observers believe the White House press corps has succumbed to Bush's charm, or at least the need to be deferential to a wartime leader.

Journalism is a profession with historically low pay scales but an artistic quality to the work. It also has, in a country built on a tradition of press freedom and a heritage of rebellious practitioners of that freedom, the appeal of being a watchdog over the powerful. "Afflict the comfortable and comfort the afflicted" is one of the hoariest of clichés in this tradition. In such a profession, few journalists would admit to being swayed by a news subjects' charm into writing favorable stories. Some might acknowledge, that, yes, in theory, a reporter might write more favorably about a source who was "one of the guys." But reporters who speak in those terms sound like examples for the Third Person Effect, an academic media theory that means basically that people will attribute unfavorable characteristics to other people but not to themselves.

Everyone interviewed for this book who was familiar with Bush's days with the Rangers said he had good press relations and got good coverage. There is no doubt Bush got on well with individual sportswriters. They found him to be honest, accessible, and passionate about the game. But it's impossible to tell whether these good relations derived from his press strategy, because the Bush ownership was so successful at running the team that there wasn't much negative stuff to cover. During Bush's first term as president, almost 10 years after he left the Rangers, the team was at or near the bottom of the standings after some disastrous free agent moves. Sportswriters and fans recalled the Bush years as the glory days of the franchise when a beautiful stadium was built, the iconic Nolan Ryan was acquired, and the team was turned into a contender.

"It was a brilliant group," Rogers said of the Bush partnership. "They came in at a good time like it was preordained, but of course it was not preordained. You have to have a long memory to recall how bad that franchise was, and the legacy for that group is the ballpark, which really gives them a chance to compete, and had they not gotten that ballpark, they would have definitely been right there with the Minnesota Twins and the Montreal Expos, organizations whose future long term is still jeopardized by facilities."[80]

The franchise, under previous owner Eddie Chiles, was a "laughingstock," but the club "of the last 20 years, you would have trouble going around all the major league teams and finding more successful groups over their tenure than the Bush/Rose group," said Rogers. "They took something that was horrible and turned it into something that was pretty darn good."[81]

Good times equals good stories and good press relations. Bush might have had a "honeymoon" with the sports press during his entire ownership because the franchise was steadily making progress, Rogers concluded.[82]

Sherrington agreed that there was not much controversy during the Bush tenure.[83]

Bush's time as governor was similar to this period with the Rangers in that he met or at least tried to meet all of his campaign pledges (he was thwarted by the legislature on his school funding reform program). Although he followed a popular governor in Ann Richards, Bush was also extremely popular, being reelected in 1998 with more than 70 percent of the vote.[84] Again, in such a successful atmosphere, it is difficult to say whether positive press relations were due to Bush's towel-snapping ways or the general good atmosphere that prevailed in Texas at that time.

Certainly, as comments by Texas journalists indicate, Bush assiduously courted the Texas press. But journalists by and large said that if Bush's personality influenced coverage at all, it was very subtle. On the other hand, a source gets nowhere by being rude to reporters.

"My motto is, reporters are like dogs. If you stroke 'em, feed 'em, talk softly to 'em, they'll lick your hand," the *American-Statesman*'s Dave McNeely said. "And if you shout at 'em and throw sticks at 'em, and they get a chance, they'll bite you in the ass."[85]

Garcia addressed the question of whether the charm offensive worked by turning it around. "You're not going to get anywhere by insulting us all the time. We're human beings, too." As editorial page editor, he sometimes gets people who submit an op-ed column and insult him by telling him, "You don't have the guts to print this." Such challenges don't work, Garcia said. "With Bush . . . certainly we didn't sit down and plot this [good press relationship]. I think that with me, anyway, I saw a combination of a good guy trying to do the right thing. I didn't buy everything he was peddling, but I really liked the forward thinking on Mexico." Bush never made conflict personal or tried to use his position as governor to intimidate, Garcia said. "I think that goes a long way."[86]

Not long enough to kill a negative story, however. "I think it is human nature that if you like somebody or someone, you probably would be human and tend to at least give them the benefit of the doubt, than if you really detested the guy," said Austin television reporter Spelce. But that human sympathy wouldn't extend to a hard news story. "Most reporters will, if they've got the story, they're going to go with it, and they may bend over backwards to get his comments or side of the story, but they are going to go with the story."[87]

Spelce said that sometimes critics who claim a reporter is being soft don't understand the purpose of the story. For instance, he was castigated for an interview he did with George H. W. Bush and George W. Bush while they were bass fishing. It was a feature story on the father-and-son relationship, yet Spelce said he received a lot of negative comments about him "throwing softball questions" instead of asking about the economy. "Of course, that wasn't the purpose of the interview, but I can see where someone watching that interview would say, 'Why didn't you try to nail him? You had both of them there in the boat, Spelce, they couldn't run away from you.'"[88]

Ratcliffe said that whether the towel snapping has an effect depends upon the individual reporter. Recall that Ratcliffe turned down Bush's request to go fishing with him. "If you socialize with someone you are going to give them a break when you shouldn't—or will you compensate by being too hard on them? It depends upon the personality of the reporter. Some reporters, if they like somebody, will pull their punches. Other reporters will say, 'I like them, and, gee, everyone knows I like them; I am just going to have to hit them a lot harder.'" He concluded, "I mean, you know, I like Bush, but I did quite a few negative stories on him—some that he was really unhappy with."[89]

The *Star-Telegram*'s Jay Root said: "I don't think I covered him any different than anyone else, and I really mean that. We were fair but tough. I think that there are other [politicians] who are just as personable. I do think that they [the Bush administration] were very cognizant of the importance of dealing with—have a good press and they took great care to not needlessly irritate reporters."[90]

Root said the Texas capital press was criticized for giving Bush a free ride, but he thought the national press acted like they were covering a celebrity when they came to Austin to cover the beginning of his presidential campaign. The mood was that the national press would show the Texas press how it's done. "Then there was the press conference when he announced he would run, it was half Texas press and half national press, and it had a very celebrity focus, a feel-good process," Root recalled. "All the questions were 'How's your Mom? What does your Dad think of you running?'—very softball questions from the national press."[91]

The only reporter interviewed for this project who admitted a source's personality can affect coverage and backed it up with an example was the *Dallas Morning News*'s Wayne Slater. "We reporters like to think that it doesn't make any difference—that our relationship with somebody will not affect in any way our coverage, but I'm here to tell you that it does affect our coverage; the ability to get access to the people we talk to, the ability to sort of relate to them—their success in ingratiating themselves to us certainly doesn't get all good stories, but I think creates an environment where a reporter is more likely, if he understands the source he is writing about, is more likely to give that person the benefit of the doubt," Slater said. "Now what that doesn't do is buy you all good coverage, and I don't think Bush has gotten all good coverage."[92]

Slater watched Bush use some of the same ingratiating style he employed as governor with the national press when he embarked on the 2000 presidential campaign. "What Bush did—because I think instinctively he knew it was a good thing to do, but also because he was also acting in concert with Karen Hughes, who understood the media and was really his media image person adviser and he trusts her—what he began to do was work the press from day one. I can remember him going up and down the aisles of the airplane for months. He would want to meet everyone on the plane. He would talk baseball if that was their interest. He learned if they were married, if they had kids; he'd learn their interests."[93]

Slater's example of how such relations can pay off was the way the campaign press covered the discovery of Bush's arrest for drunk driving when he was 30 years old. The story was first reported five days before the 2000 election by a Maine television station that had been tipped off by a Democratic operative that Bush had been arrested for drunken driving in 1976. In such a close race, the news was a potentially devastating story for Bush's campaign, which was based in part on bringing honor back to a White House that had been besmirched by Clinton's immoral behavior and lies. Bush had often admitted to having a reckless youth, but he had never mentioned the DUI arrest. He had to have suspected it would come out at some time during the campaign. His response at a news conference following the report claimed that he did not reveal it because he did not want his daughters and other young people to know about his behavior and emulate it.

Slater inadvertently became part of the story because he had said in an interview several months earlier that he had once asked Bush if he had ever been arrested other than in the already reported episode of his theft of a Christmas wreath as a college prank. Bush had said no, but looked like he was going to elaborate when Karen Hughes cut off the interview. Slater's anecdote, coupled with the revelation of the DUI, changed the Maine story from an embarrassing fact that had not been disclosed to a story about a politician who had lied to a reporter. "The issue then became one of character, which we do in the press. If someone lies, it's not really the lie, it's about the character of someone who would lie—that's the issue," Slater said.[94]

The issue for Slater became whether to call Bush a liar or to try to deal with it in a more fair way. "I largely gave him a pass on that because my relationship with him told me—and when reporters would ask me, 'Did he lie to you?' I would never use the word 'lie' because my relationship with him was . . . to give him the benefit of the doubt because I think he was going to go ahead and tell me the truth before an aide cut him off."[95]

Bruni, however, wrote that he gave Bush a pass, putting the DUI information low in the story instead of in the lead, because the release of the information so close to the election seemed unfair. Bruni heard Bush muttering to aides that the initial DUI story was a dirty trick, but Bush apparently appreciated the *Times*'s low-key treatment of the story because the second day after the story broke he told Bruni, "You're a good man."[96]

Most reporters, like Bruni, didn't so much think they were doing Bush a favor as trying to be fair. Root, for example, said there was no way to prove that Bush had really lied because Bush's campaign denied that he had denied being arrested.[97] Ratcliffe agreed with Root's assessment. "The problem everyone had with that story was that you just couldn't flat out say he lied because you just couldn't get inside Bush's head," Ratcliffe recalled. "Did Bush intentionally lie, or did he misstate, or what? That was just a very hard one."[98]

Hutcheson, for one, thought the press corps did hit the DUI story hard. "Because the idea of being in the tank for any candidate is so repugnant, I think you could even argue that there is a reverse effect that 'God, I really like this guy. Oh, man, I better not be seen as being in the tank for him. I got to be tough here, I got to put whatever my personal feelings are aside and be tough here,'" Hutcheson said. Hutcheson could not think of a specific example in which he let a source's personality influence him. "If there is an effect, it's really on the margins. You know, the pressure in the business, the whole ethic of the business, is you can't let personal feelings pro or con influence you. I just think that overwhelms any sort of personal thing."[99]

The trouble in analyzing the press coverage is that media critics can't get inside the heads of reporters, who of course by human nature are not going to admit a professional failing like being soft on a news source. Because the *Times* is considered the country's paper of record and is the one that the TV networks and the other papers follow, its downplayed treatment of the DUI story "pretty much killed it off," Slater said. "I wonder, though, how many people who wrote about this or dealt with it the next day kind of gave Bush the benefit of the doubt because they felt, 'He's a pretty good guy, and I don't believe in my heart that he's a liar. How could the guy who's talked to us be a liar?'"[100]

The effect of personality on press coverage could be debated from now until the end of the republic, but one thing seems clear: The atmosphere changed markedly once Bush was elected. CBS anchor Bob Schieffer perhaps put it best: "You can't be one of the guys when you're president of the United States."[101]

Although Bush tried to court the national press during the campaign, he was suspicious of them. One of Bush's complaints about the national press, as opposed to the Texas press, was that the reporters lacked a sense of humor. His friend Clay Johnson told a Texas reporter that Bush said the national reporters were "real serious, real grim. Their jaws were tight. It's not very friendly, very adversarial."[102] He campaigned on a pledge to unite the country, and much was made of the bitter political divide that existed when he ran for reelection in 2004. But Bush was not naïve about the prospects of changing the culture. In his last interview with Texas reporters before his inauguration, he was "relaxed and jovial" but contrasted what the presidency would be compared to his governorship. "No question Washington is a different environment," Bush told the group at a session at the Midland airport, his beaver Stetson hat laid casually on the table in front of him. "And that's why it needs a different attitude, starting with the president. It's a tougher place, and it's a meaner place than Austin."[103]

Because of Bush's lifelong relationship with the press, and especially his observations of his father's presidential press relations, he was ready.

8

SHAVING THE EAR HAIR

How closely do reporters scrutinize the people they cover? When the source has a famous name and is the popular governor of a large state, even personal grooming and speech are examined like tea leaves. Late in Bush's first term, the Austin press corps took note of subtle changes in the governor's habits that some reporters speculated were signs he would run for national office.

"He shaved his ear hair, which I know is irrelevant," said Wayne Slater, only half-joking. "He used to have just globs of ear hair, and I noticed in about 1998 he shaved his ear hair, and we in the capital press said, 'He's running for president,' because it's clear he's going for something beyond that. I know it's odd. Maybe more to the point, he quit cursing in private, by and large."[1]

Slater, who had been covering Bush since the early 1990s, had found him to be very open to reporters through his first term as governor. "Now, I noticed in about 1999—he ran for reelection against Gary Mauro in '98—in '99 he really began to change the way he talked," Slater said. "He didn't use as many curse words, especially the f-word, which he used often in conversation, and I think he was much more cautious, I sensed, the way he talked around us, around me, in private. I think he realized there were higher stakes here, and he wasn't sure how to navigate those waters that were ahead of him even if he was the son of a president."[2]

Bush, who was familiar with the way the media had reported on his grandfather and father, was no doubt aware of the probing that awaited him should he announce his candidacy for president. If the Texas press was speculating about ear hair, the national press could be expected to go even deeper.

The years between 1998, when Bush's landslide reelection as governor made him a serious contender for the Republican nomination, to 2000, when he was elected as president, was a transition period in Bush's press relations. He already knew what the press was like, and he knew what he had to do; the only question was whether he could do it.

Bush's previous success with the media had been based on two things: natural charm and knowledge of the news topics so that he could deliver a coherent, consistent message. The charm was a given, a God-given talent that some people have for connecting with others almost immediately. On the other hand, the knowledge of the subjects reporters wanted to talk about was something Bush had to learn. When Bush was working for his father's various campaigns, he was not the front man on issues but rather a spokesman for the man's character and campaign strategy. Many times he was not the interview subject himself but the gatekeeper for reporters who wanted access.

When Bush dealt with the sports press in Dallas–Fort Worth, he was working in an area he had been studying since he was a Little League catcher in Midland who had memorized the New York Yankees' starting lineup. But when he initially ran for governor, he was on less certain ground, and it showed in his first interviews. Bush had to learn the issues and then face the particular beat writers covering those issues—beat writers who have their own quirks as certainly as politicians do.

Make no mistake about it, sportswriters are professional journalists who try to break stories and often cover the legal and business problems of sports as well as the games, but they do realize they aren't covering national security. "I try to take my job very seriously, but it is just fun and games, basically, and I think George understood that," *Morning News* sports columnist Kevin Sherrington said when asked about the difference between Bush and the sports press and Bush and the White House press.[3]

Covering the statehouse attracts reporters who are deadly serious about what they cover. They have to be, because they are covering an area that directly affects readers—in many cases, much more directly than the national government—but doesn't have the glamour of covering the federal government. The state government press corps tends to be competitive and knowledgeable, but small enough for a source like Bush to get to know individual reporters quite well. The White House press corps, on the other hand, is considered by many to be the pinnacle of the profession. It draws some of the best reporters in the world, and the people who claw their way to that beat are fiercely competitive. The sheer size of the press corps covering the White House makes it difficult for the president to cultivate individual reporters.

At all levels of journalism, charm helps sources to a certain degree, as does the ability to deflect questions—a talent many sources develop through long practice in being interviewed. Sources who are interviewed frequently, whether they are politicians, athletes, or entertainers, often learn to anticipate what questions reporters are likely to ask and what sound bites will satisfy them. But this interview savvy and savior faire only goes so far in feeding the media beast. The circling sharks are going to want more than chum. They may eventually swamp an unseaworthy boat and devour the fisherman if they don't get what they want.

"You deal with reporters in two different ways," Slater explained. "One, 'Hey, how are you doing?' You make a personal relationship. But [two,] we're here to talk about you and your issues and how you would govern and so forth, so you better be able to say, 'Okay, here's my plans, and here's my agenda.' And there are politicians who can do the latter. Al Gore can talk about his agenda; he's not very good at dealing with the press. I've dealt with politicians at the state level who are pretty good at dealing with the press but are terrible at the agenda. And it's a problem for them."[4]

Skilled politicians can cover up their lack of knowledge for a time by responding to a certain question by a technique called "bridging"—essentially ignoring the question and appearing to answer by giving a canned response to an unrelated subject. But skilled reporters, particularly ones at the state or national level, quickly figure out the politicians' ignorance. "In those kinds of environments, the press comes away [with the idea] you don't know what you're talking about; you just faked an answer," Slater said. "Yes, you're facile with the give-and-take, but you really don't know what you're talking about. You're really not very good at this, and so the press begins to establish a collective sense that you don't know something, and that quickly becomes part of the conventional wisdom of a politician."[5]

Slater cited Texas governor Rick Perry as an example of a politician who can't seem to answer questions to reporters' satisfaction, sometimes answering a specific question by talking about something else. "The attitude among the press corps is, I think, [that] he's not really very bright and he's not really answering our questions, and as a result when you get stories about whether or not he's beholden to special interests and so forth, the predisposition is, yeah, he probably is because he's not a very bright guy . . . and that becomes a self-fulfilling prophecy, and I think he's been burned and will be burned by those types of stories."[6]

The best politicians are good at both befriending the press and answering questions. One example is Bill Clinton, who Slater said "dazzled" reporters with his knowledge of issues yet also appeared to focus on them as individuals. Bush, when he first ran for governor, appeared to be closer to Perry than Clinton in terms of press relations. Bush, as a Harvard MBA graduate and baseball executive, was confident in his knowledge of sports and business but shaky on his grasp of state government. Political adviser Karl Rove had arranged tutoring sessions for Bush when he began contemplating running for governor. Instructors included Mike Toomey, a former Republican state legislator who advised Bush on state government and the budget, and another legislator named Bill Ratliff, who was an expert on school finance.[7]

Bush had not quite mastered all the intricacies of state government or even his own plans for his potential administration when he first started formal campaigning. *Bush's Brain*, which Slater wrote with James Moore, describes a meeting with Texas political reporters in November 1993 after Bush had made a speech about education to a group of school administrators in San Antonio. When a reporter asked Bush a couple of specific questions while he was smiling and shaking hands "with a kind of breezy confidence," Bush couldn't answer them. Bush's confidence turned to nervousness, as he "shifted from foot to foot, his brain swimming."[8]

A campaign aide told Bush, who knew he had stumbled, "Look, you are the son of a president. You've got an MBA from Harvard. You want to be governor. You can stand in front of these Capitol reporters for 20 minutes and take their questions, because if you can't, what are we doing?"[9]

Still, the episode showed Bush wasn't ready for the press in terms of talking about his new subject—state government. "If very quickly it is determined by reporters that you don't know what you're talking about, you're dead," Slater said. "He may have been the friendliest guy in the world, but it was very clear he didn't know the size of the budget, and he didn't fully understand really how health and education spending were allocated . . . then he was quickly going to come across as a rube, and we were going to do it."[10]

Bush stayed away from the metro and Austin capital press and instead toured small cities like Navasota, Henderson, and Yoakum, where he visited businesses and hunting clubs, and he even walked in Stamford's Cowboy Reunion Parade. It was, Moore and Slater concluded, "a brilliant piece of political engineering."[11]

The *Houston Chronicle*'s Ratcliffe, another veteran Bush observer, agreed with their assessment. "You know, Bush brought to the table these natural skills of being able to talk to people, be easygoing to people, but even coming in to state government he really didn't know that much about what was going on, and Rove set out a program of educating Bush on government issues, and in particular the ones they were going to concentrate on in the '94 campaign . . . tort reform and things like that," Ratcliffe said. "So I think there is some justification for what Wayne and Jim do with Rove being 'Bush's brain,' I mean he was the guy who set up Bush University over at the governor's mansion when they needed to educate Bush on a bunch of national issues, and they brought in experts from all over the country to try to teach the guy stuff most people learn over 30 years in a 30-day period."[12]

Learning a new set of topics and then having to face a new set of reporters—this time the most competitive if not the most skilled in the business—created anxiety for Bush in the same way he had experienced when he had moved from dealing with the sports press to the state capital press.

"It's funny because I think I saw that same kind of thing, the same kind of cycle, where he has confidence in his abilities, his gut instincts in dealing with the press, until . . . every time he reaches a new level, he's got to, one, be educated about the subject he's talking about, but, two, sort of regain his confidence, reestablish his confidence," Slater recalled. "He did that in the governor's race after . . . sort of learning the subject, and then by summer he was very, very good in his understanding of the subject and then just his natural ability of being able to talk and be a good guy just kicked in."[13]

Bush's campaign staff was nervous about how he would do at his first national press conference to kick off his campaign.[14] Most of the national heavyweights were there, including the *New York Times*'s Bush-hating Maureen Dowd, sitting in the front row menacingly in sunglasses, and the loud and domineering Chris Matthews, a former Democratic political aide who now made his living shouting at politicians and other unfortunates on a MSNBC talk show.

Mark McKinnon, Bush's television media consultant, later said: "You could smell the fear in the air. You could sense the press just ready to put him through his paces and see if he was ready. He was up there on the high wire for the first time without a net and some of us in the campaign were very nervous and I think he was, too. It was a new jungle and new animals."[15]

But after an initial stiff five minutes, observers could see Bush lighten up. He called to the MSNBC host: "Matthews. It's good to see the larger personalities are starting to show up."[16]

Slater compared it to Bush's initial meetings with the Texas political press. "This was absolutely déjà vu," Slater said. Bush was now not only confident of his ability to talk to the national reporters, many of whom he knew from his father's administration, but was also confident in his knowledge of the issues. "He had gained a confidence from his private schooling on national and international events that he could give as well as get from these reporters. And so I watched that kind of—very quickly—sort of transition and after that it was successful. But the key here was, if he doesn't think he knows what he's talking about or [have] the confidence to talk to reporters, he is very, very, bad. And as a result, he had to be trained, I think, but on policy, not on how to deal with reporters."[17]

Bush knew how to deal with reporters, and he proceeded to work his charm on them during the presidential campaign, joking with them like he had with the sportswriters covering the Texas Rangers. Stuart Stevens, a Bush campaign aide, recalled Bush taking a phone call from the Associated Press's Ron Fournier, a reporter respected by the staff because of his objectivity. Bush looked at Stuart and winked as he told Fournier that he had decided not to run for president after all, telling him the story would make his career. "I gave you a scoop, Fournier, what else do you want?" Bush said.[18]

Bush mugged for the reporters, doing an impression of Mini-Me, a character in the Austin Powers series, an outrageous spoof of James Bond spy movies. He even served reporters drinks on the campaign plane, a photo of which was displayed appropriately under the headline "The Charm Offensive" on the cover of *Brill's Content*, a short-lived journalism review.[19]

The mood on the campaign plane was captured well by Alexandra Pelosi in a documentary entitled *Journeys with George*.[20] Pelosi, who is the daughter of Nancy Pelosi, a California Democratic congresswoman who became the minority leader and a virulent Bush opponent during Bush's presidency, created a fascinating portrait of the campaign that is entertaining while at the same time being informative and balanced. The movie is like a book of Bushisms; the audience can interpret it as showing a human, good-guy Bush or a buffoonish, cynical politician Bush.

Knight-Ridder's Ron Hutcheson said he recommends the movie to anyone who wants to know about the campaign.[21] Slater added, "It's not the movie I would have made, but God bless her, it really gives you a sense of what it was like on the plane."[22]

Toward the end of the documentary, one reporter tells Pelosi that he thinks the press succumbed to Bush's charm and that the reporters consequently did not do an adequate job of covering the campaign. Such a judgment is almost impossible to prove, for if you could show Bush got more favorable coverage than Gore, how could you isolate the variable that caused the favorable coverage? Nevertheless, the charm offensive portrayed in the *Journeys with George* portrait is the image that has stuck to the campaign, and certainly with some justification.

Adam Clymer, the *New York Times* reporter who Bush called a "major-league asshole" over a public address system he thought was turned off, nevertheless saw the more amiable side of Bush on the campaign plane. "You know, he was friendly without being forthcoming," Clymer said. "I mean, I think in fact he profited in that campaign because he was in a substantial way much more accessible than Gore. Gore stayed away from the press. Bush, you know, wandered around, threw a football, cracked jokes, asked where—when people returned to the campaign—asked where they'd been, joked about it; that kind of stuff."[23]

What kind of impact did it have?

"I don't know that it exactly buys you a break, although with some people it probably does," Clymer said. "But the contrast . . . I mean if both candidates had been as withdrawn as Gore, or both candidates had been as amiable and accessible as Bush I think the coverage would have been more even. . . . I think Gore got picked on for allegedly lying or making things up, and all Bush ever got picked on for were some of his more bizarre mistreatments of the English language—and they tended to get reported as a matter of good fun."[24]

Slater traveled with Gore at times and had an assessment similar to Clymer's. Slater said the press in general did not like the vice president. "He seemed a sort of chilly technocrat," Slater said. "I was really surprised as I got on the press plane with this other group, it was really night and day; it was a kind of a dyspeptic group. The press covering him were kind of unhappy. Many of these guys were real Washington veterans because they were covering the vice president. But they were kind of unhappy; they didn't like him, you know, and it was such a stark difference between the reporters, who, although they may or may not have liked Bush's politics, really *liked* the guy. And he worked at this throughout the time."[25]

The problem in analyzing Bush's presidential press coverage is that this *Journeys with George* imagery has continued as a frame through which many critics view his administration's press relations. But the towel-snapping relationship that Bush had with the press for most of his life (except when he was his father's gatekeeper) could not and did not survive his own ascendancy to the Oval Office. The presidency is too demanding and the White House press corps too big and too competitive for the president to have the type of personal relationships with journalists that would influence coverage.

Journalists who have covered Bush at various levels of his career have noticed him adapt his game to the different levels of the press. "I think he has evolved," said Ed Clements, a radio journalist who has covered Bush since his days in the oil business in Midland. "He is in a whole different arena than he was as a guy running for Congress, even as governor and then as a president because still when he was governor, he was accessible. He did not have any adversarial role about the press. I think the national press is just a different game than a local press or even the state press."[26]

Clements cited Bush's annual press Christmas party for the Austin press as an example of the easygoing relationship. "We would always take my two children—who, some of their prized possessions now are pictures of them with the Bushes—and I think it was just a more relaxed situation," Clements said. "People pulled for George Bush when he was in Midland and Austin, I believe. There was not this 'I'm going to get you; I'm going to expose you'—that sort of type of attitude. And if you were fair to George Bush—this was even when he was a candidate in 1978—and were fair reporting on something he was involved with in town, he would be very fair to you, very fair to you."[27]

Slater said he has noticed two George Bushes in terms of his relationship with the press. "One is the George Bush before he went to Washington—or more precisely the George Bush pre-1999—and the George Bush post-1999," Slater said. "Once he became a candidate for president—seriously a candidate for president, even before he formally announced it—he became a somewhat different person."[28]

Hutcheson said that when he saw *Journeys with George*, he too was reminded of the difference between covering Bush as candidate and Bush as president. "There's a sharp line for me between Bush and the press during the campaign and Bush and the press during the presidency,"

Hutcheson said. "And you know once a guy becomes president, your chances to personally interact just fall off sharply, whereas during the campaign I talked to him all the time, and there would be times where he would come sit down beside me on the plane and we would sit and chat, and you just don't get those opportunities with the president of the United States very often."[29]

As president of the White House Correspondents' Association, Hutcheson was able to sit next to Bush at the group's annual dinner in 2003. Hutcheson said he enjoyed it because Bush is such a personable guy, and they had a lot to talk about because they had things in common, such as their fondness for Austin and the fact they knew many of the same people in Texas government. The dinner and Pelosi's movie reminded Hutcheson that "in the White House, it's a very impersonal affair . . . you interact, you ask questions, you see him, but you don't sit down and talk like a couple of people, like you and I would talk."[30]

One of the first times Hutcheson interviewed Bush was when Bush was governor and went to Washington to attend a meeting. Slater was flying up with Bush from Washington, and Hutcheson, who was working for the rival *Fort Worth Star-Telegram* at the time, was anxious to get a story, "scared to death Slater had beaten the crap out of me." He rushed to the convention hotel to try to get some sort of story about the convention's kickoff. Hutcheson caught Bush in the lobby, and when he asked for a interview, Bush said he was going to interview a prospect to head the Texas office in Washington, but that Hutcheson could come up to his room and talk.[31]

"So we go up to his hotel room," Hutcheson recalled. "He's changing his shirt while he's talking to me. The guy who's doing the interview comes in—it's like a suite—and [Bush] says, just wait out here. So we're back there just talking. . . . Finally I said, 'Well, I got what I need, thank you,' and as I'm going down the elevator, I'm thinking, boy, this guy has got to get better control of his time." Reflecting on Bush's precisely scheduled White House, Hutcheson added, "Well, he sure has managed that." Hutcheson agreed with Slater's thought on the contrast between the Governor Bush and the President Bush, saying, "It definitely was a different deal."[32]

The difference between the White House and statehouse beats is well known to reporters. Although to the general public the term "White House correspondent" no doubt implies the reporters are regularly talking with Bush, the reality is so different that more than a few reporters turn down the assignment. Interestingly, both Ratcliffe and Slater declined opportunities to cover Bush in the White House because of the restrictive nature of the job.

Slater had dreamed of being a White House correspondent when, as a college student in the 1970s, he had worked one summer at the San Clemente Inn, next door to Richard Nixon's Western White House in Southern California. Slater watched the press corps come and go and thought it would be a great job. By the time he had covered a presidential campaign, he changed his mind. He traveled all over America and to other countries, but rarely saw anything other than the events he covered. Slater, as senior political writer for the *Morning News*, has a comfortable ninth-floor office with a window overlooking downtown Austin and is only a five-minute walk from the Texas Capitol. By contrast, he knew a White House "office" would be a tiny cubicle from which he would be called to briefings. "It is a grind," Slater said of covering the White House. "It's a grind day in and day out, and the morning gaggle–it's just not something I wanted to do."[33]

During the last week of the 2000 race, Don Evans, a Bush friend who became commerce secretary, asked Ratcliffe if he was going to come to Washington to cover the White House for the *Chronicle*. "I told him no, because I realized that what they were going to do was sequester Bush away from the press, and I felt the job would really be a glorified stenographer position. And Don says, 'Well, you're right about that.'"[34]

The life of a White House reporter is indeed a strange one, and not at all like the image viewers get from television, watching the correspondents pepper Bush with questions at news conferences or as he is walking past the press line on the way to his helicopter. Television viewers are used to seeing reporters gravely doing their stand-ups with the White House in the background, the implication being that they are intimately familiar with what goes on inside the mansion.

In fact, the press quarters are cramped, the hours are bad, and the traveling schedule is too hectic to allow them to see much of the dramatic sites they visit. Jim Lo Scalzo, a photographer for *U.S. News & World Report*, described the White House briefing room, with its littered papers and trash and soundmen sleeping with their feet propped on chairs, as resembling "an adult movie theater after the lights come on."[35] Traveling with the president was less cramped but was often disorienting because of the schedule.

Lo Scalzo wrote that on one trip covering Clinton, he looked out a hotel window at a dreary scene and wondered why Florence did not look more charming. He picked a matchbook off the dresser and realized he was in Bulgaria, not Italy. The president, to Lo Scalzo, was seen for 10-second photo ops or as a "distant blur ducking into a limousine." He only saw the front of Air Force One on a courtesy tour given by a steward when the president was not aboard. Reporters leaping out of the press van at a presidential event "are a horrible, panting, sweating stampede—the personification of everyone's worst impression of the media, bumping into stanchions and abandoning colleagues who couldn't keep up," he wrote.[36]

A journalist's news organization might be impressive, but that doesn't mean the reporter will have much contact with Bush. Paul Koring, for example, is a Canadian journalist who has worked all over the world for the *Toronto Globe and Mail*, one of the country's premier newspapers. Koring is one of three White House reporters for the *Globe and Mail*, which bills itself as Canada's national newspaper, yet the Canadian reporters are at the level of waiting hopefully for callbacks from their telephone queries. At the time Koring was interviewed for this book, he had yet to ask Bush a question.[37]

If Bush has a personal relationship with any reporters, it is a very small group, Koring said. "You'll see him in news conferences—and I've been sitting in the room—you know, where he'll point at so-and-so and say 'Skip,' or 'Fred,' or 'Jill,' and whether that relationship is actually substantive or whether it's all glib and for the cameras, I don't have a clue, because I'm definitely not one. He doesn't know my name," Koring said. "And I don't think I know anybody in the foreign-based media—this is a bit of a stretch because I'm not certain of this—but I cannot recall a single instance of him having that kind of apparent familiarity with anybody who wasn't an American, which—now I'm speculating—if you're president, makes sense. There aren't a lot of voters in Bulgaria or Canada or France."[38]

Koring has worked in the Middle East and Europe as well as North America covering various heads of state. He said the sheer size of the White House press precludes the more intimate types of relations between leader and press that he has seen in other countries. "American presidents aren't accessible, period," Koring declared. "Some of it's a security issue. . . . The U.S. president's relationship is just entirely different. On the one hand, you've got the sort of death watch pool that's there all the time. And on the other hand, there is no ongoing familiarity, and you've got this monster press."

He continued: "I mean, what is the Washington press corps? Is it all these weird sort of organizations like mine? We're not in every capital in the world, but we're in Washington. Compare that with—and this may not be a terribly good comparison—but you compare that with the Canadian prime minister with a couple hundred reporters in town—the entire press corps might be a couple hundred people. So does he have to struggle to [know] a couple of dozen of them by name? And when he gets on a plane, it's not like there's two press planes following. We're actually talking about the same plane now. And it's not a plane that's sort of divided by security bulkheads. So, yeah, he actually walks down the aisle and there are kind of side conversations. Now that might exist in the Washington press corps, and it may be the handful of people who are closest are actually having a Coke with him at Camp David. I simply don't know."[39]

It may seem odd for a White House correspondent to speculate about the workings of the White House, but Koring's experiences are more typical than not. In some ways, the elite group of American reporters on Air Force One might as well be on the trailing press planes for all the access they get to the president.

"It's just a different world when you get on board Air Force One, and you know the cabin in front of you is the Secret Service, so there is no way you are going to walk up and talk to George Bush," Hutcheson said. "He's not going to walk back because early on they said he would do that if we went off the record, but nobody—well, there was a division in the press corps about that—but the fundamental conclusion was no, because he's president, so when he comes back he's got to be on the record now. We would take the candidate off the record, but not the president."[40]

In such an atmosphere, where every comment or joke could end up being a negative story, Bush knows he has to restrain himself. "Meeting you with a tray full of drinks after the last event of the day, that's a charm offensive, no doubt about it," Hutcheson said. "But the fact is, he's a towel-snapping guy, and the other fact is, as president, he restrains that side; he's in a different role, he knows that people expect him to act presidential, so although I think that sometimes that's not the way he wants to act, he does—and especially around us."[41]

Texas Monthly editor Paul Burka said he thought Bush was suspicious of the national press since his father lost the 1992 election. Burka said Laura Bush told him they quit watching the national television news at that time. "He does hate the national media," Burka said. "No question about it."[42]

Burka, like Slater and Ratcliffe, noted that Bush avoided the state capital press on his first run for governor because his campaign saw them as a threat. "Once he got here, he was so successful as governor that access was very good," Burka said. "He had regular press conferences. . . . He was very easy to have access to, I thought. And then all that changed with the national press; the press was not only a threat, but they viewed them as an enemy."[43]

According to Burka, the Bush campaign was "very bitter" about the *New York Times* story about Bush complaining that he was tired of traveling during the 2000 campaign.[44] That was the same story, written by Frank Bruni, that had generated a small controversy when Karen Hughes poked fun at Bruni for writing the piece and then taking some time off himself. Bush continued to towel snap the reporters during the campaign and even made up with Bruni, but his manner since becoming president is quite different.

"I think he went up there [to Washington] with a chip on his shoulder, went up there prepared to dislike them," Burka said. "They went up there with a view of controlling the media and controlling access."[45]

The *Washington Post*'s Dan Froomkin speculated that Bush may have found it easier to relate to the Texas press than the Washington press. "Just offhand, it seemed to me back when he was a baseball owner, he saw people in the press who loved baseball," Froomkin said. "Back when he was governor, at least he saw the press people who were Texans. Now he looks at these guys and he has nothing in common with them."[46]

Bush's suspicion of the White House press appears justified, given the mocking tone of some of the pool reports on his activities. The pool consists of a small group of about a dozen reporters who follow the president virtually everywhere—what Koring called the "death watch." One reporter writes a pool report, which is sent to a White House press aide and then distributed to the rest of the press. The *Washington Times*'s Bill Sammon, who has written four books about Bush, described pool reports about Bush that the White House staff believed were disrespectful. One report by the *Washington Post*'s Dana Milbank noted that Bush told reporters that a meeting with congressional leaders would get a lot done for America. The report, which sarcastically referred to Bush as "our hero," noted, "The president and the caucus got so many things done for America so quickly that the hour-long meeting lasted only 45 minutes."[47]

Sammon described Bush chatting with reporters after taking an early morning jog with one member of the pool, Dick Keil of Bloomberg News. Bush cut off the conversation rather quickly. "Bush was well aware that these friendly chats could turn treacherous," Sammon wrote. "During a similar encounter on a golf course five weeks earlier, Francine Kiefer of the *Christian Science Monitor* repeatedly asked him if he was 'taking any naps in the afternoon.' Bush saw it as an attempt to perpetuate the widely reported story that he was spending too much time vacationing on his Texas ranch. *USA Today* had even commissioned a poll showing that 55 percent of Americans believed the four-week break was too long. The president knew that if he acknowledged taking even an occasional nap, the press would have a field day. So he refused to rise to the bait. Instead of answering the question, Bush suggested the elitist press resented having to cover his working vacation."[48]

CBS anchor Bob Schieffer, whose brother Tom was an executive with Bush in the Rangers organization, said Bush doesn't distrust *all* reporters. "People say that he's kind of antipress and all that," Schieffer said. "I think he's anti *some* press because I think he's just, like, given up on them. Rightly or wrongly, he believes they're not ever going to give him a fair shake—I mean that's his opinion, not mine. And most presidents come to that conclusion somewhere along the line. It's very difficult for them to have a good relationship with the press because everything they do is under scrutiny and second-guessed, which in a funny kind of way is like being a baseball owner multiplied by a thousand . . . because running a sports team is very much like politics because everything you do is second-guessed, everything you do is reported on a day-to-day basis. So, in a way, I think that has given Bush a certain kind of tough hide." Schieffer added that he thinks Bush brushes off most of the criticism. "I think he actually likes reporters and gets a kick out of the give-and-take from time to time."[49]

Although Bush banters with the press, he usually ignores media demands for more access and criticism of his policies. Liberal cartoonist Gary Trudeau mocked Bush's National Guard service by offering a $10,000 reward for anyone who could prove he had served with Bush in Alabama—a series of "Doonesbury" strips that made him a Pulitzer Prize finalist in 2004. Although Bush angrily contacted Trudeau about a cartoon during George H. W. Bush's vice presidency that asserted the older Bush had put his manhood in a blind trust,[50] Trudeau never heard from George W. Bush about the National Guard strips. "One of the many lessons he drew from his father's presidency was to never empower critics by acknowledging them," Trudeau said.[51]

It was not necessarily a lesson learned by Bush, who had been dealing with the press long before Trudeau started mocking his father, but rather an indication of how he has adapted his changing media relations to his changing roles. He was friendly with the sports press and the Austin capital press. His relationship was close enough that occasionally he would even let a source know when he thought a story was wrong. But in Washington, the more a politician reacts to stories, the more trouble he creates for himself.

This characteristic of Washington is evident even to a nonpolitician like famed movie director Robert Altman, who with Trudeau made the HBO miniseries *Tanner '88* about the 1988 presidential campaign. Altman said avoiding the press was what he learned from making the series. "What I learned was not to talk too much to the press," Altman told *U.S. News & World Report* when the series was re-aired during the 2004 campaign. "You step in potholes. Everybody's looking for a sound bite, not a story."[52]

Former Bush press secretary Ari Fleischer wrote that one of Bush's greatest strengths was his ability to ignore media criticism, especially concerning the war on terror. "He had faith and confidence in the mission and the abilities of our military to carry it out," Fleischer wrote. "He didn't waver in the face of skeptical questioning. He kept his sights on the long-term goal of defeating the Taliban and routing Al Qaeda, no matter how long it took. He didn't like the press's impatience, but he never let it get to him. He wouldn't let it change his policies."[53]

The White House press secretary each day usually has what is called "the morning gaggle," which is a low-key morning briefing of reporters where no television cameras are allowed. Bush almost daily wanted a summary of Fleischer's press briefings as a way of knowing what was on the minds of reporters and "about the controversy du jour and how the press were approaching it." Fleischer wrote that Bush spent part of each morning checking out the headlines and stories that interested him, but he only occasionally watched television news or talk shows. "For the most part, he counted on me and Karen Hughes or Dan Bartlett, the communications director, to fill him in, but he didn't lose any sleep over what was on TV," Fleischer wrote. "He presumed most of it would be highly opinionated and largely negative, and he expected the communications staff to deal with it."[54]

Bush doesn't deal with any favorite reporter, either. Since at least the time of Andrew Johnson, who forged a special professional relationship with the *Cincinnati Commercial*'s Joseph B. McCullagh in the late 1860s, some presidents have had particular reporters they rely on to get their stories out. Kennedy, for example, gave special access to the *New York Times*'s Arthur Krok.[55] But according to Hutcheson, the current relationship is all business. "He's just a very private man," Hutcheson said. "I'm sure there are always these stories about past presidents calling their favorite reporters at night; I just don't picture Bush doing that or have heard of that ever happening."[56]

Before Bush hurt his knee, he would invite reporters, including Hutcheson, to jog with him. When Bush started riding a bike because of knee trouble, he would sometimes invite reporters along for rides, but Bush isn't thrilled when the ride is turned into a story, said Hutcheson. "I think there's an element of 'We're just going to go out and ride bikes,'" he continued. "The thing about Bush is he so zealously guards his private time, and so when he lets someone into his private time—and unlike most presidents, he views, he thinks he can draw a lot sharper line between 'private' and 'public' than certainly the press ever thinks and than some previous presidents have thought."[57]

G. Robert Hillman, a White House correspondent for the *Dallas Morning News*, wrote a feature story about Bush's exercise habits at his Crawford ranch, but it was based on an interview with Mark McKinnon, not Bush. Hillman included quite a bit of detail about what trails Bush likes to ride, the model of his bike, and the fact that he wears a heart monitor and listens to country music on an iPod while he rides. McKinnon said Bush burns about 1,000 calories on the ride but made up for it with a big lunch. When Hillman asked what Bush had for lunch, McKinnon dismissed the question with "Off-limits."[58]

Reporters started feeling that access to Bush was off-limits even before the 2000 election was over, giving them a sense of powerlessness. During the legal battles over the Florida recount, a CNN anchor asked the network's Austin correspondent what Bush was doing. The frustrated reporter replied, "Your guess is as good as mine."[59] During the 2004 campaign, Bush often bypassed the White House press in favor of local newspapers in battleground states. In one case, Bush invited reporters from local Ohio newspapers on board his campaign bus for interviews while reporters from the *New York Times* and the *Washington Post* were on another bus in the caravan.[60] Bush's strategy paid off with a win in Ohio, a state that turned out to be the key to the election.

Critics of the White House press charge that when reporters do get access to Bush, they don't ask him tough questions about the war or potential administration scandals. The critics include a wide assortment of pundits, professors, and political hacks. Even members of the White House press have engaged in a surprising amount of self-flagellation over supposedly giving Bush a free ride. The critics have offered several theories for the allegedly softball coverage, although most revolve around the reporters' desire to look good in the eyes of the public, something a hard-nosed watchdog journalist is not supposed to worry about.

One theory, which has already been explored earlier in the chapter, is that Bush and the correspondents have a good-ol'-boy locker-room relationship, and reporters would never put their buddy on the hot seat. Another school of thought is that when Bush entered the White House, the reporters were suffering from their own Clinton fatigue. Worn out from eight years of Travelgate, Whitewater, Monica Lewinsky, ad nauseam, they felt that with Bush they "could breathe easier."[61] Todd Gitlin, a journalism and sociology professor at Columbia University and frequent media critic, wrote that the press had been distracted from covering serious issues even before Clinton and Lewinsky, overcovering such events as the O. J. Simpson trial and Princess Di's fatal car accident. Nevertheless, the press was easier on Bush's potential donor scandals than Clinton's scandals because it would have looked mean to criticize "a chief executive who was so, well, unchief like."[62]

Gitlin wrote that reporters were also afraid of being labeled "liberal" and "unpatriotic." The Bush family, according to Gitlin, has been playing the label game since George H. W. Bush ran for president, "boxing journalists about the ears," in "a game they routinely win as long as reporters, cowed by the 'liberal media' charge, turn themselves into megaphones for the right-wing noise machine." The reporters become stenographers to avoid complaints, but stenography benefits sources who want to "obfuscate," he concluded.[63]

The pressure to be stenographers for the administration in times of war is almost overwhelming. During World War II, for example, the U.S. War Department did not have much trouble censoring stories because the reporters largely censored themselves. The war was universally considered a just war of defense against tyranny, and journalists wanted to contribute to the effort.[64] Similarly, the terrorist attacks on 9/11 were widely viewed as attacks justifying a strong military response. A scholarly analysis of the editorial pages of the *Washington Post* and the *New York Times* in the month between September 11 and October 7, 2001, when the military campaign began in Afghanistan, showed that the editorials became more supportive of the administration position over the time period studied and that not one of the editorials explicitly criticized the Bush administration's plans. The authors wrote that the positions of these two influential papers would be noticed and considered by many smaller media.[65]

Paul McMasters, First Amendment ombudsman for the First Amendment Center in Arlington, Virginia, told *Presstime* that reporters "care about Sept. 11, rightfully," but "didn't really probe into the ramifications of the USA PATRIOT Act on civil rights, failed to really cover the FOI exemptions in the Homeland Security Act, fumbled the coverage of peace protests and failed to question the executive orders of President Bush on classification and openness."[66]

Even political cartoonists gave Bush a break in the aftermath of 9/11. Mike Luckovich of the *Atlanta Journal-Constitution* said he shrunk Bush's ears in caricatures after 9/11 partly because he believed everyone "was in this together" now. "I still want to skewer him in cartoons, but I think he deserves to have a little smaller ears," Luckovich said.[67]

The cease-fire did not last long. The *American-Statesman*'s Ben Sargent recalled that a few weeks after 9/11, he asked another cartoonist, "Are we ready to stop drawing World War II posters yet?" "I haven't backed off," Sargent said. "[Bush's] face has gotten a little more strange. A reader called and said she was canceling her subscription because I made him look like a chimpanzee. I wanted to write back [and say] I didn't make him look like a chimpanzee; God made him look like a chimpanzee."[68]

But even if some of the cartoonists were again ready to attack Bush, some of their bosses were still a little squeamish about running antiwar cartoons. The *San Diego Union-Tribune*, which supported the war, compromised with cartoonist Steve Breen and ran his drawing of Bush, National Security Advisor Condoleeza Rice, Defense Secretary Donald Rumsfeld, and Vice President Dick Cheney on "Mount Rush to War" in the paper's Sunday roundup section rather than the featured spot on the editorial page. The *Record* of Hackensack, New Jersey, rejected David Margulies's drawing of Bush holding the Oscar for "Best Performance in a Misleading Role" because the editor thought it was too flippant—not because he disagreed with the sentiment. The *Pittsburgh Post-Gazette* rejected Rob Rogers's panel comparing 9/11 to "slaughtering Native Americans, Slavery and nuking Japan," because it was too soon after the attack and feelings were still raw. And the *Atlanta Journal-Constitution* rejected Luckovich's drawing of happy faces on coffins as a sign of administration spin because it might be interpreted as mocking soldiers rather than the administration.[69]

Koring said that Bush benefited from the natural pattern of initial support for a leader when he first assumes office and later from patriotism when the country was attacked. But Koring said all Western media tend to do this, not just the White House press corps. "This doesn't apply to all individuals, but I think there is a collective media relationship that doesn't always follow a pattern. . . . The Canadian media kind of fell in love with [Pierre] Trudeau when he was first elected and the British media kind of fell in love with Maggie Thatcher when she was first elected and the American media kind of fell in love with—'fell in love with' is probably too strong a term—was enamored by, slightly bedazzled by, whatever the right word is, with Ronald Reagan when he first came to office," Koring said. "There is probably a natural equilibrium of relationship between a Western media and a political leader that is adversarial in nature. That tends to kind of swing like a pendulum, swing from adversarial to not adversarial enough, if you are measuring on some cosmic scale, and when societies are under particular stress or have been particularly shocked, I think both the body politic and the media tend to swing to not being adversarial enough."[70]

Longtime White House UPI correspondent Helen Thomas said simply that the performance of the press corps was "lousy" when asked about its coverage of Bush. "They haven't asked the questions that should have been asked," she said. "We never should have had the credibility gap we have now on why we went to war. Everything they said was not true. It was up to the reporters to challenge the information. The Congress didn't challenge, either. So we're deeply into a war we shouldn't have been in. Unprovoked. Illegal. Immoral."[71]

Hutcheson, however, said one of his "pet peeves" is the criticism that the White House press corps has not been tough enough on Bush. "That idea—and it mainly comes from the left—that we're lapdogs because we don't ask hard questions, well, you can ask a question like Helen Thomas did the other day: 'Why are we killing people in Iraq? Why are we killing innocent people in Iraq?' And then [Presidential press secretary] Scott [McClellan] starts talking about how we're trying to battle insurgents and terrorists. And Helen Thomas says, 'They're just trying to defend their own country.' All right, so there you go, the left says, 'Great, that's what the media should be doing.'

"Well, it's not a debating contest. Our job is to elicit information, and you're never going to elicit information from George Bush by confronting him. There are ways to ask difficult questions, but if you go straight at him with a difficult question like that, you're not going to get anything besides boilerplate. He's very good at hitting the tape button and playing the tape, and the real challenge is to ask him a question that will get him to go beyond that, and I guarantee you don't get him to do that by coming on like a Helen Thomas or a Michael Moore or somebody like that."[72]

Hutcheson cited as an example an interview of Bush by an Irish journalist shortly before the president went on a European trip. "She really got in his face. It was really an entertaining interview, in a way you can elicit that to piss him off, which sometimes can be kind of journalistically useful—she did. She basically said flat out, 'We hate you in Europe'—that kind of thing, and Bush got his back up, and it didn't go anywhere.

"A week later I asked essentially the same question in a much more gentle way and got a much more thoughtful response. . . . It's all in how you ask the question, because when he responded to me, the [answer] was along the lines about, 'Yeah, it does bother me, and yeah, I have thought about it,' and then eventually wound up with the boilerplate, but there was at least an acknowledgement that, 'Yes, I recognize that there is validity to the question,' whereas when you come to him at his face, he goes straight into the defensive crouch and kind of says, 'What kind of question is that?'"[73]

But Thomas said that reporters failed to hold Bush accountable. "You can force him, because you can keep writing the president has not fulfilled his accountability, and write it early and often of how he has avoided questions that should have been asked and should be asked, and at some point you smoke them out," she said. "There's a blackout in the news, and it is affecting every human life in the country—in all the world, in fact. You should press—that's the kind of power a president has."[74]

Ultimately, every source, whether a president, a police officer, or a person on the street has the power to say no to a reporter. No journalist can compel a source to talk. It's true that a prestigious journalist or even a not-so-prestigious journalist working for a prestigious organization has a megaphone that a source might want to use. Journalists even have a certain amount of power in that they can produce stories about a source whether the source cooperates or not. As Robert Novak said, there are two types of people in Washington: sources and targets.[75]

Fleischer has a unique perspective because he worked for Bush and worked closely with Thomas and Hutcheson. He devoted an entire chapter of his memoir to his relationship with Thomas, referring to her as his "sparring partner" because of her confrontational questions. Fleischer wrote that he respected her as a justifiable "icon in American journalism" and that they got along well on a personal level. But he noted that during Bush's term she was a columnist and was therefore more free to state her opinions than a straight news reporter is. For example, when she was quoted as saying Bush was the worst president in American history, Fleischer called her about it and she simply affirmed the statement.[76]

Fleischer described Hutcheson as "one of the most thoughtful reporters" he'd ever met, and noted that he used a "savvy" way to elicit a comment from Bush about Iraq by asking him how being a member of the Vietnam War generation would affect his thinking.[77]

Fleischer indicated the friendly approach worked better than the in-your-face attacks. He cited as an example how the press harassed Bush for some information about how he would decide whether the government would fund stem cell research. Bush took his time on the decision, gathering information for more than a month during the summer of 2001, before 9/11 dominated all national debate. According to Fleischer, reporters shouted at Bush every time they saw him whether he had made up his mind.[78]

"I often thought how differently I'd approach the topic if I was a reporter," Fleischer wrote. "If the press *wanted* him to ignore their questions, asking him about stem cell first was the best way to have him walk away and take no questions. If, instead, they had lured him into taking questions with a different first topic, then popped the stem cell question, they might have gotten more from him."[79]

The debate about how to handle Bush as a news source and whether the press was doing its job reached a crescendo following Bush's March 6, 2003, prime-time press conference. The self-flagellation of some of the reporters who were at the press conference was almost as denigrating as the criticism from left-wing pundits. As such, it is worth examining the press conference in detail. The next chapter will illustrate how Bush deals with the group that many consider to be the toughest reporters on the planet.

9

EATING THE ZOMBIES

Ask Knight-Ridder's Ron Hutcheson about Bush's March 6, 2003, press conference—or more appropriately criticism that the press conference was a scripted event in which the press corps was complicit with the administration—and his voice gets louder and he admits the issue is a hot button for him. "That pisses me off," Hutcheson said, referring to charges that reporters told Bush in advance what questions they would ask. "That's just a total misunderstanding of, first, what Bush meant when he made a joke, which is what it was."[1]

Bush made the joke, which backfired on him, when he turned down one reporter's question to instead go to CNN's John King by saying, according to the White House transcript: "We'll be there in a minute. King, John King. This is a scripted—(laughter)."[2]

Hutcheson said the event was scripted only insofar as Bush had a list of reporters and was following long-established protocol in who would get the first questions. "Basically, like any president, he goes in there with some idea of who he is going to call on, and part of that is, you know, the first seven questions, seven or eight, are strictly protocol—you know, you call the wires, you call the networks," Hutcheson said. "So once you get through AP, Reuters, you got the four networks we have today, with Fox and CNN thrown in there, there's seven questions right there that you got to do, and then he's got some other people that he feels like, 'I need to call on this guy this time or this guy this time.' And that's what he meant from 'This is all scripted here.' He had that list."[3]

Helen Thomas, who had covered the White House longer than any other reporter on duty at the time of the press conference, acknowledged that the first two questions traditionally would go to the wire services. And when she worked for United Press International, she and the reporter for the Associated Press, the other main wire service, would rotate who got the opening question. "The regulars are called on, as well they should be because they're manning the barricades seven days a week, and they should get first crack—those who are covering every minute and every day, instead of walking in from the cold at a presidential news conference," Thomas said. "The president is pretty familiar with the people who cover him regularly."[4]

Thomas said that although there has always been a tradition of calling on representatives of certain news organizations, Bush's press conferences are more scripted than those of other presidents she has covered. "He has a list of reporters to call on, which is rather unusual," she said. When reminded that the crowd laughed at Bush's scripting remark, Thomas said: "Well, it was a joke, but it was true. I mean he was trying to be funny because he knew it was so bizarre."[5]

Many media observers did not take Bush's remark as a joke. The *New York Press*'s Matt Taibbi was so disgusted with what he thought was a softball press conference that he wrote, "The entire White House Press corps should be herded into a cargo plane, flown to an altitude of 30,000 feet, and pushed out, kicking and screaming, over the North Atlantic."[6] Even some of the White House beat reporters agreed that their group had done a poor job. ABC News reporter Terry Moran, quoted in a *New York Observer* piece titled "Bush Eats the Press," said the president was not "sufficiently challenged" in the press conference and made the journalists look like "zombies."[7]

In most horror movies, the zombies eat their victims, not the other way around. But Bush is a president dubbed "the Great Polarizer" by *Time* magazine, and it is not surprising that others see the press as the soulless monster looking to feed on presidential flesh.[8] Brent Bozell, a conservative media critic, wrote that the reporters asked tough questions, including one by Moran that "lectured" Bush that international opinion perceived the United States as "an arrogant power." "The standard for the event's worth, then, was not whether Bush was held accountable to his audience, but whether the press pounded him sufficiently," Bozell wrote.[9]

The debate over whether reporters pounded Bush or were merely zombie slaves hypnotized by his presidential charm intensified after the seminal prewar press conference, which has come to symbolize the idea that reporters are easy on Bush. About six months after the press conference, *American Journalism Review*, for example, used a description of the event to lead a nine-page cover story, "Are the News Media Soft on Bush?"[10] A letter to the editor in a subsequent issue of the magazine castigated the White House press corps, saying the reporters should have refused to hold a press conference if they had to submit questions in advance. The writer, Kenny Goldberg, a health reporter for KPBS in San Diego, said the press conference was "the most pathetic example of journalism I've ever seen" and criticized the reporters for asking most of their questions about Iraq rather than the economy.[11]

The criticism of Bush's press coverage continued throughout 2003 and into the election year. Critiques appeared from the left and the right and in a variety of publications. Allan Wolper wrote in *Editor & Publisher* that "it seems the Bush White House is wearing down the press."[12] *Salon.com* media critic Philip J. Trounstine, writing a little more than a year after the press conference in an article suggestively titled "Bush's Press Slaves," argued that the media should be harder on the president.[13] Tom Wicker blamed the press for failing to probe Bush's reasons for invading Iraq.[14] Columnist Richard Reeves rejoiced when Bush was attacked by John Kerry early in the presidential campaign because "We haven't seen that in a while—neither press nor politicians have laid a glove on the 'war president.'"[15] But columnist and former Republican speechwriter Peggy Noonan chastised the press for being unfair to Bush.[16]

The debate is not easy to resolve because it's hard for the debaters to be neutral about politics. "It's the eye of the beholder," CBS White House correspondent Bill Plante said when asked about criticism of the prewar press conference. "I mean it depends on who's doing the assessing. A lot of people who disagree with this president's policies, or any president—we got the same complaint with Clinton—the people who disagree believe you should hector the president and go after him hammer and tongs and scream."[17]

But Plante said the form of a presidential press conference places some limits on the White House reporters. "There's a certain decorum, and this president just about refuses to take follow-up questions, and there's nothing much you can do," Plante explained. "I mean, you can yell and scream; it won't get you anywhere, except uninvited to the next one. But even if you didn't care about that, it still wouldn't produce any results."[18]

One of the problems with analyzing the success of presidential press conferences is that the press and the president want different results from them. The president wants to convey a message and an image to the public. The press wants to hold the president accountable for his actions. The dominant party has seesawed back and forth, depending upon the man in the White House and the character of the reporters covering him. Both sides have advantages and disadvantages in the press conference.

The president has the biggest advantage because he decides whether to hold the press conference at all, although the press often tries to shame the president into holding more press conferences by writing about his lack of accessibility. The president also has an extensive press office that can prepare him for the questions he will likely face. Although the press conference appears to be an open forum for reporters, the president maintains control through things like scheduling and deciding who asks questions. Because there are large numbers of journalists involved, the opportunity for follow-up questions is reduced, and presidents find press conferences easier to control than one-on-one interviews.[19]

Reporters, however, are not powerless. They get to choose their questions, and the public nature of the event forces the president to answer them or else appear ignorant, devious, or both. Many reporters consider open presidential press conferences "sacrosanct" because they protect the collective interest of the White House press corps. The journalists achieve an important status as a group that most would never achieve as individuals, and the president's ability to "divide and conquer" by favoring certain reporters is greatly reduced.[20]

Reporters seem to have gotten the upper hand over the past 50 years, although the advantage in the early years went to the president. Theodore Roosevelt is generally considered to be among the first and best at handling this forum. In Roosevelt's tenure, the sessions were a kind of "club" that only the most privileged reporters could attend, but by the 1980s press conferences had become more of a show for the public, and "their intrinsic value to a thoughtful reporter" had declined.[21] Some research on presidential press conferences indicates that reporters became much more aggressive and less deferential during the intervening 30 years between the Eisenhower and Reagan administrations.[22] William S. White blamed television for adding "sheer theater" to press conferences and argued that TV tends to favor the more aggressive reporters over thoughtful journalists.[23]

One scholar wrote that the "adversarial relationship appears to be a well-established fact of life" and reporters have turned the event into an irritating and embarrassing situation for modern presidents, who are finding other ways to communicate with the public.[24] For example, research shows that presidents are progressively giving more speeches while holding fewer press conferences.[25]

The press conference is unlikely to disappear because it serves a useful function for the president, who can demonstrate to the public his command of the issues, or at least his fearlessness in facing an adversarial press, which makes him look sympathetic even if he struggles with their questions. Presidential scholar Martha Joynt Kumar noted that although various modern presidents have experimented with changes in the format of the press conference in terms of location, time, and other elements, the event has continued "to be an enduring publicity forum for chief executives."[26]

The press conference has also proven to be an enduring benefit to the public. One scholar concluded that the institution is a "vital servant" of democracy because it contains aspects of leadership, accountability, information, and image-building in one venue and serves both the president and the press.[27] Another argued that although the president "holds most of the cards" because he arranges the press conference and chooses the questioners, the press conference "still retains enough spontaneity that it can serve public and press well."[28] The forum especially serves the public because it shows the president "in action under conditions likely to illuminate his mind at work and his techniques. . . . [Press conferences] stand alone as firsthand records of presidential 'action' and reflection."[29]

Helen Thomas strongly believes the news conference is a public duty for the president. "Presidential news conferences are the only forum in our society where the president can be questioned on a regular basis, and if the president isn't questioned—I mean, this sounds memorized, but I've said it so often—if the president isn't questioned, he can be a dictator, he can be a king, he can rule by executive order, and that's not the way democracy works," she said. "So presidents should be questioned early and often on everything they do. He can be subpoenaed by Congress, true, but they're not going to do that unless it's a critical, dire situation. But we should be asking him why he does certain things—give a rationale and so forth."[30]

When asked if reporters should have posed more questions to Bush at the prewar news conference, Thomas said: "Absolutely, even though they knew the die was cast and he was going. He wanted to go to war—we all knew that for a couple of years. But it was very important to pin him down, and they didn't."[31]

Did the White House correspondents pin him down, or did Bush towel snap them into submission? The question for the prewar press conference is important because it is the event that for many critics symbolizes the failure of the White House press corps. Answering the question in an objective way is difficult, but one scholar has provided a thoughtful approach. Carolyn Smith explained a method for analyzing presidential press conferences in her aptly titled 1990 book, *Presidential Press Conferences: A Critical Approach*,[32] which provides a useful framework for examining the interaction between Bush and the White House reporters.

Smith argues for evaluating a press conference from the perspective of both the press and the president in order to judge its merits more completely. She says that most press conference critics evaluate them from the viewpoint of either the press or the president. They then evaluate the press conference based on one of two standards: whether the president was persuasive or whether the press held the president accountable. She argued that critics should instead evaluate the quality of the press conference from both sides. Every good press conference should reflect the inherent tension between the two sides; the press should be neither hostile nor fawning.

Smith writes that the first step in evaluating a press conference is to determine the agenda of the session, which is a combination of the agendas of the president and the press.[33] The heart of Smith's approach is the second step: analyzing the quality of the press questions and the president's responses to them.[34] Lastly, Smith calls for examining news coverage and public reaction to the press conference to try to determine its effects.[35] What follows is an examination of Bush's March 6, 2003, press conference based on these steps.

A president's agenda, or purpose, for a press conference may be evident from his opening statement or the news cycle leading to the session, or the president may have a hidden agenda, hoping to diffuse a potential controversy by addressing it obliquely in the session. Press conferences can also be "institutional," having no apparent purpose other than to maintain contact between the president and the press.[36] In the case of the prewar press conference, Bush's agenda was clearly to persuade the public of the necessity of war if Saddam Hussein did not comply with a UN resolution demanding that he disarm. The press conference was among a series of speeches and public appearances by various members of the administration, including Bush, to make the case that Iraq must be disarmed.

The press conference was held the day before the UN's chief weapons inspector, Hans Blix, was to deliver an updated report on Iraq. Bush, in a rather lengthy opening statement of 15 paragraphs, first briefly mentioned the capture of one of the planners of the 9/11 attacks, Khalid Sheikh Mohammed, but then immediately referred to Blix's upcoming report as "an important moment in confronting the threat posed to our nation and to peace." Bush said there was only one question to ask: "Has the Iraqi regime fully and unconditionally disarmed, as required by Resolution 1441, or has it not?"

Both David Gergen, a former Clinton adviser, and William Kristol, editor of the conservative *Weekly Standard*, agreed that Bush's question framed the upcoming debate over invading Iraq around an absolute standard of compliance with the resolution, rather than whether Blix reported that Iraq was making progress toward compliance.[37]

Some observers believed Bush needed to make his case for war to both the American people and the country's allies. For example, NBC reporter Tim Russert said Bush needed to answer two questions: Why Iraq? and Why now?[38] However, others thought Bush had already made his case in previous speeches, and the purpose of the press conference was largely to reassure the American people that he had carefully considered his decision.[39]

Bush's opening statement contained no new information but instead repeated arguments he had made in previous speeches, including one to the American Medical Association that focused on Medicare reform.[40] His tone was so somber that it was commented upon by numerous critics. *Washington Post* columnist Tom Shales wrote that Bush was too grim: "There were times when it seemed every sentence Bush spoke was of the same duration and delivered in the same dour monotone, giving his comments a numbing, soporific aura."[41] But Kristol praised Bush because "he didn't seem reckless, he didn't seem impetuous."[42] Different viewers took away different impressions, but it is clear that Bush tried to set an extremely serious tone through his mannerisms and speech.

White House communications director Dan Bartlett confirmed that Bush scheduled the press conference because he knew what the majority of the questions would be and he wanted to answer them. "We think the public will see the thought and care and attention he's given to a lot of the different questions that are being asked about the diplomatic side and the military side and the potential post-Iraq issue. These are all legitimate questions that he has answers for and wants to talk about."[43]

The questions on the journalists' agenda are easy to discover by reading the front pages of major newspapers for a few days before the event. The best reporters will ask questions based on current stories because obscure questions and the president's answers to them will not make news.[44] In the case of the March 6, 2003, press conference, the most newsworthy topic was obviously the crisis over Iraq. Major U.S. newspapers often carried multiple stories on the crisis in the week preceding the press conference. The journalists' agenda is also shown by the first few questions of the press conference, which are usually asked by senior reporters and set the tone for the event.[45] The first question, a rambling paragraph that actually included three questions, and the second question, a follow-up, essentially asked Bush how soon the United States would go to war. Although the next question concerned North Korea, 21 out of the 23 questions concerned the crisis with Iraq.[46]

The heart of press conference analysis, according to Smith, is an examination of questions and answers. A good press conference will have compelling questions and persuasive answers. "The best press exchanges are those which reveal that the president is exercising legitimate leadership and the press is exercising its legitimate watchdog role," Smith wrote.[47]

As mentioned above, the first question of this press conference was a poorly worded five-line statement that sought to pin Bush down on a date for war. It also strongly hinted the reporter's own position through the phrasing, "And what harm would it do to give Saddam a final ultimatum?" Smith would likely have disapproved of this opening; she notes that questions for new information are "usually unproductive" and that "the advocacy question has no legitimate place in a presidential press conference."[48] In this case, Bush ignored the question, vaguely stating the administration was in the "final stages of diplomacy" and repeating the argument he had made in his opening statement. Although several critics of the press conference decried the lack of follow-up questions,[49] the next reporter restated the question, "Are we days away?" but Bush, as one would expect for military reasons, refused to give a specific date for war, saying, "We are days away from resolving this issue at the [UN] Security Council."

This exchange was fairly representative of the rest of the press conference. The reporters exercised their watchdog role by asking Bush questions on various aspects of the upcoming war, but the questions were often overlong and poorly worded and seemed to advocate an antiwar position. Some questions were ones that Bush obviously could not answer. One could hardly have expected Bush to say, "We will attack in three days." Had Bush wanted to issue an ultimatum, he would have done so in a speech, as he did in fact several days later when he warned Saddam Hussein to leave Iraq.

The third question was better phrased but took the president off the topic that was on everyone's mind. "If North Korea restarts their plutonium plant, will that change your thinking about how to handle this crisis, or are you resigned to North Korea becoming a nuclear power?" Bush answered the question appropriately, reaffirming that the issue was important to the United States and its allies and that he believed the best course was the current one of "multilateral" negotiations.

The next reporter made the biggest mistake of the night from the standpoint of holding the president accountable. A natural follow-up would have queried Bush about an apparent inconsistency: Why a multilateral solution for North Korea but not for Iraq? This type of question—asking about inconsistencies—is often the best for holding a president accountable for his policies, according to Smith.[50]

Instead of following this line of reasoning, the reporter instead asked Bush why some U.S. allies did not think the Iraqi threat was imminent when they were privy to the same intelligence data. The question was important and legitimate and set up a controversy Bush could settle. But like many others, it was too long—10 lines in the transcript—and indicated the reporter favored the Canadian proposal to give Hussein more time. The phrases "that would give you a little bit of a chance to build more support" and "Is that something the government should be pursuing?" show bias and weaken the reporter's legitimacy. The rambling nature of the question allowed Bush to answer the easier part first and demonstrate his resolve by saying: "We, of course, are consulting with our allies at the United Nations. But I meant what I said, this is the last phase of diplomacy." Bush brushed aside the intelligence issue by repeating that there were a number of allies involved in the coalition.

A follow-up question on the intelligence issue would have been justified, and the next questioner did follow it after a fashion, but in a confused, roundabout way and with another suggestion of advocacy. The reporter first asked Bush what he was "waiting to hear or see" before deciding on war. This question was a poor one because Bush would have revealed this already if he intended to; instead, he just repeated his earlier statements that Hussein must disarm. The second part of the question referred to peace protestors and seemed to attack Bush by quoting their idea "that the U.S. was a threat to peace" and mused, "I wonder why you think so many people around the world take a different view of the threat that Saddam Hussein poses than you and your allies." This question was legitimate and challenged Bush. The president's response was measured. He acknowledged the view of the protestors and agreed that he did not want war. But Bush reasserted forcefully that he believed disarming Hussein was necessary. "The risk of doing nothing, the risk of hoping that Saddam Hussein changes his mind and becomes a gentle soul, the risk that somehow—that inaction will make the world safer, is a risk I'm not willing to take for the American people," Bush said.

The next exchange became the most controversial part of the press conference when Bush made the aforementioned joke about the press conference being scripted. Bush was joking about the process of calling reporters from a list—something Bill Clinton, George H. W. Bush, and Ronald Reagan had done as well[51]—and correspondents acknowledged he was joking by laughing at his aside. Presidents practice before press conferences and know the identity of the reporters they call on. The spontaneity occurs because reporters are free to ask whatever they want, and indeed they did during the prewar event.

John King's question following Bush's joke was certainly not one Bush would have scripted: "How would you answer your critics who say that they think this is somehow personal? As Senator Kennedy put it tonight, he said your fixation with Saddam Hussein is making the world a more dangerous place." The topic was legitimate and phrased in a way to challenge Bush, but King made the mistake of going on too long and asking Bush to provide details on worst-case scenarios in terms of casualties and financial costs—something the president was unlikely to share. Bush answered the question by dramatically raising his hand as if taking the oath of office and saying: "People can ascribe all kinds of intentions. I swore to protect and defend the Constitution; that's what I swore to do. I put my hand on the Bible and took that oath, and that's exactly what I am going to do." The question seemed to irritate Bush, and after reiterating why he believed Hussein was a threat, he said, "The rest of your six-point question?"[52] Ordinarily, presidents look bad when they show displeasure in a press conference. But King looked worse in the exchange by asking a question that implied the president would go to war to avenge his father. The phrasing seemed to be a personal attack on the president, something Americans instinctively dislike.[53]

The next question was another lengthy, strongly worded attack question, following up on previous questions about the rift between the United States and some of its allies. The questioner was the aforementioned Terry Moran, who later called himself and his colleagues "zombies" for their weak performance.[54] Moran's question indicated he was a zombie, if the description means creatures that are out for blood: "May I ask, what went wrong that so many governments and people around the world now not only disagree with you very strongly, but see the U.S. under your leadership as an arrogant power?" The question was emotional and biased. The wording assumed that Bush had done something wrong and implied he was a poor leader. In general, the more hostile the question, the more benign the answer should be, and Bush backed off from his sarcastic response to King, instead answering Moran evenly, repeating that "a lot" of nations would be with the coalition, although he understood that France and Germany disagreed with the United States on the use of force.

"Having said that, they're still our friends and we will deal with them as friends," Bush said. "We've got a lot of common interests. Our transatlantic relationships are very important. While they may disagree with how we deal with Saddam Hussein and his weapons of mass destruction, there's no disagreement when it came time to vote on [UN Security Council Resolution] 1441, at least as far as France was concerned. They joined us. They said Saddam Hussein has one last chance of disarming. If they think more time will cause him to disarm, I disagree with that."

The next question was one of the shortest of the evening—one sign of a good question—and was effective in that it tried to hold the president accountable for past rhetoric, in this case his famous statement that he wanted Osama bin Laden "dead or alive." The reporter asked if the Iraq operation would be a success if the United States did not capture Hussein "dead or alive." Bush tried to evade the question by responding that the regime would change, "and replacing this cancer" would create a better government. The reporter repeated the question in an even more economical phrasing, and Bush repeated that the "regime" would change. The question was legitimate and phrased well, but Bush could have answered it better by stating more forcefully that the administration goals did not depend upon the capture of one man. His answer made him seem evasive.

The subsequent question followed up on other queries about the necessity of the war. It was a poor question because it was long, confusing and referred to the reporter's own opinion: "Mr. President, to a lot of people, it seems that war is probably inevitable, because many people doubt—most people, I would guess—that Saddam Hussein will ever do what we are demanding that he do, which is disarm." The reporter cited polls and attacked Bush by suggesting that many people don't believe him: "A lot of people . . . who agree that he should be disarmed, who listen to you say that you [Bush] have the evidence, but who feel they haven't seen it, and who still wonder why blood has to be shed if he hasn't attacked us." Did the reporter want Bush to respond to poll results or explain why the United States should attack if Hussein hasn't attacked first? The bias and confrontational nature of the question made Bush look sympathetic, and the confusing question structure allowed Bush to answer any way he chose. He handled it well by referring to the reporter's statement that people believe Hussein should be disarmed but is not going to disarm—there is only way to do it, "and that happens to be my last choice—the use of force."

The next exchange was brief and effective. The reporter asked Bush if he would call for a UN Security Council vote on attacking Iraq even if he thought the United States would not win the vote. The reporter followed up immediately to get Bush to confirm his answer. Bush did so in memorable language: "No matter what the whip count is, we're calling for the vote. We want people to stand up and say what their opinion is about Saddam Hussein and the utility of the United Nations Security Council. And so, you bet. It's time for people to show their cards, to let the world know where they stand when it comes to Saddam." It was a good question that elicited new information, and the whole exchange took fewer lines in the transcript than several of the long-winded previous questions.

The following question was also brief and effective, pursuing the UN theme by asking Bush what would happen if the United States attacked without UN approval. The reporter's biased phrasing, asking Bush if he would be "worried" if the United States was seen as "defiant" of the United Nations, actually worked well by provoking Bush to a revealing response about his thinking. "No, I'm not worried about that," Bush said immediately. He added that although the United States had been working through the United Nations, U.S. security was paramount. "When it comes to our security, we really don't need anybody's permission," Bush said.

Another reporter then followed the theme of asking about the reaction of allies, specifically Turkey's hesitancy to allow troops to attack from its territory. The first part of the question suggested casualties would be higher without Turkey's cooperation, an opinion that Bush could be expected to dismiss, and he did, saying he was "confident" it would not be a "hardship." The second half of the question was more effective, asking Bush if he would stop backing Turkey's entry into the European Union if it didn't cooperate on the war. Bush answered unhesitatingly that he would continue to support Turkey, which he described as a "friend."

After fielding several tough questions in a row trying to get Bush to explain aspects of the possible war, Bush was next asked a rambling question about his faith that critics later cited as an example of a "softball" because it let Bush expound on his Christianity.[55] But the reporter was really trying to get Bush to swing and miss at a curve. The first half of the confusingly worded question referred to critics of Bush's policy: "Mr. President, as the nation is at odds over war, with many organizations like the Congressional Black Caucus pushing for continued diplomacy through the UN, how is your faith guiding you?" The question suggested the reporter's attitude that there was discrepancy between faith and support for the war, but it was so poorly worded the president could answer however he wanted. The former baseball executive hit the question out of the park, answering emotionally, "My faith sustains me because I pray daily." Bush skillfully connected himself with the millions of his fellow citizens who are religious: "One thing that's really great about our country, April, is there are thousands of people who pray for me that I'll never see and be able to thank. But it's a humbling experience to think that people I will never have met have lifted me and my family up in prayer. And for that I'm grateful. That's—it's been a comforting feeling to know that is true. I pray for peace, April. I pray for peace." The exchange definitely favored the president, but not because the reporter was trying to be his foil. The question was poorly constructed, although it was a legitimate attempt to make Bush comment on the role of his faith in the crisis, an important topic given his emphasis upon it in his campaigns.

The next reporter raised another good topic, asking Bush whether the war would lead to more terrorism and instability in the Middle East. The reporter challenged Bush by prefacing the question with a reference to disagreements with Bush's ideas, "As you know, not everyone shares your optimistic vision of how this might play out." Bush refused to be baited and answered evenly that, "It's hard to envision more terror on America than September the 11th, 2001." Bush, focusing on his main purpose for the press conference, said he had "thought long and hard about the use of troops" but concluded the cost of inaction was more dangerous than war and that a better world would develop after the liberation of Iraq. The question and answer were both reasonable.

The following question, at first glance, appears to be a waste of valuable time in a rare presidential press conference. The reporter asked whether the president would give enough warning to let weapons inspectors, humanitarian workers, and journalists out of Baghdad before the war started. Although the question in a way appeared to be self-serving because it asked about the safety of reporters, it induced Bush to essentially declare that he would not launch a surprise attack. Several previous questions had tried to nail Bush down on how soon a war might commence, and Bush had evaded them. But in this exchange, he confirmed: "Of course. We will give people a chance to leave." Although not a dramatic exchange, this answer put Bush on the record for the coming course of events.

Another reporter sought to put Bush on the record for the financial cost of the war but awkwardly tied it to Bush's rhetoric about tax cuts. "Sir, you've talked a lot about trusting the American people when it comes to making decisions about their own lives, about how to spend their own money. When it comes to the financial costs of the war, sir, it would seem that the administration, surely, has costed out various scenarios. If that's the case, why not present some of them to the American people so they know what to expect, sir?" It would have been legitimate to ask Bush whether he would be compelled to change the tax cut because of military costs, and the reporter could have constructed an either/or question to force Bush to make a stand on the record. Instead, the question attacked Bush's rhetoric and was almost a pleading for information. Bush handled the question easily, saying he would send a supplemental spending bill to Congress if the United States did go to war. Bush turned the topic back to 9/11, reminding the reporter that the United States had already suffered significant financial costs from terrorists. The president made the reporter look insensitive when he answered that human life, freedom, and security—"those are immeasurable costs. And I weigh those very seriously, Ed." Bush had made the financial cost of the war, which was a legitimate question, a minor side issue.

The next question was wasted. The reporter said he wanted to follow up on the earlier question about North Korea. Unfortunately, the reporter did not follow up but asked essentially the same question in different words, querying Bush about his attitude toward negotiations over North Korea's nuclear program. Bush, as one would expect, repeated a variation of his earlier answer—that the administration was making progress on the issue.

After that came a question that was factually inaccurate because it stated the United States entered the Vietnam War with the goal of "regime change." The United States, of course, was trying to prevent the toppling of South Vietnam's regime in that ill-fated war. Nevertheless, the question challenged Bush "to assure [the American people] that you will not lead this country down a similar path in Iraq." Bush either didn't notice or chose to ignore the reporter's embarrassing ignorance of history, but instead called it a "great question" and seized on it to distinguish the difference between the Vietnam War and the upcoming operation, using the word "clear" three times in five lines to describe the war's mission to disarm Iraq: "Our mission is precisely what I just stated," Bush said. "We have got a plan that will achieve that mission, should we need to send forces in." The question was legitimate and forced Bush to go on the record that he would not let Iraq turn into a quagmire. Bush's response showed determination and his understanding of the potential problem.

The final question's poor construction allowed Bush to wrap up the press conference the way he wanted. The reporter tried to ask Bush about his attitude toward a possible deadline being added to the UN resolution, but unwisely gave Bush an out by including the phrase "I know you don't want to tip your hand." Bush immediately responded, "You're right, I'm not going to tip my hand," and concluded the event by saying it was up to Hussein to stop the war. "He's the person that can make the choice of war and peace," Bush said. "Thus far, he's made the wrong choice. If we have to, for the sake of the American people, for the sake of the peace of the world, and for freedom to the Iraqi people, we will disarm Saddam Hussein. And by we, it's more than America. A lot of nations will join us."

The immediate effect of Bush's performance on the news agenda can be ascertained by looking at media coverage. Most news stories emphasized Bush's statements on talks at the United Nations and often quoted his statement that the United States did not need the UN's permission to invade. Wolf Blitzer of CNN said that the press conference "dispelled" any idea that Bush would hesitate to attack Iraq if it did not disarm and described Bush as "a man who refused to deviate from his stance."[56] The *New York Times* led with the "permission" quote, saying that Bush "vowed that he would press for a vote on a new resolution at the United Nations in the next few days."[57] The *Washington Post* had a very similar lead about the UN negotiations, stating that Bush "left no doubt that he would act to oust Iraqi President Saddam Hussein even without the blessing of the world body."[58] Bush was successful in getting the media to report that he was a determined leader who was ready to wage war regardless of the actions of the United Nations. Media accounts reported Bush's position that disarming Iraq was crucial to U.S. security.

However, Bush was unsuccessful in persuading opposing editorial page boards and pundits to back him. Those who criticized Bush before the press conference continued to do so. The *New York Times* argued on its editorial page that the United States should not attack without broad international support, and the *Washington Post* likewise editorialized that diplomacy should be given another chance.[59] The *Times*'s Maureen Dowd, a frequent Bush critic, ripped him after the press conference as the "Xanax Cowboy," a "scary" president who tried to sound reasonable but appeared "tranquilized."[60]

On the other hand, those who agreed with the president found no reason to change their opinion after his scrum with the press. The *Dallas Morning News*, for example, editorialized that "Mr. Bush convincingly made the case for war."[61] Jay Nordlinger, writing in the conservative *National Review*, argued that he could not imagine anyone doing better than Bush had done. "He did everything right, said everything right, thought everything right."[62]

The media opinion leaders remained polarized, but the public did not. A *New York Times*/CBS News poll taken two days after the press conference showed 44 percent of respondents favored military action against Iraq "soon," compared to 36 percent two weeks earlier. The poll showed 58 percent of Americans thought the United Nations was doing a poor job, which was up 10 points from the previous month, and 55 percent said they would support an invasion without UN approval. The *Times* concluded that the results "suggest that President Bush has made progress, at least at home, in portraying Saddam Hussein as a threat to peace while rallying support for a war over rising objections from the international community."[63]

The poll showed that Bush had achieved what he wanted from the press conference. He and other members of his administration had been making their case for disarming Iraq for many months. Little new information was revealed at the press conference. He could not reasonably expect to change the minds of the leaders of France or Germany nor could he expect to sway many partisans from the unfriendly side of a polarized body politic. That was never his intent. But Bush did show that he was a resolute leader determined to oust Hussein unless Iraq disarmed. Bush, through his language and mannerisms, demonstrated he was serious and was not going to war like a cowboy shooting up Dodge City. A majority of the country, the audience he wanted to reach, believed him.

Some members of the working press engaged in a round of self-flagellation and were given some additional vicious strokes of the rhetorical lash from pundits on the left side of the political spectrum. A detailed analysis of the questions and answers at the press conference shows that, although many of the questions were poorly worded, the White House reporters tried to do their job of holding the president accountable. They concentrated on the Iraq crisis, as they should have. It's true that they didn't ask questions about Osama bin Laden, Medicare, or the drug Ephedra—all front-page stories the week before the press conference—but they shouldn't have. No power of the national government is more serious than war, and that was the topic on everyone's mind.

The reporters covered all of the proper topics about Iraq: the costs of war (both financial and human), the participation of Turkey, the resolution before the UN Security Council, the effect on the rest of the Middle East, and even whether Bush would attack Iraq because he was "fixated" on the country. The last question alone should put to rest the absurd idea that the press corps, as the *New York Press* indelicately wrote, "grab[bed] its ankles" for Bush.[64] Many of the questions were prefaced with hostilely worded or at least challenging statements quoting positions critical of Bush's policies. But Bush was able to evade or ignore many of these questions because they were so long as to be incoherent or because they appeared to advocate a position, making reporters look biased and the president sympathetic.

The long questions actually affirmed Bush's own oft-stated opinion of press conferences. "Bush has said many times—I first heard him say this in 2000—that one of the reasons he doesn't like news conferences is that he thinks the reporters are just preening for their editors or their audience, and they're looking to come up with a 'gotcha' question," said Bill Plante. "Now, there's just enough truth in that to give it some standing, although certainly in my view it isn't entirely the case. So that's another reason that he prefers other venues, other platforms than news conferences to get something out."[65]

The most effective question, at least in terms of prompting Bush to give newsworthy information, was a simply worded question asking whether Bush would push for a Security Council vote. Had other reporters done less grandstanding and more straightforward questioning, they might have gotten better answers. But the fact remains that they did quiz Bush on the appropriate topics in a challenging manner and forced him to go on the record on several items, such as promising the war would not turn into a quagmire. The press conference was not perfect, but the press did hold Bush accountable, and Bush did communicate his ideas and his determination. The public was served.

Unfortunately, the critique of the press conference as a scripted, softball event was being repeated months afterward in magazines ranging from *Columbia Journalism Review* to *Vanity Fair*,[66] which suggests that a lowering of the professional reputation of the White House press and an increase in the reputation of Bush as a press manipulator were a pair of long-term results of the press conference. Bush's towel-snapping humor—his tendency to, as Hutcheson said, pull off the façade of the formality of presidential press relations[67]—gave ammunition to critics of both his administration and of the people who work hard to cover his policies. Bush's throwaway line about the press conference is one of the most remembered exchanges of the event.

"He was joking, but it's one of those things that has reverberated off the walls ever since," Plante noted. "People tend to believe that he knows what questions we're going to ask anyway. But . . . in a way he does. Because in the modern presidency, at least since Eisenhower, news conferences are preceded by practice sessions at which the staff asks the questions they think the press will ask to give the president a chance to practice. The staffs usually enjoy this a lot. They get to pretend, and even though they are pretending, it gives them a chance to be irreverent, even if they're snarkey. I remember Mike Deaver telling me once after a Reagan news conference, he said, 'We got every single question you guys asked . . . except the one from Sarah McClendon.'" McClendon had asked an obscure question about a military base in Texas that took Reagan and everyone else by surprise.[68]

The only way the press corps could have surprised Bush would have been to ask a narrow off-topic question, like McClendon had with Reagan. But the purpose of the press conference was to talk about Iraq, and that's what the reporters asked about. Anyone following the news for the previous few weeks could guess what the questions would be. Bush could more than guess. He had a professional staff to prep him and give him suggested answers. Furthermore, he had years of experience in handling press questions.

Criticizing the event as being scripted indicates a serious misunderstanding of presidential press relations. The criticism certainly didn't hurt Bush, who benefited in the 2004 campaign from charges that the press was biased against him. Ultimately, the critics only hurt the reputation of the press, the very institution best able to hold the president accountable.

10

NO ONE WILL DO IT BETTER

On a bookshelf in Wayne Slater's office in Austin sets a framed photo of then governor George W. Bush writing the *Dallas Morning News* reporter a check for five dollars. On the check itself, which is also framed, Bush wrote in the "memo" section that it was for a "Lost bet (CA)."

Bush wrote the check shortly after the final U.S. Supreme Court decision officially made him president-elect in 2000. Before the election, Bush had bet Slater that he would win the state of California. Bush lost California heavily, but Slater did not remind Bush of the wager until the tension of the controversial recounts was over. Slater joked that Bush owed him for losing California, and Bush immediately had his aide bring his checkbook so he could pay up. The check, despite the frame, looks remarkably ordinary with the simple heading "George W. and Laura Bush" at the top, as if it were from the checkbook of a Sears athletic department salesman, a job Bush held one summer when he was in college.

But when a man becomes president, everything about him becomes noteworthy, and his checks are usually worth more as memorabilia than the dollar amount written on the face. When Bush went to the White House, he was unable to preserve that joking, "I'll bet you five bucks I win California" relationship with the press that he had enjoyed most of his life. But he was able to keep his own towel-snapping attitude toward the press—to have fun, ignore what the critics thought and always, always remember that he had the power in the relationship. He would snap the towel, but he was too nimble to be hit by any who dared to snap back.

The presidential press relationship, it turns out, is surprisingly simple. The president has most of the power in the relationship because he controls access to himself and his staff. The problem is trying to control the type of large, diverse, and creative staff that serves a president and resisting the temptation to respond to the maelstrom of media noise that surrounds the White House. Bush, however, entered the White House already understanding how reporters work at all levels—from covering a YMCA electric train race in Midland, Texas, to a State of the Union address in Washington, D.C. And Bush, unlike many of his predecessors, was not overly concerned with press criticism of his actions. The best example of Bush's attitude is press conferences. Bush does not hold them because White House correspondents, journalism professors, or assorted media scolds say it's a good thing to hold them. Bush schedules them, to paraphrase the language he directed at terrorists following 9/11, at a time and place of his choosing.

Furthermore, Bush uses his iron personal discipline to reveal only what he wants to reveal in interviews and to rigidly stay on the message that he has determined ahead of time is the idea he wants to convey to the public. Bush uses his personally inspirational management style and Harvard Business School training to ensure that one of the most loyal White House staffs ever assembled stays on the same message.

The press and press critics—including pundits, journalism professors, and journalists who work for industry publications—have been unable to adjust to this reality. They have gotten used to reporters either hounding presidents out of office like Lyndon Johnson and Richard Nixon, or snipping and snarling at them for so long that the president spends most of his term like a treed raccoon—alive but in no position to do anything. Bob Woodward, who with Carl Bernstein helped bring down Nixon, has made a career out of mining scandals in subsequent presidencies, and even wrote a book, *Shadow*, detailing how all presidents following Nixon have had to deal with the legacy of Watergate.[1]

But no scandal or controversy has been able to stop Bush from governing. The press has been unable to "lay a glove" on Bush, to use the phrase of columnist Richard Reeves.[2] The experience has proved maddening to the point that the members of the media industry, like rats trapped in a cage without food, have started devouring each other. The "fear and loathing" that gonzo journalist Hunter S. Thompson used to describe the

1972 election campaign now seems to apply to journalists more than to politicians, campaign aides, or voters. Thompson, a rabid Bush critic, shot himself in 2005, no doubt unrelated to Bush's triumph over the press. Still, his death seemed to symbolize the state of the media in the first year following Bush's reelection.

Examples of press self-loathing during the Bush administration abound, but two instances suffice to represent an era when the press's performance is scrutinized as much as the president's. The best example is the reaction to the March 6, 2003, press conference. The previous chapter detailed some of the numerous critiques of the correspondents' performance and how even a member of the White House press corps believed the reporters were zombies. Such criticism misstates not only what happened at the press conference but also overstates the importance of the press.

Knight-Ridder's Ron Hutcheson said the criticism was unfair because Bush was himself a zombie at the press conference, and the reporters were responding to his demeanor. "It was clearly one of those deals where he was determined to show he was somber and serious, and as a result, it was soporific," Hutcheson said. "And I mean I thought [the criticism] was absurd . . . that's the downside of the press thinking we're the stars of the show. We're not. We're the bit players. It's the president who is the star of the show, and the president was as flat as a pancake that night and no amount of whiz-bang questions is going to change anything."[3]

Hutcheson said Bush wanted to show he was serious about the monumental issue of war, but that did not make for good television, or a good press conference. "At that press conference, I think we did the best we could with a guy who just wasn't going to play that day," Hutcheson said.[4]

Hutcheson's choice of words is appropriate. Bush holds the towel, and he decides when and how to play. Reporters are left to snap their much smaller towels at each other, whether it's over their performance at a prime-time press conference or in the much less publicized daily briefings, the source of the second example of how the press has morphed from investigator to target of investigation.

One regular at the press briefings in 2005 was a man working under the name of Jeff Gannon for a then little-known Web organization called Talon News Service. White House observers began to suspect Gannon's credentials because he always seemed to be tossing softball questions to press secretary Scott McClellan, to the point that he appeared to be a fail-safe for the administration side whenever a briefing was getting too uncomfortable. The fact that the Talon website was funded by a Republican activist added to the controversy. Eventually, left-wing Internet bloggers revealed that Gannon's real name was Jeff Guckert and that his picture appeared on websites advertising for a gay escort service. Although the White House press corps did not break the story, the mainstream press eventually covered the saga, generating another round of soul searching by journalists and criticism by pundits. Gary Trudeau naturally picked it up for "Doonesbury," writing a series of strips in which one of his long-running reporter characters goes to work for the White House as a shill in the press pool.

The administration denied any role in giving Guckert special treatment or using him as a mole.[5] The White House Correspondents' Association reacted by passing a resolution endorsing "inclusiveness" in credentialing reporters while stating that it wanted to remain independent of the White House and its credentialing procedures.[6] Indeed, journalists have always been loath to regulate their profession because it carries the taint of licensing, which is considered by most to be an unacceptable infringement on press freedom. Questions about whether Guckert was a shill and who outed him, both as a conservative and a gay man, obscure the fact that Bush didn't need a spy in the press corps. When the president controls the number of press conferences, determines how they are structured, and, perhaps most important of all, exerts self-control over his own responses to questions, a shill is less effective than whipping the towel at a real pro.

Because Guckert was not working for a mainstream news organization and had been brought down by bloggers also working outside the mainstream, one might be tempted to dismiss the tawdry episode as internecine warfare outside the "real press." But in the Internet age, such distinctions are irrelevant. People are getting increasing amounts of information from new media like blogs; a blogger was given a permanent White House press pass for the first time in March 2005.[7]

"Gannongate" illustrated that the searchlight for scandal has been turned from the administration to the press. Through the spring of 2005, the juiciest scandals during the Bush years, and the ones that brought down the mighty, usually have involved the press (including bloggers in that definition) investigating the press, not the administration. Secretary of Defense Donald Rumsfeld did not resign over the Abu Ghraib prison scandal, but CBS executives fired several people and demoted anchor Dan Rather following the broadcasting of a fake memo denigrating Bush's National Guard service.

The ridiculous Gannon/Guckert saga, rather than being damaging to Bush, made the press corps appear not only biased but just plain weird—at least to anyone who bothered to follow the story. A little more than a month after the scandal broke, I mentioned it in a journalism history class of about 25 students at the University of North Texas. Not one of the students—almost all journalism majors, some of whom were at the time working for campus media—had heard of the story. Perhaps the lack of awareness could be attributed to the indifference of the typical college undergraduate; still, it is likely the episode was a nonstory for most Americans. It was noteworthy only for those in the media and media observers who obsess over national politics.

In the historical context of presidential press relations, Gannongate was not really unusual—apart from its soap opera aspects—because getting reporters to ask specific questions that the president wants to answer is nothing new. Franklin D. Roosevelt, for example, had press secretary Stephen Early tell some chosen reporters ahead of time what questions he wanted asked.[8] The public, while perhaps not versed in the history of American presidential press relations, no doubt sensed, if they noticed the scandal at all, that it was the sort of thing to be expected in Washington and responded with a collective shrug.

In similar fashion, media observers and media workers shook their heads and professed shock that the Bush administration used video press releases to promote favorable stories. The Bush administration did substantially increase funding for that activity over what the Clinton administration spent, but it is a tactic that was certainly not pioneered by Bush. At any rate, everyone from the Boy Scouts to breweries to, yes, even media companies, avail themselves of press releases and public relations campaigns when they want to be represented in the "court of public opinion," as the professionals say. As of this writing, "scandals" about Guckert, video news releases, and the administration paying three syndicated columnists for consulting work or promoting administration ideas had again failed to lay a glove on the president. The White House issued perfunctory statements about the issues as they came up, with Bush rarely commenting on them personally. The spread of democracy in the Middle East, the death of the pope, and Bush's push to reform Social Security made the stories in early 2005 about Bush's press relations and policies seem trivial.

The enormities of the issues Bush has tackled or had thrust upon him since he was elected in 2000 are, in fact, staggering. Bush's change of U.S. foreign policy to endorse preemptive war and his attempts at major reforms of FDR's New Deal legislation are by themselves enough to secure him a spot as one of the most influential presidents of the last 50 years. It is not surprising that various writers have compared Bush (both favorably and unfavorably) to Woodrow Wilson, Abraham Lincoln, Harry S. Truman, and Franklin Roosevelt. In our microwave, instant-messaging culture, speculation started within days of the election about who would run in 2008 and who among Republicans could best continue Bush's policies. A number of writers touted an all-female race of Bush secretary of state Condoleeza Rice versus former first lady and current U.S. senator Hillary Clinton. Pundits even began speculating whether conservatives would draft Vice President Dick Cheney—who had said since the 2000 campaign that he had no ambition beyond the No. 2 spot—as the best person to carry on the Bush legacy.[9]

It's appropriate, then, if still early, to speculate on Bush's legacy of press relations and where he ranks among his fellow presidents. The problem with comparing presidents is that the presidency, the press, and the interaction between the two has changed over time. Both Bush and FDR, for example, mobilized the country after sneak attacks and focused their administrations on fighting their respective wars. But in the pre-Watergate era, journalists and the American people were more trusting of the government, making FDR's management of the press much easier than Bush's and the historian's task of comparing the administrations much harder. The task is further complicated because the substance of a president's press coverage largely depends on the problems he faces and his ability to handle them, rather than his relations with journalists.

"Events dominate everything," Slater said, explaining that even if a politician establishes a rapport early on, as Bush did during the charm offensive in the 2000 campaign, bad news like increasing casualties in Iraq will trump any press strategy. "The press will always step back and assume its fundamental role, which is to report the truth as we see it as best we can about anything that we're covering, whether we like the guy or not. Whether we instinctively want to give him the benefit of the doubt, we fall back on that role, as the critics say—pack journalism. We'll all just snarl and bark and act in concert to go after a politician in trouble."[10]

A president who can survive disastrous events and beat back the snarling pack is a president who is adept at press relations. A president is not a dictator but must earn election and govern by persuading the public to vote for him and the Congress and the often recalcitrant bureaucracy he heads to cooperate with him. A president can survive and thrive only through communication skills. If the measurement of success is getting his message across, getting elected and getting policies enacted in the face of a snarling pack of media hounds, Bush ranks among the best presidents ever at handling the press.

Let's first look at elections. In every contest except his reelection as Texas governor in 1998, Bush faced major obstacles, yet he won all of them save his 1978 congressional campaign—and he made that one close, even though he was a rookie going against a seasoned politician. In 1994 he defeated incumbent Ann Richards, who was a popular figure in Texas and a national star for the Democratic Party. In 2000 he defeated an incumbent vice president who was running at a time of peace and prosperity. But perhaps his greatest triumph came in 2004 when he won reelection during what looked like a quagmire in Iraq, a sluggish economy, and a sense among a significant portion of the population that the country was heading in the wrong direction. Furthermore, Bush faced a well-funded, well-organized group of opponents who loathed him with an irrational fervor that went beyond typical electioneering.[11] On top of all that, a majority of the members of the mainstream press wanted him to lose. Evan Thomas of *Newsweek*, who later reduced his numerical estimate but did not change his opinion, said most of the press favored Kerry and it was worth 10 points to the Democrat in the campaign.[12]

Many in the media were convinced that Bush would lose in any case. In an interview several months before the 2004 election, Slater said that he himself thought Bush would win, but that other journalists he trusted disagreed, based on their close analysis of polling data. "All the smart guys think he's going to lose," Slater said.[13] The *American-Statesman*'s Arnold Garcia said before the election that he too thought Bush would lose unless he started getting some good news, although he added that: "He is also extremely lucky. I've always said that boy is born under a star."[14] David Broder, a longtime *Washington Post* political columnist, wrote in August that Bush would need that luck because of the war and the economy. "If Bush can win re-election . . . he will truly be a political miracle man," Broder wrote.[15] Following the election, *Texas Monthly*'s Paul Burka, who noted that he voted for Bush, wrote that by every objective measure Bush should have lost.[16]

The election, then, was a dramatic victory for Bush and an affirmation of his press strategy: stay on message; ignore scandals except for brief, expected responses; control access; craft an image; stop leaks. The press tried to light the fire of scandal but could never get enough air for any damaging story to truly take hold. Like a candle placed under a glass jar, the story would quickly sputter and disappear without the oxygen of reaction from a White House that refused to play along.

Bush's electoral success is a fact. The evaluation of Bush's policies will likely be debated for as long as histories are written about the United States. Bush has already shown he plays for big stakes, implementing a radical new foreign policy of preemptive war and at home trying to reform the "third rail" of American politics–Social Security. Early in his second term, Bush focused his presidency on the war on terror and Social Security reform, and historians will ultimately judge him on those issues, especially the former. Regardless of the success of those endeavors, even Bush critics concede he has been a leader in those areas.

Liberal columnist Michael Kinsley, for example, wrote shortly after the Iraq invasion that, right or wrong, Bush had demonstrated he was a leader by persuading the American people of the necessity of the war.[17] Bush's March 6, 2003, press conference and other speeches, as mentioned in the previous chapter, shifted public opinion on the necessity of war and indicated his mastery of press relations. The litany of bad news from the war during the 2004 campaign was not enough to trump Bush's message to stay the course under his leadership. To be sure, if the economy and the war had spun out of control during the campaign, no amount of press relations would have saved Bush's presidency. But a leader has to be able to communicate to the people through the media, and in Bush's case, through a hostile media, in order to get them to follow him. By that standard, Bush, again, has been a master of media relations.

By the spring of 2005, Bush's push for Social Security reform was facing serious opposition. Congressional Democrats, although a minority, were threatening to hold up Bush's judicial appointments through the use of the filibuster. Iraqis were developing a democratic government but were still beset by suicide attackers. Later in the year, a disastrous hurricane destroyed much of New Orleans, and critics blamed the Bush administration for slow rescue and relief efforts there. In October, even many of his staunch conservative supporters criticized him for his nomination of his own lawyer, Harriett Miers, to the Supreme Court. Bush had not completed the first year of his second term, and pundits were questioning whether he could accomplish much of anything in the remaining three years.[18]

By November, Bush's approval rating was at 35 percent, the lowest of his presidency.[19] The December issue of the left-wing *American Prospect* featured a cover of an oafish-looking cartoon Bush with wide eyes and simian lips being speared in the rear end by a fork next to a headline proclaiming, "HE'S DONE." The accompanying article argued that although Bush would be president for three more years, his image as a latter-day Winston Churchill responding to 9/11 was over, and along with it, "his presidency as we have known it."[20] The article claimed that historians who "chronicle the fall of the Bush presidency" would study this period as the time when it collapsed.[21] How historians will evaluate the Bush presidency is anyone's guess, but it's doubtful they will mark 2005 as its collapse because Bush started hitting back at his critics in a series of speeches explaining his conduct of the war, and before the *American Prospect* was off the newsstands his approval rating had increased to 40 percent.[22]

Of course, Bush's ratings could go back down again. If they stay under 50 percent and the Republicans lose one or both houses of Congress in the 2006 midterm elections, it is not inconceivable that an emboldened Democratic House of Representatives could impeach Bush over allegations of the misuse of intelligence in the run-up to the war.

But the nightmare scenario for Bush seems unlikely because he is a skilled politician who learns from his mistakes and knows how to communicate to the public despite a hostile press. On October 25, 2005, the *New York Times* had published a downbeat story marking the two-thousandth American soldier killed in the Iraq War. The story included a profile of Marine Corporal Jeffrey B. Starr, 22, who had been killed in a firefight during his third tour. The story quoted a letter found on Starr's laptop in which he predicted his own death, "A third time just seemed like I'm pushing my chances."[23] Only two days later, conservative blogger and political columnist Michelle Malkin wrote, based on an interview with Starr's uncle, that the *Times* had left out important details from the letter.[24]

Bush also quoted Starr in an emotional speech November 30 at the U.S. Naval Academy, where he outlined the importance of the war and his strategy for winning it. Calling Starr one of the "fallen heroes," Bush quoted a different passage from Starr's last letter: "(I)f you're reading this, then I've died in Iraq. I don't regret going. Everybody dies, but few get to do it for something as important as freedom. It may seem confusing why we are here in Iraq, it's not to me. I'm here helping these people, so they can live the way we live. Not (to) have to worry about tyrants or vicious dictators. Others have died for my freedom, now this is my mark."[25]

Bush concluded, "There is only one way to honor the sacrifice of Corporal Starr and his fallen comrades—and that is to take up their mantle, carry on their fight, and complete their mission."[26] He didn't mention the *New York Times*.

Bush had snapped the towel full in the writer's face, but it was unlikely he was worried about the newspaper's coverage. At a White House Chanukah party the next month, conservative author David Horowitz noticed that Bush looked fit and acted cheerful, greeting Horowitz with a bear hug. Horowitz wrote on his blog that the brief encounter had energized him for his own battles: "In the moment I had his ear I said, 'Thank you for taking all those arrows for the rest of us.' Graciously, he said 'You take more than I do,' which I don't, and said so. Then as I was walking away he called out, 'Don't let them get to you.' I called back, 'Don't you either,' and he replied in a strong voice, 'I won't.'"[27]

The bet here is that Bush's great strength in handling the press—his ability to not let the media noise get to him—will see him through his second term and that he will leave office in 2009 at least as popular as Bill Clinton did in 2001. If Bush leaves office more like Carter (or Nixon) than Clinton it will be because of disastrous historical events that—as Slater said—trump everything. Certainly the pattern for every second term since LBJ's presidency is scandal and ineffectiveness. But if any president can break that pattern through adept handling of the press, it is Bush.

What will the Bush presidency mean for future press relations? Two changes have occurred or at least accelerated during Bush's first five years in office. The first change is the dramatic weakening of the mainstream press in comparison to alternative media. The second change is the ascendancy of the president over the press in their long-running battle for dominance of their relationship. The decline of the mainstream press, while perhaps not caused directly by Bush, has been exacerbated because the divisiveness of his presidency has generated more rabid, partisan response to the news and more interest in partisan media outlets. The decline of the mainstream press has helped Bush dominate in his relationship with journalists, although he was well equipped through experience to handle them when he arrived in Washington.

A pair of events held within eight days of each other in the Dallas–Fort Worth metroplex illustrates the changes during the Bush years.

On March 8, 2005, a group of journalistic heavyweights gathered in Fort Worth to honor one of their own. Former NBC anchor Tom Brokaw, *Washington Post* investigative reporter and author Bob Woodward, PBS anchor Jim Lehrer, and *New York Times* columnist Tom Friedman appeared on a panel to discuss the state of the media during a day-long celebration of the naming of the new Texas Christian University journalism school after CBS anchor Bob Schieffer.

Schieffer had been recently named to temporarily succeed Dan Rather, who left the anchor's chair in disgrace following his reporting of what turned out to be fake National Guard records that denigrated Bush's service. CBS News president Andrew Heywood gave a brief speech at the naming festivities, but Rather—like Schieffer, a Texan who made it big—was conspicuous by his absence.

Although Rather's name was scarcely mentioned—appropriately, since it was Schieffer's day—the panel donned the journalistic hair shirt regarding coverage of the Bush era. The journalists acknowledged that the press could have covered the administration's march to war better and pressed officials for more details. They also, under questioning from the audience, admitted that the public perceived the mainstream media as biased against the administration. Lehrer and Woodward said this perception could be addressed by better explaining that the role of the media is to critically cover the government. Brokaw mocked the Fox News slogan of "fair and balanced," saying he had swampland to sell to anyone who believed it, although he added he had no problem with its "being there," and that Fox did provide some information with its "spin." But Brokaw and Lehrer downplayed the significance of Fox, saying it had smaller ratings in comparison to the big three networks.

Eight days later, in a speech to the Dallas World Affairs Council, former Bush press secretary Ari Fleischer said the press was indeed biased against conservatives. But he said the most significant press bias was toward conflict—that the press always takes the Devil's Advocate role in covering the presidency and emphasizes bad news over good. Fleischer suggested that Fox was successful precisely because viewers were unsatisfied with the bias of the mainstream networks.

The contrasting views presented at the two panels illustrated how journalists and public officials see each other. Journalists are skeptical of public officials; public officials believe journalists always assume the worst to create conflict. But the panels also indicated that many members of the mainstream press don't get what is happening to their industry. The Schieffer panel represented a roll call of the mainstream media—networks and major newspapers that are becoming increasingly irrelevant to the public. Instead of admitting that bias exists in the media, they mock upstarts like Fox. Their solution to what they see as the public's "perception" of bias—note they don't acknowledge real bias—is to lecture the public about the importance of the media. For them not to acknowledge the problem of bias or the threat of alternative sources like Fox is willful self-delusion.

A national survey showed that the majority of journalists are liberal,[28] and studies of the 2004 campaign showed the coverage was biased against Bush.[29] Rather's "Memogate" was only the most visible example of coverage that at the least showed an eagerness to publish negative material about Bush. Despite survey and anecdotal evidence, most journalists, including Rather, refused to admit that personal beliefs impacted their coverage of Bush and the war. The relentless harping on Bushisms, the *New York Times*'s October-surprise nonstory about missing ammunition in Iraq, the emphasis on the Abu Ghraib prisoner abuse scandal compared to scant coverage of terrorist atrocities—an analysis of the way all of these issues were covered could take up another book. Fair or not, they collectively created an atmosphere of a press that had a distinctly anti-Bush bias. It's no wonder the public shrugged over Gannongate and the video news releases; the press has become the boy crying wolf regarding Bush.

It's also no surprise the public started ignoring those cries and the media claims that they were reporting objectively. In fact, the Bush years may well signal the end of objectivity—the idea that mainstream news organizations are neutral except in editorials. The public, if it ever did buy the notion of objectivity, certainly doesn't buy it now, as evidenced by the way it is selecting its news purveyors. The 2004 political conventions showed that the conservative Fox network dominated the ratings during the Republican convention, and the liberal CNN dominated during the Democratic convention.

It is time for journalists to embrace the change that is happening, because it is beyond their control. Defenders of objectivity say people need neutral views, and if they get their news only from sources that cater to their own biases, they will be uninformed. But who says in an information society with myriad satellite television channels, websites, and print and Internet newspapers, people will not look at multiple sources to test the accuracy of their favorite source? Wouldn't viewers still retain some skepticism of their partisan sources, knowing that they are partisan? At least with each news organization stating its political slant, the consumer could disagree with the news source while at the same time respecting its honesty. In the current environment, news consumers are taught to not only question the accuracy of a news story but also the motivation of the individual journalist who reports it.

Those who resist this tide run the risk of being drowned by it. A cartoon that appeared at about the time the Internet was gaining popularity showed a group of newspaper journalists as dinosaurs, pounding on typewriters and telling each other not to worry about the mammals working nearby on a website. In fact, mainstream media have turned out to be dinosaurs not because of technology but ideology—they cling to their ideal of objectivity without being objective. They need either to abandon it for the chimera it is or else seek diversity not just in race and gender but in political philosophy. If they don't want ideological balance in the newsrooms, then the media companies should pick a stand and market themselves accordingly. They already do it based on age, gender, and race, creating publications for youth, such as *Redeye* and *Red Streak* in Chicago, and *Al Día* for Hispanics in Dallas. It's not much of a jump to market the publication to a political viewpoint. Call it politigraphics instead of demographics. Skeptics may say that media organizations that adopt such an approach will lose a significant part of the audience that disagrees with their politics. But if the success of Fox is an indication of the future, they are already losing audience due to perceived bias.

The above argument is not to say that George W. Bush by himself is the cause of the decline of objectivity. But Bush's presidency, beginning with the bitter Florida recount and continuing with angry division over the war in Iraq, has surely accelerated the changes, and Bush was a great part of it whether he intended to be an agent of change or not. Ultimately, Bush's success at message discipline and controlling access to sources was a sort of towel snapping of the watchdog press that generated an effect similar to that of snapping a towel at a real dog. The press dogs became meaner, and in the case of Memogate, so desperate to bite the teasing president that they violated journalistic conventions to publish a story that was not true. The public found it could no longer trust the watchdog, which had turned out to be a rabid pit bull.

Some in the press pack turned into whining poodles, perhaps in some ways more repulsive to the public than a rabies-stricken hound. Reporters and media critics kept a constant score of Bush's press conferences, comparing them to the number held by his predecessors. While there are valid reasons for asserting that presidential press conferences are important—it is a chance to make the president think on his feet in front of the public—it is doubtful the average citizen values them as much as journalists do.

Hutcheson acknowledged the difference between the public's perception of Bush's accessibility and what the press experiences in trying to cover him. He said the public actually sees Bush a lot on TV answering questions or giving speeches; it's just not in the format that reporters would like to have.

"Obviously in my role as president of the presidential correspondents' association, I'm pressing for as many press conferences as we can get, but I also know that for the average person out there, when Bush is on TV taking questions from the press, they don't make a huge distinction whether it's in a so-called formal press conference at night or whether it's two questions at the end of a meeting with a foreign leader," Hutcheson said. "They see a president taking questions, and they wonder what all the carping is about."[30]

The selective access of the press to Bush is part of the sophistication of the Bush administration's press relations, Hutcheson said. "It would be one thing if Bush just went silent for two weeks and you never saw him. But he does public events almost every day and takes questions every couple of days. Usually there are cases where he does go silent, but they are rare," Hutcheson said.[31] Bush often holds press events with foreign leaders, which also heightens the appearance of accessibility.

"Now granted, the problem is that two questions for the U.S. media, two questions for the foreign media, and that's it, so you don't get a lot of follow-up; you tend to get the news-of-the-day question—you know, like, 'What do you think about what Putin said about Ukraine'—not a real examination with multiple questions about U.S. policy, but it still looks as if he's very accessible to the media, and I think that's a deliberate thing, too," Hutcheson said. "So in that whole debate about formal press conferences, I think that gets overlooked. It makes it much harder to push our position on that when he is in fact taking a lot of questions; it is just not in a form that is conducive to a fuller exchange of information."[32]

From the administration's point of view, there is no reason to expose the president more often to the pounding of a formal press conference. Fleischer said in his speech in Dallas and in his memoir that one of the main problems with the press is that its emphasis on conflict leads reporters to try to bait officials or trap them into saying something controversial. Fleischer cited several examples in his book where he would have liked to have given the press more information but knew he had to be careful because anything he said might be used against him. When a person's words are constantly being twisted, there is little incentive to volunteer information.

Bush's great strength in dealing with the press is that he observed his father's White House and came to office with a lot of confidence in how to deal with the press. Hutcheson explained: "He decided, 'I set the rules. I don't play by Washington's rules about you've got to do this; you've got to do formal press conferences because that's the way it's been done.' He's just going to play by his own rules, and that's what he's done."

Will future presidents play by Bush's rules?

The *New York Times*'s Adam Clymer didn't think so. "I don't think it's likely to be a template that the Democrats will follow, simply because the Democrats' view of the press is misguided—but it's more useful for the press. It's the 'Why aren't you on our side on this one? We expect you to be on our side.' And so they are constantly explaining themselves and trying to persuade the press that we should be on their side. And so they are never going to be as distant as these [Bush] guys."[33]

Clymer said the next Republican president may try to copy Bush's press strategy, but that will depend upon the nominee. "If John McCain becomes the president, there's no way in the world his administration would be like this. McCain loves reporters. He sometimes jokes we're his core constituency."[34]

CBS anchor Bob Schieffer, however, said the pattern for presidential press relations has been one of increasing control no matter who is in the White House. Schieffer said Bush runs a disciplined White House, and that it's more difficult for reporters to get information out of the Bush White House than it was for them to get information out of the Clinton administration. But Schieffer added that Clinton's White House was more difficult for reporters than George H. W. Bush's.[35]

"What has happened is we have all become extremely sophisticated in managing information," Schieffer said. "I mean, when I first came to Washington, most congressmen didn't even have a press secretary. Now we have media coaches, we have talking points, we have information plans . . . and what happens is that every White House has learned from the people who came before them, and so the result of that is it has become harder with each succeeding administration to get information out of the White House. . . . This is just the latest version."[36]

But Bush's press relations are not like the annual upgrades of computer software or the rollout of new car models, where improvement is almost imperceptible. Bush's White House has marked a major change in the relationship between the president and the press. Journalists fear that this shift in power—the president realizing he sets the rules and can communicate with the people without catering to the press—will be the legacy of Bush's press relations.

"I think he is setting a template that other presidents are going to want to follow," Hutcheson said. "The message he has sent is that the White House controls things, not the press, so the press can say, 'Oh, you've got to do press conferences.' Or another fight that's been going on is the size of the pool. They can just say, 'Well, no, it's going to be this number of people.'

"'Well, it's always been this number,' [the press would respond].

"'Too bad. It's going to be this number because we don't like this ragtag operation.'"[37]

Although future presidents may try to emulate Bush, they probably will not be as successful because Bush's extraordinary discipline is unique. "I think everyone's going to try to mimic it, and I think just about everyone is going to fail," Hutcheson said, noting that Bush has an unusual ability to get loyalty from his staff.[38]

CBS's Bill Plante echoed Hutcheson's comment. "All presidents try to control the message," he said. "These people are simply better at it than most of the others. What does them in every time, in my experience, is the internal fighting inside the administration, because somebody who is working at cross-purposes to someone else is going to seek out the media, whether it's one reporter or more than one, to usually spread the bad news about his opponent. That's what does them all in, and most presidents find themselves unable to cope with it. This one is—just because of his personality and the way he runs things—seems to be able to head that off. Or maybe he just has an exceptionally loyal staff. Whichever."[39]

Is this dominance of the presidential press relationship by the president good for democracy? Perhaps not. On the other hand, the dominance of the press since LBJ's tenure and the increasing emphasis on conflict are not good, either. Does the citizen benefit when public servants are afraid to speak for fear that any statement will be used to create conflict? Better to be silent, as Fleischer and others often conclude. In pre-Watergate days, the press probably went too far in the other direction, covering up Kennedy's affairs and FDR's ill health. The public doesn't need a press corps that applauds the president, as it did FDR at his first news conference.[40] But neither does it need a press that reflexively assumes the posture of the opposition to the government. Until the press can find a middle ground between fulsome praise and carping criticism, it is likely to become increasingly distrusted by a public that knows the press isn't always right and the government isn't always wrong.

Perhaps a good place to start would be for the press to stop complaining about the Bush administration's supposed lack of cooperation with journalists. Fleischer noted that some reporters assume the administration considers them the enemy.[41] Bush has often said that he believes the press has a vital role in our democracy. He has also said the war on terror is crucial to American survival. Is it possible that any controls on information put in place by the Bush administration were not a war on the media but on terror? Instead of comparing the Bush administration to Soviet Communists,[42] perhaps journalists should give the president the benefit of the doubt and not assume every action is done for nefarious purposes. Journalists should try to meet the president halfway in negotiating better relations, and they can do this by toning down their own rhetoric and simply doing their job.

When asked to evaluate the White House press corps coverage of Bush, Plante said: "Well, it's never good enough. I mean, I'll say that without hesitation. But I think the fault is always ours, even if this White House, or any White House, makes it difficult—less accessible."[43]

Plante said that compared to the Reagan, George H. W. Bush, and Clinton administrations, the George W. Bush White House is more difficult to cover because Bush is a top-down manager who has demanded and received loyalty so there are no leaks—the best source of stories. "But is that their fault?" Plante asked. "No. I mean, I don't believe it's useful or accurate to say, 'Well, they've got the place so locked up that they are doing the American people a disservice.' It's up to *us* to find ways to determine what's happening.

"And there are still ways. You talk to Capitol Hill, where there are many, many different points of view [and] very little hesitancy, usually, in expressing them. And they hear things. I mean, they know what the legislative shop at the White House is telling Republicans. You know, even the Democrats know. Or you can call over to the agencies. They often—people at the agencies often have their own agendas and timetable and will be happy to help you if it will advance what they want. So it's up to us to work harder when things are not spilling out as easily."[44]

Schieffer had similar thoughts. "Each succeeding administration gets more disciplined and it gets harder to get the straight facts, but there's nothing illegal about that," Schieffer said. "The politicians are there to deliver their message; the challenge for reporters, and the burden for us, is to get to the truth and to give people a second source that they can check on to compare what we're saying with what the government is saying."[45]

In a democracy, journalists and politicians should want the same thing—good government—even if the practices of their respective professions sometimes put them at odds. In theory, then, the two should be able to have a cooperative, respectful relationship. Presidential scholar Louis W. Liebovich, in a book published shortly after the 2000 election, traced the various reasons the relationship had deteriorated since Kennedy's term. He suggested that one skilled president could restore the relationship, although he made no prediction about Bush's tenure.[46]

Still, given Bush's success with sportswriters and the Austin capital press, it seemed reasonable in 2000 to think Bush might be that president. Indeed, by the middle of his first term, many observers thought Bush was using his towel-snapping personality to get positive coverage. As it turns out, both thoughts were wrong.

When the Liebovich idea that one president could restore good press relations was mentioned to Slater, he immediately said of Bush, "He ain't the guy." Slater explained that although Bush had developed some good relations during the 2000 campaign, his years in office had created some bad feelings because of the lack of access for the press and the clampdown on information. The reservoir of good feelings would not be there when Bush needed a break, Slater said, because he had squandered the earlier good feelings, and bad news about Iraq or anything else would trump any personal relationships.[47]

But Slater's relationship with Bush is a perfect example of how reporter–source interaction changes when a man moves from something even as high profile as the governor of Texas to the presidency. The same types of personal associations Bush had with Texas reporters are virtually impossible in the bubble of the White House. Bush couldn't restore the presidential–press relationship because it can't be restored. The White House press corps is too big and the presidency is too demanding for it to ever return to the days of JFK.

The change didn't seem to matter much to Bush. In fact, Bush demonstrated during the 2004 campaign that he didn't need the mainstream press. He kept interviews with the White House press corps to a minimum and communicated to the public through speeches and local interviews. The election result speaks for itself.

Kent Hance, the only man to ever beat Bush in an election, said Bush had "great people skills," but that being friendly with the press once a politician gets beyond the local level can be a detriment rather than a help. At higher levels, reporters are afraid of being seen as favoring a politician and will be even harder on ones with whom they are friendly, Hance explained.

"Bush likes people," said Hance, who is now a Republican lawyer in Austin and has visited Bush in the White House. "But it's a different situation . . . in dealing with the press. It's not—You have to realize, they're not your friend, they're not your enemy. They're there to do a job. Now, you may have some that you think are your friends or you think are your enemy, but 95 percent of them are there to do a job to report what they're seeing. And just because they're nice and friendly with you doesn't mean they're going to write the story in a way that's friendly to you, and just because they're nice and friendly doesn't mean that they're not going to ask tough questions. . . . You're going to get some questions that you think are unfair questions, but you can't let them know it bothers you, and you got to answer them. It may not be fun, but you got to do it."[48]

Almost 30 years after Hance gave Bush his first personal lesson in politics, Bush has perfected the art of handling journalists. Bush understands their job as well as any president ever has. Bush is friendly but maintains his distance. Bush controls his staff's press relations. Bush stays on message, even when tempted to respond to critics. Bush plays by his own rules in conducting interviews and press conferences.

Towel snapping the press doesn't mean you have locker room camaraderie with reporters. Towel snapping the press means you keep them in their place.

NOTES

PREFACE

1. Tom Reichert, James E. Mueller, and Michael Nitz, "Disengaged and Uninformed: 2000 Presidential Election Coverage in Consumer Magazines Popular with Young Adults," *Journalism and Mass Communication Quarterly* 80, no. 3 (Autumn 2003): 519–520.
2. Louis W. Liebovich, *The Press and the Modern Presidency: Myths and Mindsets from Kennedy to Election 2000* (Westport, CT: Praeger, 2001), 193.
3. Chuck Todd, "Air Force Won," in *Midterm Madness*, ed. Larry J. Sabato (Lanham, MD: Rowman & Littlefield, 2003), 35–45.
4. Michael Kinsley, "The Power of One," *Time*, 21 April 2003.

CHAPTER 1: FRIENDS FOR A LONG TIME

1. Wayne Slater, interview by author, 18 August 2004, Austin, Texas.
2. Dana Milbank, *Smashmouth: Two Years in the Gutter with Al Gore and George W. Bush—Notes from the 2000 Campaign Trail* (New York: Basic Books, 2001), 317.
3. Bill Minutaglio, *First Son: George W. Bush and the Bush Family Dynasty* (New York: Three Rivers Press, 1999), 238.
4. Tracy Ringolsby, telephone interview by author, 25 November 2002.
5. Randy Galloway, interview by author, 19 June 2002, Arlington, Texas.
6. Phil Rogers, telephone interview by author, 18 March 2003.
7. Gerry Fraley, "Just Venting," *Dallas Morning News*, 10 June 2003.
8. Kevin Sherrington, "Rogers Stands Out on Long List of Issues," *Dallas Morning News*, 1 July 2005.
9. Bob Schieffer, telephone interview by author, 17 March 2005.
10. Galloway, interview.
11. Jim Reeves, telephone interview by author, 24 June 2002.

12. Reeves, interview.
13. Peter Schweizer and Rochelle Schweizer, *The Bushes: Portrait of a Dynasty* (New York: Doubleday, 2004), 21–23.
14. Schweizer and Schweizer, *The Bushes*, 9.
15. James Spada, *The Bush Family* (New York: St. Martin's Press, 2004), 14. Although George W. Bush may not be one of the grandchildren in the photo, it does illustrate the level of family involvement, which would have included the future 43rd president.
16. Minutaglio, *First Son*, 40.
17. Slater, interview.
18. Evan Thomas and the staff of *Newsweek. Election 2004: How Bush Won and What You Can Expect in the Future* (New York: PublicAffairs, 2004), xix.
19. Elizabeth Mitchell, *W: Revenge of the Bush Dynasty* (New York: Hyperion, 2000), 132.
20. Mitchell, *W*, 118.
21. Minutaglio, *First Son*, 143.
22. Minutaglio, *First Son*, 111–112.
23. Minutaglio, *First Son*, 121.
24. Ed Clements, telephone interview by author, 11 October 2004.
25. Clements, interview.
26. Clements, interview.
27. Mel Tittle, telephone interview by author, 27 July 2004.
28. Minutaglio, *First Son*, 216–223.
29. Dave McNeely, interview by author, 13 October 2004, Austin, Texas.
30. Slater, interview.
31. John Blake, interview by author, 7 April 2003, Arlington, Texas.
32. Blake, interview.
33. Tucker Carlson, "Devil May Care," *Talk*, September 1999.
34. Bill Plante, telephone interview by author, 16 December 2004.
35. Arnold Garcia Jr., interview by author, 17 August 2004, Austin, Texas.
36. Slater, interview.
37. Jay Root, interview by author, 13 October 2004, Austin, Texas.
38. Slater, interview.
39. Howard Kurtz, *Spin Cycle: How the White House and the Media Manipulate the News* (New York: Touchstone, 1998), 25–29.
40. Slater, interview.
41. Robert Reno, "George W. Bush Is Reagan's Heir," *Newsday*, 12 November 2002, a28.
42. Ron Hutcheson, telephone interview by author, 17 December 2004.
43. R. G. Ratcliffe, telephone interview by author, 10 November 2004.
44. Plante, interview.
45. Plante, interview.
46. Helen Thomas, telephone interview by author, 16 December 2004.
47. George W. Bush, White House press conference, 4 November 2004, official transcript available at www.whitehouse.gov/news/releases/2004/11/20041104-5.html.
48. Hutcheson, interview.
49. Thomas, interview.
50. Bush, press conference transcript.

CHAPTER 2: NOT HIS FATHER'S (OR GRANDFATHER'S) PRESS RELATIONS

1. Neal Spelce, telephone interview by author, 8 September 2004.

2. Walter R. Mears, *Deadlines Past: Forty Years of Presidential Campaigning; A Reporter's Story* (Kansas City, MO: Andrews McMeel, 2003), 3.

3. Spelce, interview.

4. Spelce, interview.

5. John Tebbel and Sarah Miles Watts, *The Press and the Presidency: From George Washington to Ronald Reagan* (New York: Oxford University Press, 1985), 3.

6. Tebbel and Watts, *The Press and the Presidency*, vi.

7. Louis W. Liebovich, *The Press and the Modern Presidency: Myths and Mindsets from Kennedy to Election 2000* (Westport, CT: Praeger, 2001), xii–xiii.

8. Liebovich, *The Press and the Modern Presidency*, xi, xii.

9. Bob Woodward, *Plan of Attack* (New York: Simon & Schuster, 2004), 132.

10. Mark J. Rozell, *The Press and the Bush Presidency* (Westport, CT: Praeger, 1996), 171–176.

11. Mark Hertsgaard, *On Bended Knee: The Press and the Reagan Presidency* (New York: Farrar, Straus & Giroux, 1988), 5–8.

12. Liebovich, *Press and the Modern Presidency*, 171–172.

13. Mickey Herskowitz, *Duty, Honor, Country* (Nashville, TN: Rutledge Hill Press, 2003), xvi, xviii, 14.

14. Herskowitz, *Duty, Honor, Country*, 54–55.

15. Herskowitz, *Duty, Honor, Country*, 157–158.

16. Peter Schweizer and Rochelle Schweizer, *The Bushes: Portrait of a Dynasty* (New York: Doubleday, 2004), xiv.

17. Herskowitz, *Duty, Honor, Country*, 114.

18. Bill Minutaglio, *First Son* (New York: Three Rivers Press, 1999), 41.

19. Herskowitz, *Duty, Honor, Country*, 211.

20. Herskowitz, *Duty, Honor, Country*, 80–81.

21. Herskowitz, *Duty, Honor, Country*, 56–57.

22. Herskowitz, *Duty, Honor, Country*, 136–140.

23. Herskowitz, *Duty, Honor, Country*, 141–142.

24. Herskowitz, *Duty, Honor, Country*, 79.

25. Herskowitz, *Duty, Honor, Country*, 69–72.

26. Minutaglio, *First Son*, 222.

27. Spelce, interview.

28. Rachel Smolkin, "The Crowded Bus," *American Journalism Review*, April 2003, 38–43.

29. Dave McNeely, interview by author, 13 October 2004, Austin, Texas.

30. Smolkin, "Crowded Bus," 40.

31. Mears, *Deadlines Past*, 172.

32. Marlin Fitzwater, *Call the Briefing! Bush and Reagan, Sam and Helen: A Decade with Presidents and the Press* (Holbrook, MA: Adams Media, 1995), 11–12.

33. Fitzwater, *Call the Briefing!*

34. Michael Duffy and Dan Goodgame, *Marching in Place: The Status Quo Presidency of George Bush* (New York: Simon & Schuster, 1992), 54–55.

35. Duffy and Goodgame, *Marching in Place.*

36. John Robert Greene, *The Presidency of George Bush* (Lawrence: University Press of Kansas, 2000), 147–148.

37. Greene, *The Presidency of George Bush,* 148.

38. Herbert S. Parmet, *George Bush: The Life of a Lone Star Yankee* (New York: Scribner, 1997), 420.

39. Parmet, *George Bush,* 128–130.

40. George [H. W.] Bush, *Heartbeat,* ed. Jim McGrath (New York: Scribner, 2001), 326–327.

41. Fitzwater, *Call the Briefing!,* 11–12.

42. S. Robert Lichter, "Consistently Liberal: But Does It Matter?" *Forbes MediaCritic* 4, no. 1 (Fall 1996): 26–39.

43. Lichter, "Consistently Liberal."

44. Eduardo Porter, "Do Newspapers Make Good News Look Bad?" *New York Times,* 12 September 2004, available at www.nytimes.com/2004/09/12/business/yourmoney/12view.html?ei=5006&en=662.

45. Mears, *Deadlines Past,* 264.

46. Fitzwater, *Call the Briefing!,* 329.

47. George Bush, *Heartbeat,* 325.

48. Fitzwater, *Call the Briefing!* 331.

49. Fitzwater, *Call the Briefing!* 263–264.

50. Fitzwater, *Call the Briefing!* 352–353.

51. Bush, *Heartbeat,* 256.

52. Bush, *Heartbeat,* 322.

53. Greene, *Presidency of George Bush,* 147.

54. Bush, *Heartbeat,* 325.

55. Bush, *Heartbeat,* 328.

56. Frank Bruni, *Ambling into History: The Unlikely Odyssey of George W. Bush* (New York: HarperCollins, 2002), 8–9.

57. Wayne Slater, interview by author, 18 August 2004, Austin, Texas.

58. McNeely, interview.

59. Peter Goldman, Tom Mathews, Thomas M. DeFrank, Mark Miller, Andrew Murr, and Patrick Rogers, "Face to Face in Prime Time," *Newsweek,* 1 November 1992.

60. Bill Sammon, *Fighting Back: The War on Terrorism—From Inside the Bush White House* (Washington, D.C.: Regnery, 2002), 5–6.

61. Karen Hughes, *Ten Minutes from Normal* (New York: Viking Penguin, 2004), 113.

62. McNeely, interview.

63. Records of Texas Governor George W. Bush, State Archives, Austin, Texas.

64. Spelce, interview.

65. Slater, interview.

66. George W. Bush, interview by Brian Lamb, C-SPAN, 25 January 1999, available at Governor George W. Bush Records, State Archives, Austin, Texas.

67. Seth Mnookin, "The Charm Offensive," *Brill's Content* 3, no. 7 (September 2000): 76–81, 128–129.

68. Chris Usher, telephone interview by author, 17 January 2005.

69. Usher, interview.

70. Peter Goldman, Thomas M. DeFrank, Mark Miller, Andrew Murr, and Tom Matthews, with Patrick Rogers and Melanie Cooper, *Quest for the Presidency* (College Station: Texas A&M University Press, 1994), 586.

71. Lou Dubose, Jan Reid, and Carl M. Cannon, *Boy Genius: Karl Rove, the Brains behind the Remarkable Political Triumph of George W. Bush* (New York: PublicAffairs, 2003), 158–160.

72. Lichter, "Consistently Liberal," 26–39.

73. Adam Clymer, telephone interview by author, 16 June 2005.

74. Clymer, interview.

75. Clymer, interview.

76. McNeely, interview.

77. McNeely, interview.

CHAPTER 3: MESSAGE DISCIPLINE BEFORE IT WAS COOL

1. Chris Usher, telephone interview by author, 17 January 2005.

2. Lou Dubose, Jan Reid, and Carl M. Cannon, *Boy Genius: Karl Rove, the Brains behind the Remarkable Political Triumph of George W. Bush* (New York: PublicAffairs, 2003), 17.

3. Donald F. Kettl, *Team Bush: Leadership Lessons from the Bush White House* (New York: McGraw-Hill, 2003), 84.

4. Kettl, *Team Bush*, 93, 97.

5. Bill Plante, telephone interview by author, 16 December 2004.

6. Dana Bash, panel discussion, Association for Education in Journalism and Mass Communication convention, San Antonio, Texas, 11 August 2005.

7. Julie Mason, panel discussion, Association for Education in Journalism and Mass Communication convention, San Antonio, Texas, 11 August 2005.

8. John Blake, interview by author, 7 April 2003, Arlington, Texas.

9. Jay Root, interview by author, 13 October 2004, Austin, Texas.

10. Neal Spelce, telephone interview by author, 2004.

11. Howard Kurtz, *Spin Cycle: How the White House and the Media Manipulate the News:* (New York: Touchstone, 1998), 105.

12. Ken Auletta, "Fortress Bush," *New Yorker*, 19 January 2004, 55.

13. Marlin Fitzwater, *Call the Briefing! Bush and Reagan, Sam and Helen: A Decade with Presidents and the Press* (Holbrook, MA: Adams Media, 1995), 326.

14. Richard W. Waterman, Robert Wright, and Gilbert St. Clair, *The Image-Is-Everything Presidency: Dilemmas in American Leadership* (Boulder, CO: Westview Press, 1999), 61.

15. Kurtz, *Spin Cycle*, xiv.

16. Kurtz, *Spin Cycle*, 107.

17. Kurtz, *Spin Cycle*, 110.

18. Kurtz, *Spin Cycle*, 288.

19. Usher, interview.

20. Wayne Slater, interview by author, 18 August 2004, Austin, Texas.

21. Dana Milbank, *Smashmouth: Two Years in the Gutter with Al Gore and George W. Bush—Notes from the 2000 Campaign Trail* (New York: Basic Books, 2001), 31.

22. Kenneth T. Walsh, "A Case of Confidence," *U.S. News & World Report*, 17 November 2003.

23. Walsh, "A Case of Confidence."

24. David Frum, *The Right Man: The Surprise Presidency of George W. Bush* (New York: Random House, 2003), 26–27.

25. Frum, *The Right Man*, 55.

26. Karen Hughes, *Ten Minutes from Normal* (New York: Viking Penguin, 2004), 85.

27. Hughes, *Ten Minutes from Normal*, 85–86.

28. Slater, interview.

29. R. G. Ratcliffe, telephone interview by author, 10 November 2004.

30. Dubose, Reid, and Cannon, *Boy Genius*, 69–70.

31. Slater, interview.

32. Dave McNeely, interview by author, 13 October 2004, Austin, Texas.

33. Slater, interview.

34. Slater, interview.

35. Clay Robison and R. G. Ratcliffe, "Richards Defends Her Drug Czar, Derides Attack on Nominee by 'Phantom Candidate' Bush," *Houston Chronicle*, 20 April 1994.

36. George W. Bush, *A Charge to Keep* (New York: Perennial, 2001), 31.

37. Patricia Kilday Hart, "Little Did We Know . . . ," *Texas Monthly*, November 2004, 76–84.

38. Kilday Hart, "Little Did We Know . . . ," 80.

39. Kilday Hart, "Little Did We Know . . . "

40. David House, telephone interview by author, 27 September 2004.

41. House, interview.

42. Arnold Garcia Jr., interview by author, 17 August 2004, Austin, Texas.

43. Root, interview.

44. Ratcliffe, interview.

45. Dubose, Reid, and Cannon, *Boy Genius*, 188.

46. Frank Bruni, *Ambling into History: The Unlikely Odyssey of George W. Bush* (New York: HarperCollins, 2002), 48.

47. Clay Robison, "Campaign 2000: Reports About 'Rats' and Dyslexia All Part of 'Bizarre' Day for Bush," *Houston Chronicle*, 13 September 2000.

48. Clay Robison, "Bush Will Need More Than Expectations," *Houston Chronicle*, 20 June 1999.

49. R. G. Ratcliffe, Clay Robison, John Gonzalez, and Cragg Hines, "Campaign 2000: Bush Dogged by Questions About Fire in Belly for Presidential Race," *Houston Chronicle*, 13 February 2000.

50. Clay Robison, "Election 2000: Bush Eyeing Democrats for High-level Positions," *Houston Chronicle*, 29 November 2000.

51. Dubose, Reid, and Cannon, *Boy Genius*, 179–180.

52. Linda Chavez, "It's Debate Time," *Townhall.com*, 29 September 2004, www.townhall.com/opinion/columns/lindachavez/2004/09/29/13166.html.

53. Ari Fleischer, *Taking Heat: The President, the Press, and My Years in the White House* (New York: William Morrow, 2005), 41.

54. Fleischer, *Taking Heat*, 41–42.

55. Fleischer, *Taking Heat*, 42.

56. Frum, *Right Man*, 48.

57. Ron Suskind, *The Price of Loyalty: George W. Bush, the White House, and the Education of Paul O'Neill* (New York: Simon & Schuster, 2004), 149.

58. Suskind, *The Price of Loyalty*, 91–93.

59. Suskind, *The Price of Loyalty*, 150.

60. Suskind, *The Price of Loyalty*, 157.

61. Edwin Chen, telephone interview by author, 17 December 2004.

62. Chen, interview.

63. Dan Froomkin, telephone interview by author, 17 February 2004.

64. Plante, interview.

65. Evan Thomas and the staff of *Newsweek. Election 2004: How Bush Won and What You Can Expect in the Future* (New York: PublicAffairs, 2004), xxiv.

66. Thomas, *Election 2004*, 28.

67. Mike Allen, "Bush's Isolation from Reporters Could Be a Hindrance," *Washington Post*, 8 October 2004.

68. Ken Auletta, "Kerry's Brain," *New Yorker*, 20 September 2004.

69. Auletta, "Kerry's Brain."

70. Ron Hutcheson, telephone interview by author, 17 December 2004.

CHAPTER 4: PLUGGING LEAKS

1. Arnold Garcia Jr., interview by author, 17 August 2004, Austin, Texas.

2. Helen Thomas, *Thanks for the Memories, Mr. President* (New York: Scribner, 2002), 76.

3. R. G. Ratcliffe, "Media Access Bites Dust on Presidential Trail; Bush's Relationship with Journalists Changed Drastically During the Race as Free Flow of Information was Restricted," *Houston Chronicle*, 17 December 2000.

4. John W. Dean, *Worse than Watergate: The Secret Presidency of George W. Bush* (New York: Little, Brown, 2004), 58.

5. Dean, *Worse than Watergate*, 59.

6. George [H. W.] Bush, *Heartbeat*, ed. Jim McGrath (New York: Scribner, 2001), 254.

7. Bush, *Heartbeat*, 255.

8. Bush, *Heartbeat*, 255–256.

9. Chuck Cooperstein, telephone interview by author, 24 March 2003.

10. Randy Galloway, interview by author, 19 June 2002, Arlington, Texas.

11. Gerry Fraley, telephone interview by author, 22 November 2002.

12. Phil Rogers, telephone interview by author, 18 March 2003.

13. Ratcliffe, "Media Access Bites Dust."

14. Jay Root, interview by author, 13 October 2004, Austin, Texas.

15. Garcia, interview.

16. Clay Robison, "Bush's Secrecy Coloring Enron Scandal," *Houston Chronicle*, 3 February 2002.

17. Wayne Slater, interview by author, 18 August 2004, Austin, Texas.

18. Lou Dubose, Jan Reid, and Carl M. Cannon, *Boy Genius: Karl Rove, the Brains behind the Remarkable Political Triumph of George W. Bush* (New York: PublicAffairs, 2003), 239.

19. Dubose, Reid, and Cannon, *Boy Genius.*
20. Ratcliffe, "Media Access Bites Dust."
21. Ratcliffe, "Media Access Bites Dust."
22. Charles Layton, "Miller Brouhaha," *American Journalism Review*, August–September 2003, 30–35.
23. Ratcliffe, "Media Access Bites Dust."
24. Ronald Kessler, *A Matter of Character: Inside the White House of George W. Bush* (New York: Sentinel, 2004), 251.
25. David Frum, *The Right Man: The Surprise Presidency of George W. Bush* (New York: Random House, 2003), 71–73.
26. Neal Spelce, telephone interview by author, 8 September 2004.
27. Frum, *Right Man*, 28–29.
28. Karen Hughes, *Ten Minutes from Normal* (New York: Viking Penguin, 2004), 100–101.
29. Hughes, *Ten Minutes from Normal.*
30. Michael Fletcher, "Cabinet Members Required to Put in Time at White House," *Dallas Morning News*, 31 March 2005.
31. Fletcher, "Cabinet Members Required to Put in Time at White House."
32. Ron Hutcheson, telephone interview by author, 17 December 2004.
33. Fleischer, *Taking Heat*, 40.
34. Edwin Chen, telephone interview by author, 17 December 2004.
35. Zach Fox, "Bush's Press Conferences Too Scripted, Author Says," *Daily Trojan*, 9 April 2004, available at www.dailytrojan.com/home/index.cfm?event=displayIssueArticles&issue_date=04%2F09%2F2004.
36. Ron Suskind, *The Price of Loyalty: George W. Bush, the White House and the Education of Paul O'Neill* (New York: Simon & Schuster, 2004).
37. Matt Davies, cartoon, *U.S. News & World Report*, 26 January 2004, 8.
38. Richard A. Clarke, *Against All Enemies: Inside America's War on Terror* (New York: Free Press, 2004), x.
39. Christine Todd Whitman, *It's My Party Too: The Battle for the Heart of the GOP and the Future of America* (New York: Penguin, 2005).
40. Christine Todd Whitman, interview by Sean Hannity and Alan Colmes, *Hannity & Colmes*, Fox News, 27 January 2005; edited transcript available at www.foxnews.com/story/0,2933,143440,00.html.
41. Frum, *Right Man*, 270–271.
42. Chris Usher, telephone interview by author, 17 January 2005.
43. Usher, interview.
44. Usher, interview.
45. Usher, interview.
46. Usher, interview.
47. Amanda Ripley, with Mark Thompson, "An Image of Grief Returns," *Time*, 3 May 2004.
48. Ripley, "An Image of Grief Returns."
49. Tracy Ringolsby, telephone interview by author, 25 November 2002.
50. Ken Paulson, "Too Free?" *American Journalism Review*, September 2002, 30–35.
51. Ken Paulson, "Upon Further Review," *American Journalism Review*, August–September 2003, 60–65.

52. Hughes, *Ten Minutes*, 267.
53. Fleischer, *Taking Heat*, 150.
54. Fleischer, *Taking Heat*, 151.
55. Fleischer, *Taking Heat*, 170.
56. Charles Layton, "The Information Squeeze," *American Journalism Review*, September 2002, 20–29.
57. Travis Loop, "Stepping up Secrecy," *Presstime*, September 2003, 37.
58. Michelle Mittelstadt, "AG Takes Blame for Patriot Act Confusion," *Dallas Morning News*, 2 February 2005.
59. "Impact of Ashcroft Memo Debated," *Quill*, November 2003, 41.
60. "The War of Fog in D.C.," *Editor & Publisher*, 7 April 2003, 16.
61. Robert Leger, "Secrecy Compromises Safety," *Quill*, May 2003, 4.
62. "Ashcroft's Press Pass," *Editor & Publisher*, 30 June 2003, 13.
63. Dave Astor, "*N.Y. Times* Offering 550 Cartoonists?" *Editor & Publisher*, 30 June 2003, 32.
64. Jane Kirtley, "Keeping the Door Open," *American Journalism Review*, October 2002, 86.
65. Dean, *Worse than Watergate*, 21.
66. Kirtley, "Keeping the Door Open," 60–63.
67. Kirtley, "Keeping the Door Open," 67–69.
68. Kirtley, "Keeping the Door Open," 69.
69. Seymour M. Hersh, "The Coming Wars," *New Yorker*, 24 and 31 January 2005, 40–47.
70. Tony Blankley, "Espionage by Any Other Name," *Jewish World Review*, 19 January 2005, available at www.jewishworldreview.com/0105/Blankley011905.php3.
71. Michael Ledeen, "The Hersh File," *National Review Online*, 21 January 2005, www.nationalreview.com/ledeen/ledeen200501210807.asp.
72. Bob Woodward, *Bush at War* (New York: Simon & Schuster, 2002); Bob Woodward, *Plan of Attack* (New York: Simon & Schuster, 2004).
73. Wesley Pruden, "The Lesson Missed in the Graveyard," *Washington Times*, 23 April 2004.
74. Stephen Graubard, *Command of Office: How War, Secrecy, and Deception Transformed the Presidency from Theodore Roosevelt to George W. Bush* (New York: Basic Books, 2004), 548–549.
75. Fred Barnes, review of *Bush at War*, *Townhall.com*, n.d., www.townhall.com/opinion/books_entertainment/reviews/FredBarnes/140584.html.
76. Howard Kurtz, *Spin Cycle: How the White House and the Media Manipulate the News* (New York: Touchstone, 1998), 67.
77. Dean, *Worse than Watergate*, 55.
78. Layton, "Miller Brouhaha," 32.
79. Michael Duffy, Matthew Cooper, and John F. Dickerson, "Collateral Damage," *Time*, 24 May 2004, 30–33.
80. Hughes, *Ten Minutes*, 144–145.
81. Mark Steyn, "Plame Security Breach? It just ain't so, Joe," *Chicago Sun-Times*, 17 July 2005, available at www.suntimes.com/output/steyn/cst-edt-steyn17.html.
82. "Month in Review," *Editor & Publisher*, February 2005, 49.

83. Todd J. Gillman, "Bush PR Spending Doubled Over Term, Analysis Shows," *Dallas Morning News*, 28 January 2005.
84. Gillman, "Bush PR Spending Doubled Over Term."
85. Chen, interview.

CHAPTER 5: THE DARK SIDE

1. R. G. Ratcliffe, "Campaign 2000: Remark Aimed at Reporter Might End Up Biting Bush," *Houston Chronicle*, 5 September 2000.
2. Adam Clymer, telephone interview by author, 16 June 2005.
3. Clymer, interview.
4. Clymer, interview.
5. Clymer, interview.
6. Clymer, interview.
7. Clymer, interview.
8. Clymer, interview.
9. Clymer, interview.
10. Dana Milbank and Jim VandeHei, "Resistance to Bush Comes at a Heavy Cost," *Dallas Morning News*, 21 March 2003.
11. Edwin Chen, telephone interview by author, 17 December 2004.
12. Helen Thomas, *Thanks for the Memories, Mr. President* (New York: Scribner, 2002), 81.
13. Herbert Lee Williams, *The Newspaperman's President* (Chicago: Nelson-Hall, 1984), 190, 195.
14. Thomas, *Thanks for the Memories*, 24, 31.
15. Howard Kurtz, *Spin Cycle: How the White House and the Media Manipulate the News* (New York: Touchstone, 1998), 71–72.
16. James Jefferson, "Clinton Rips Media, Ken Starr After Opening of Presidential Library," *SFGate.com*, 19 November 2004.
17. Kurtz, *Spin Cycle*, 83.
18. Fred Barnes, "Clinton's Good News," *Forbes MediaCritic* 4, no. 1 (Fall 1996): 18–21.
19. Barnes, "Clinton's Good News."
20. Kurtz, *Spin Cycle*, 231.
21. Peter Schweizer and Rochelle Schweizer, *The Bushes: Portrait of a Dynasty* (New York: Doubleday, 2004), 114–115.
22. Schweizer and Schweizer, *The Bushes*, xiii.
23. Schweizer and Schweizer, *The Bushes*, xiv.
24. Thomas, *Thanks for the Memories*, 145.
25. George [H. W.] Bush, *Heartbeat*, ed. Jim McGrath (New York: Scribner, 2001), 68, 322.
26. Thomas, *Thanks for the Memories*, 150.
27. Thomas, *Thanks for the Memories*, 153.
28. Schweizer and Schweizer, *The Bushes*, 384.
29. Clay Robison, "Barbara Bush Too 'Nervous' to View N.H. Debate," *Houston Chronicle*, 3 December 1999.
30. Barbara Bush, *Barbara Bush: A Memoir* (New York: Lisa Drew Books, 1994), 442. Emphasis in original.

31. Bush, *Barbara Bush.*
32. Bill Sammon, *Fighting Back: The War on Terrorism—From Inside the Bush White House* (Washington, D.C.: Regnery, 2002), 129.
33. Ron Hutcheson, telephone interview by author, 17 December 2004.
34. Hutcheson, interview.
35. Bill Minutaglio, *First Son: George W. Bush and the Bush Family Dynasty* (New York: Three Rivers Press, 1999), 208–209.
36. Paul Waldman, *Fraud: The Strategy behind the Bush Lies and Why the Media Didn't Tell You* (Naperville, IL: Sourcebooks, 2004), 6–7.
37. Minutaglio, *First Son*, 190–191.
38. Kent Hance, interview by author, 14 October 2004, Austin Texas.
39. Minutaglio, *First Son*, 191.
40. Elizabeth Mitchell, *W: Revenge of the Bush Dynasty* (New York: Hyperion, 2000), 180.
41. Hance, interview.
42. Minutaglio, *First Son*, 221–222.
43. Minutaglio, *First Son*, 223.
44. Wayne Slater, interview by author, 18 August 2004, Austin, Texas.
45. Randy Galloway, interview by author, 19 June 2002, Arlington, Texas. *Fortunate Son* refers to the gossipy biography by convicted felon Mark Hatfield, who reported a variety of unconfirmed rumors about Bush, including that he did public service to get out of a cocaine rap. Hatfield's biography predated Kitty Kelley's salacious tome *The Family* by about five years.
46. Galloway, interview.
47. Galloway, interview.
48. Galloway, interview.
49. Galloway, interview.
50. Gerry Fraley, telephone interview with author, 22 November 2002.
51. Fraley, interview.
52. Jim Reeves, telephone interview by author, 24 June 2002.
53. Arnold Garcia Jr., interview by author, 17 August 2004, Austin, Texas.
54. Garcia Jr., interview.
55. Slater, interview.
56. Slater, interview.
57. R. G. Ratcliffe, telephone interview by author, 10 November 2004.
58. Clay Robison, "Prince of Public Office is Loss of Some Privacy," *Houston Chronicle*, 23 August 1999.
59. Ratcliffe, interview.
60. Slater, interview.
61. Slater, interview.
62. Karen P. Hughes to Suzanne Gamboa, October 4, 1996, Press Office, Records, Texas Governor George W. Bush, Archives and Information Services Division, Texas State Library and Archives Commission.
63. James Moore and Wayne Slater, *Bush's Brain: How Karl Rove Made George W. Bush Presidential* (Hoboken, NJ: John Wiley & Sons, 2003).
64. Slater, interview.
65. Slater, interview.
66. Slater, interview.

67. Lou Dubose, Jan Reid, and Carl M. Cannon, *Boy Genius: Karl Rove, the Brains behind the Remarkable Political Triumph of George W. Bush* (New York: PublicAffairs, 2003), 72.

68. John Brady, *Bad Boy: The Life and Politics of Lee Atwater* (Reading, MA: Addison-Wesley, 1997), 111.

69. Karen Hughes, *Ten Minutes from Normal* (New York: Viking Penguin, 2004), 135–136.

70. Frank Bruni, *Ambling into History: The Unlikely Odyssey of George W. Bush* (New York: HarperCollins), 74–75.

71. Ibid., 75.

72. R. G. Ratcliffe, Clay Robison, John Gonzalez, and Cragg Hines, "Campaign 2000: Bush Dogged by Questions About Fire in Belly for Presidential Race," *Houston Chronicle*, 13 February 2000.

73. R. G. Ratcliffe and Clay Robison, "Campaign 2000: Ex-N.H. Governor Backs Bush; Meanwhile, Newspaper Says Texan Belittled Granite State Voters," *Houston Chronicle*, 29 January 2000

74. Ari Fleisher, *Taking Heat: The President, The Press, and My Years in the White House* (New York: William Morrow, 2005), 182–186.

75. Zach Fox, "Bush's Press Conferences Too Scripted, Author Says," *Daily Trojan*, 9 April 2004, available at www.dailytrojan.com/home/index.cfm?event=displayIssueArticles&issue_date=04%2F09%2F2004.

76. Chris Usher, telephone interview by author, 17 January 2004.

77. Usher, interview.

78. Usher, interview.

79. John W. Dean, *Worse than Watergate: The Secret Presidency of George W. Bush* (New York: Little, Brown, 2004), 170–172.

80. Joseph Wilson, *The Politics of Truth: Inside the Lies that Led to War and Betrayed My Wife's CIA Identity* (New York: Carroll & Graf Publishers, 2004).

81. Dean, *Worse than Watergate*.

82. "Appeals Court Rules Against Reporters," *Dallas Morning News*, 16 February 2005.

83. Dean, *Worse than Watergate*, 169.

84. Waldman, *Fraud*, 15–16.

85. Sammon, *Fighting Back*, 363–364.

86. Jay Root, interview by author, 13 October 2004, Austin, Texas.

87. Howard Kurtz, "A Morbid Finger On the Pulse of Politics," *Washington Post*, 12 January 2004.

88. George W. Bush, interview by Brit Hume, Fox News, 22 September 2003, available at www.foxnews.com/story/0,2933,98111,00.html.

89. "Hot Type," *Editor & Publisher*, 12 February 2001, 28.

90. Marlin Fitzwater, *Call the Briefing! Reagan and Bush, Sam and Helen: A Decade with Presidents and the Press* (Holbrook, MA: Adams Media, 1995), 211.

91. Clymer, interview.

92. Paul Burka, interview by author, 14 October 2004, Austin, Texas.

93. Burka, interview.

94. Burka, interview.

95. Burka, interview.

96. Robert Shogan, *Bad News: Where the Press Goes Wrong in the Making of the President* (Chicago: Ivan R. Dee, 2001), 4–5.

97. Hutcheson, interview.
98. Slater, interview.
99. Bush, interview.
100. Fleisher, *Taking Heat*, 358–359.
101. Hutcheson, interview.
102. Sammon, *Fighting Back*, 362.
103. Bush, interview.
104. Hutcheson, interview.
105. Clymer, interview.
106. Dan Froomkin, telephone interview with author, 17 February 2004.

CHAPTER 6: THE PLAIN TALK OF BUSHISMS

1. Kevin Sherrington and Jan Hubbard, "Rangers to Stay Here, Bush Says," *Dallas Morning News*, 19 March 1989. "Rusty" is Rusty Rose, another major investor in the team.

2. Ken Stephens, "Chiles Steps Aside after Long Sale," *Dallas Morning News*, 19 March 1989.

3. Blackie Sherrod, "Reading His Lips, Bush Looks Like Politician," *Dallas Morning News*, 20 March 1989.

4. Just a few examples include D. B. Gilles and Sheldon Woodbury, *W.: The First 100 Days, A White House Journal* (Kansas City, MO: Andrews McMeel, 2001); Kevin Guilfoile and John Warner, *My First Presidentiary: A Scrapbook by George W. Bush*, ed. Michael Colton (New York: Three Rivers Press, 2001); Jacob Weisberg, ed., *George W. Bushisms* (New York: Fireside, 2001); Jacob Weisberg, ed., *More George W. Bushisms* (New York: Fireside, 2002); *"They Misunderestimated Me!": The Very Curious Language of George W. Bush 2003 Calendar of Presidential (Mis)Speak* (Skaneateles, NY: Outland Communications, 2002); Jacob Weisberg, *George W. Bushisms 2004 Calendar* (Kansas City, MO: Andrews McMeel, 2003).

5. Paul Begala, *"Is Our Children Learning?": The Case against George W. Bush* (New York: Simon & Schuster, 2000).

6. Paul Burka, interview by author, 14 October 2004, Austin, Texas.

7. Helen Thomas, *Thanks for the Memories, Mr. President* (New York: Scribner, 2002), 61, 131.

8. *Bushisms: President George Herbert Walker Bush, in His Own Words*, comp. editors of the *New Republic* (New York: Workman, 1992).

9. Thomas, *Thanks for the Memories,* 145, 149.

10. Walter Mears, *Deadlines Past: Forty Years of Presidential Campaigning; A Reporter's Story* (Kansas City, MO: Andrews McMeel, 2003), 49–52.

11. Greg Pierce, "Inside Politics," *Washington Times*, 5 October 2004.

12. Phil Rogers, telephone interview by author, 18 March 2003.

13. Gerry Fraley, telephone interview by author, 22 November 2002.

14. Jim Reeves, telephone interview by author, 24 June 2002.

15. Randy Galloway, interview by author, 19 June 2002, Fort Worth, Texas.

16. Galloway, interview.

17. Wayne Slater, interview by author, 18 August 2004, Austin, Texas.

18. R. G. Ratcliffe, telephone interview by author, 10 November 2004.

19. Ratcliffe, interview.

20. Arnold Garcia Jr., interview by author, 17 August 2004, Austin, Texas.

21. Jay Root, interview by author, 13 October 2004, Austin, Texas.

22. Robert Novak, "Bush's Little Blooper," *Townhall.com*, 2 September 2004, www.townhall.com/opinion/columns/robertnovak/2004/09/02/12877.html.

23. Mark Crispin Miller, *The Bush Dyslexicon: Observations on a National Disorder* (New York: W. W. Norton, 2001), 15, 40.

24. Justin A. Frank, *Bush on the Couch: Inside the Mind of the President* (New York: ReganBooks, 2004), 139.

25. Frank, *Bush on the Couch*.

26. Begala, *"Is Our Children Learning?,"* 125.

27. Slater, interview.

28. Slater, interview.

29. Dana Milbank, *Smashmouth: Two Years in the Gutter with Al Gore and George W. Bush—Notes from the 2000 Campaign Trail* (New York: Basic Books, 2001), 36, 15.

30. Ratcliffe, interview.

31. Garcia, interview.

32. Slater, interview.

33. Slater, interview.

34. Edwin Chen, telephone interview by author, 17 December 2004.

35. Dave McNeely, interview by author, 13 October 2004, Austin, Texas.

36. Frank Bruni, *Ambling into History: The Unlikely Odyssey of George W. Bush* (New York: HarperCollins, 2002), 38–39.

37. Bruni, *Ambling into History*, 45.

38. Clay Robison, "Candidates Too Often Stoop to Nitpick," *Houston Chronicle*, 15 October 2000.

39. Adam Clymer, telephone interview by author, 16 June 2005.

40. Rachel Smolkin, "The Crowded Bus," *American Journalism Review*, April 2003, 38–43.

41. Ratcliffe, interview.

42. Brian S. Brooks, George Kennedy, Daryl Moen, and Don Ranly, *News Reporting and Writing* (Boston: Bedford/St. Martin's, 2002), 83–84. The anecdote mentions clearing up a presidential quote. *Which* president is not made clear in the text, but it is not George W. Bush because the anecdote has been included in editions of the text long before he took office.

43. Norm Goldstein, ed., *The Associated Press Stylebook and Libel Manual* (New York: Associated Press, 1996), 172.

44. Robert S. Brown, ed., *"They Misunderestimated Me!": The Very Curious Language of George W. Bush, 2003 Calendar of Presidential (Mis)Speak*, calendar (Skaneateles, NY: Outland Communications, 2002), quote for 23/24 August 2003.

45. Brown, *"They Misunderestimated Me!"* quote for 10 October 2003.

46. Brown, *"They Misunderestimated Me!"* quote for 13 October 2003.

47. Brown, *"They Misunderestimated Me!"* quote for 16 October 2003.

48. Brown, *"They Misunderestimated Me!"* quote for 6/7 December 2003.

49. Robert S. Brown, ed., *Presidential (Mis)Speak: The Very Curious Language of George W. Bush*, 2004 calendar (Skaneateles, NY: Outland Communications, 2003), quote for 10 March 2004.

50. Robert S. Brown, ed., *Presidential (Mis)Speak: The Very Curious Language of George W. Bush*, 2005 calendar (Skaneateles, NY: Outland Communications, 2004), quote for 4 February 2005.

51. Rob Long, "My Candidate!," *National Review*, 25 October 2004, 30, 32.

52. Slater, interview.

53. Ron Hutcheson, telephone interview by author, 17 December 2004.

54. Peter Schweizer and Rochelle Schweizer, *The Bushes: Portrait of a Dynasty* (New York: Doubleday, 2004), 150.

55. Patricia Kilday Hart, "Little Did We Know . . . ," *Texas Monthly*, November 2004, 76–84.

56. Bill Minutaglio, *First Son: George W. Bush and the Bush Family Dynasty* (New York: Three Rivers Press, 1999), 285–286.

57. Hart, "Little Did We Know . . . ," 84.

58. Hart, "Little Did We Know . . . ," 84.

59. Brown, *"They Misunderestimated Me!"* quote for 13/14 December 2003.

60. Thomas, *Thanks for the Memories*, 206–207.

61. Thomas, *Thanks for the Memories*, 215.

62. Brown, *"They Misunderestimated Me!"* quote for 11/12 October 2003.

63. Brown, *"They Misunderestimated Me!"* quote for 13/14 December 2003.

64. Bill Sammon, *Misunderestimated: The President Battles Terrorism, John Kerry, and the Bush Haters* (New York: ReganBooks, 2004).

65. Mark McKinnon, "How to . . . Sell a Candidate," *Texas Monthly*, July 2003, 66–67.

66. Karen Hughes, *Ten Minutes from Normal* (New York: Viking, 2004), 161–162.

67. Brown, *"They Misunderestimated Me!"*, 2003 calendar, quote for 29 August 2003.

68. Rudolph W. Giuliani, with Ken Kurson, *Leadership* (New York: Hyperion, 2002), 127.

69. Giuliani, *Leadership,* 190–193.

70. Miller, *Bush Dyslexicon*, 13.

71. D. M. Ryfe, "Franklin Roosevelt and the Fireside Chats," *Journal of Communication* 49, no. 4 (December 1999), 92.

72. Maureen Dowd, "Westerns and Easterns," *New York Times*, 12 September 2004.

73. Ryan Lizza, "Flip Side," *New Republic* 231, no 13 (27 September 2004): 10–11; quote on 10.

74. Hutcheson, interview.

75. Peggy Noonan, *Simply Speaking* (New York: ReganBooks, 1998), xi.

76. Garcia, interview.

77. Noonan, *Simply Speaking*, 188.

78. "Talkin' Baseball," *Dallas Morning News*, 26 February 2005.

79. John Tebbel and Sarah Miles Watts, *The Press and the Presidency: From George Washington to Ronald Reagan*, (New York: Oxford University Press, 1985), 264–265.

80. Kenneth T. Walsh, "Hunting Quayle," *Forbes MediaCritic*, Summer 1996, 62.

81. Neal Spelce, telephone interview by author, 2004.

82. Bob Schieffer, telephone interview by author, 17 March 2005.

83. Root, interview.

84. Dan Froomkin, telephone interview by author, 2005.

CHAPTER 7: TOWEL SNAPPING

1. Kevin Sherrington, telephone interview by author, 22 November 2003.
2. Sherrington, interview.
3. R. G. Ratcliffe, telephone interview by author, 10 November 2004.
4. Jim Reeves, telephone interview by author, 24 June 2002.
5. Wayne Slater, interview by author, 18 August 2004, Austin, Texas.
6. Slater, interview.
7. Wayne Slater, "Catching Bush on the Fly," *Dallas Morning News*, 7 March 2002. The incident was also captured in Alexandra Pelosi's documentary about the 2000 campaign, *Journeys with George: A Home Movie by Alexandra Pelosi* (New York: HBO Video, 2003).
8. Slater, interview.
9. Edmund Morris, *The Rise of Theodore Roosevelt* (New York: The Modern Library, 2001), 728.
10. John Tebbel and Sarah Miles Watts, *The Press and the Presidency: From George Washington to Ronald Reagan* (New York: Oxford University Press).
11. Tebbel and Watts, *Press and the Presidency*, 337.
12. Tebbel and Watts, *Press and the Presidency*, 183.
13. Tebbel and Watts, *Press and the Presidency*, 198–199.
14. Edwin Chen, telephone interview by author, 17 December 2004.
15. Helen Thomas, *Thanks for the Memories, Mr. President* (New York: Scribner, 2002), 17, 19–20.
16. Dan Thomasson, "Cheap-shot Journalism," *Quill*, January 1986, 18–21.
17. Dan Rather, interview by Joe B. Frantz, 16 April 1973, Oral History Collection, Lyndon Baines Johnson Library, Austin, Texas.
18. Thomas, *Thanks for the Memories*, 127.
19. Joe Klein, "The Secrets of Reagan's Success," *Time*, 14 June 2004, 21.
20. Mark Hertsgaard, *On Bended Knee: The Press and the Reagan Presidency* (New York: Farrar, Straus & Giroux, 1988), 47.
21. Hertsgaard, *On Bended Knee*.
22. Slater, interview.
23. Edward J. Friedlander and John Lee, *Feature Writing for Newspapers and Magazines: The Pursuit of Excellence* (Boston: Pearson Education, 2004), 149.
24. Seth Mnookin, "The Charm Offensive," *Brill's Content* 3, no. 7 (September 2000): 76–81, 128–129.
25. Gerry Fraley, telephone interview with author, 22 November 2002.
26. Reeves, interview.
27. Phil Rogers, telephone interview by author, 18 March 2003.
28. Ratcliffe, interview.
29. Ratcliffe, interview.
30. Rogers, interview.
31. Arnold Garcia Jr., interview by author, 17 August 2004, Austin, Texas.
32. Dave Montgomery, telephone interview by author, 10 December 2004.
33. Dale Hansen, telephone interview by author, 31 March 2003. Tom Hicks bought the Rangers from Bush's former partnership and also owns the Dallas Stars hockey team at the time of this writing.

34. Garcia, interview.

35. Garcia, interview.

36. Montgomery, interview.

37. Peter Schweizer and Rochelle Schweizer, *The Bushes: Portrait of a Dynasty* (New York: Doubleday, 2004), 365–366.

38. Ben Sargent, telephone interview by author, 20 August 2004.

39. Frank Bruni, *Ambling into History: The Unlikely Odyssey of George W. Bush* (New York: HarperCollins, 2002), 4–5.

40. Slater, interview.

41. Bill Sammon, *Fighting Back: The War on Terrorism–From Inside the Bush White House* (Washington, D.C.: Regnery, 2002), 31.

42. Bill Plante, telephone interview by author, 16 December 2004.

43. Ron Hutcheson, telephone interview by author, 17 December 2004.

44. Hutcheson, interview.

45. Bruni, *Ambling into History,* 18, 25–26.

46. Paul Burka, interview by author, 14 October 2004, Austin, Texas.

47. Burka, interview.

48. Bruni, *Ambling into History*, 49.

49. Hutcheson, interview.

50. Thomas, *Thanks for the Memories*, 225.

51. Thomas, *Thanks for the Memories*, 218–219.

52. Hansen, interview. This anecdote occurred around the time President Clinton was accused of granting sleepovers in the Lincoln bedroom in exchange for campaign contributions.

53. Slater, interview.

54. Slater, interview.

55. Clay Robison, "Bush Will Need More Than Expectations," *Houston Chronicle*, 20 June 1999.

56. Garcia, interview.

57. Garcia, interview.

58. Alexandra Pelosi, *Journeys with George: A Home Movie by Alexandra Pelosi* (New York: HBO Video, 2003).

59. Hutcheson, interview.

60. Garcia, interview.

61. Garcia, interview.

62. John Blake, interview by author, 7 April 2003, Arlington, Texas.

63. Ratcliffe, interview.

64. Ratcliffe, interview.

65. Schweizer and Schweizer, *The Bushes*, xiv, 269.

66. Hansen, interview.

67. Hansen, interview.

68. Fraley, interview.

69. Tracy Ringolsby, telephone interview by author, 25 November 2002.

70. Ringolsby, interview.

71. Ringolsby, interview.

72. Neal Spelce, telephone interview by author, 8 September 2004.

73. Reeves, interview.

74. Schweizer and Schweizer, *The Bushes*, 473–474.

75. Maureen Dowd, *Bushworld: Enter at Your Own Risk* (New York: G. P. Putnam's Sons, 2004), 9–10.

76. R. G. Ratcliffe, "Media Access Bites Dust on Presidential Trail; Bush's Relationship with Journalists Changed Drastically During the Race as Free Flow of Information was Restricted," *Houston Chronicle*, 17 December 2000.

77. Robert Reno, "Bush Jr. Creating His Own Image," *Columbia Missourian*, 15 November 2002.

78. Matt Taibbi, "Cleaning the Pool," *New York Press*, 12 March 2003.

79. Rachel Smolkin, "Are the News Media Soft on Bush?" *American Journalism Review*, October–November 2003, 16–25.

80. Rogers, interview. Two years after this interview, in the spring of 2005, the Expos franchise began its first season in Washington, D.C.—renamed the Nationals—after being unable to make it in Montreal.

81. Rogers, interview. Rose was Rusty Rose, another principal owner in the partnership.

82. Rogers, interview.

83. Sherrington, interview.

84. Schweizer and Schweizer, *The Bushes*, 449–450.

85. Dave McNeely, interview by author, 13 October 2004, Austin, Texas.

86. Garcia, interview.

87. Spelce, interview.

88. Spelce, interview.

89. Ratcliffe, interview.

90. Jay Root, interview by author, 13 October 2004, Austin, Texas.

91. Root, interview.

92. Slater, interview.

93. Slater, interview.

94. Slater, interview.

95. Slater, interview.

96. Bruni, *Ambling into History*, 194–196.

97. Root, interview.

98. Ratcliffe, interview.

99. Hutcheson, interview.

100. Slater, interview.

101. Bob Schieffer, telephone interview by author, 17 March 2005.

102. R. G. Ratcliffe, Clay Robison, John Gonzalez, and Cragg Hines, "Campaign 2000: Bush Dogged by Questions About Fire in Belly for Presidential Race," *Houston Chronicle*, 13 February 2000.

103. R. G. Ratcliffe, "Bush Ready If Foreign Bully Tests Resolve; Reflects on His Texas Past and Challenges of the Future," *Houston Chronicle*, 18 January 2001.

CHAPTER 8: SHAVING THE EAR HAIR

1. Wayne Slater, interview by author, 18 August 2004, Austin, Texas.
2. Slater, interview.

3. Kevin Sherrington, telephone interview by author, 22 November 2003.

4. Slater, interview.

5. Slater, interview.

6. Slater, interview. Some evidence to back up Slater's assessment of Perry is that in the summer of 2005 Perry was facing a possible challenge to his reelection from within his own party—U.S. Senator Kay Bailey Hutchison. In contrast, Bush faced no serious challenge to his nomination for a second term in 1998.

7. James Moore and Wayne Slater, *Bush's Brain: How Karl Rove Made George W. Bush Presidential* (Hoboken, NJ: John Wiley & Sons, 2003), 162–163.

8. Moore and Slater, *Bush's Brain*, 170–171.

9. Moore and Slater, *Bush's Brain*, 171.

10. Slater, interview.

11. Moore and Slater, *Bush's Brain*, 171–172.

12. R. G. Ratcliffe, telephone interview by author, 10 November 2004.

13. Slater, interview.

14. Moore and Slater, *Bush's Brain*, 238.

15. Quoted in Moore and Slater, *Bush's Brain*, 238.

16. Moore and Slater, *Bush's Brain*, 239.

17. Slater, interview.

18. Stuart Stevens, *The Big Enchilada: Campaign Adventures with the Cockeyed Optimists from Texas Who Won the Biggest Prize in Politics* (New York: Free Press, 2001), 41.

19. Seth Mnookin, "The Charm Offensive," *Brill's Content* 3, no. 7 (September 2000): 76–81, 128–129.

20. *Journeys with George: A Home Movie by Alexandra Pelosi*, directed by Alexandra Pelosi (New York: HBO Video, 2003).

21. Ron Hutcheson, telephone interview by author, 17 December 2004.

22. Slater, interview.

23. Adam Clymer, telephone interview by author, 16 June 2005.

24. Clymer, interview.

25. Slater, interview.

26. Ed Clements, telephone interview by author, 11 October 2004.

27. Clements, interview.

28. Slater, interview.

29. Hutcheson, interview.

30. Hutcheson, interview.

31. Hutcheson, interview.

32. Hutcheson, interview.

33. Slater, interview.

34. Ratcliffe, interview.

35. Jim Lo Scalzo, "Overexposed," *U.S. News & World Report*, 13 December 2004, 66–67.

36. Lo Scalzo, "Overexposed."

37. Paul Koring, telephone interview by author, 13 September 2004.

38. Koring, interview.

39. Koring, interview.

40. Hutcheson, interview.

41. Hutcheson, interview.

42. Paul Burka, interview by author, 14 October 2004, Austin, Texas.
43. Burka, interview.
44. Burka, interview.
45. Burka, interview.
46. Dan Froomkin, telephone interview by author, 17 February 2005.
47. Bill Sammon, *Fighting Back: The War on Terrorism—From Inside the Bush White House* (Washington, D.C.: Regnery, 2002), 26–27.
48. Sammon, *Fighting Back*, 33–34.
49. Bob Schieffer, telephone interview by author, 17 March 2005.
50. Peter Schweizer and Rochelle Schweizer, *The Bushes: Portrait of a Dynasty* (New York: Doubleday, 2004), 171–172.
51. Dave Astor, "Syndicates: Good Work in Bad Times," *Editor & Publisher*, 4 November 2004, 63.
52. Vicky Hallet, "The Candidate to Watch," *U.S. News & World Report*, 2 February 2004, 17.
53. Ari Fleischer, *Taking Heat: The President, the Press, and My Years in the White House* (New York: William Morrow, 2005), 207–208.
54. Fleischer, *Taking Heat*, 38–39.
55. Charles C. Clayton, *Little Mack: Joseph B. McCullagh of the* St. Louis Globe-Democrat, (Carbondale: Southern Illinois University Press, 1969).
56. Hutcheson, interview.
57. Hutcheson, interview.
58. G. Robert Hillman, "On the Bike, Bush Holds Nothing Back," *Dallas Morning News*, 27 March 2005.
59. R. G. Ratcliffe, "Media Access Bites Dust on Presidential Trail; Bush's Relationship with Journalists Changed Drastically During the Race as Free Flow of Information was Restricted," *Houston Chronicle*, 17 December 2000.
60. Mike Allen, "Bush Visits Worried Workers of the Rust Belt," *Washington Post*, 1 August 2004.
61. Lou Dubose, Jan Reid, and Carl M. Cannon, *Boy Genius: Karl Rove, the Brains behind the Remarkable Political Triumph of George W. Bush* (New York: PublicAffairs, 2003), 235.
62. Todd Gitlin, "The Great Media Meltdown," *Mother Jones*, November–December 2004, 56–59, 100; quote on 59.
63. Gitlin, "The Great Media Meltdown," 100.
64. Phillip Knightley, *The First Casualty: From the Crimea to Vietnam, the War Correspondent as Hero, Propagandist, and Myth Maker* (New York: Harcourt Brace Jovanovich, 1975), 305–306.
65. Andre Billeaudeaux, David Domke, John S. Hutcheson, and Philip Garland, "Newspaper Editorials Follow Lead of Bush Administration," *Newspaper Research Journal* 24, no. 1 (Winter 2003): 166–184.
66. Travis Loop, "Stepping Up Secrecy," *Presstime*, September 2003, 34–38 and 40–41; quote on 38.
67. Alina Tugend, "Maybe Not," *American Journalism Review*, May 2002, 50–53; quote on 53.
68. Sargent, interview.
69. Dave Astor, "Hot Toons," *Editor & Publisher*, May 2004, 50–52, 54.
70. Koring, interview.
71. Helen Thomas, telephone interview by author, 16 December 2004.

72. Hutcheson, interview.
73. Hutcheson, interview.
74. Thomas, interview.
75. David Frum, *The Right Man: The Surprise Presidency of George W. Bush* (New York: Random House, 2003), 269.
76. Fleischer, *Taking Heat*, 246–247.
77. Fleischer, *Taking Heat*, 229–230.
78. Fleischer, *Taking Heat*, 135.
79. Fleischer, *Taking Heat*. Emphasis in original.

CHAPTER 9: EATING THE ZOMBIES

1. Ron Hutcheson, telephone interview by author, 17 December 2004.
2. George W. Bush, press conference, 6 March 2003, transcript available at www.whitehouse.gov/news/releases/2003/03/20030306-8.html. In this chapter, all quotes by President Bush or reporters from this press conference are taken from this transcript.
3. Hutcheson, interview.
4. Helen Thomas, telephone interview by author, 16 December 2004.
5. Thomas, interview.
6. Matt Taibbi, "Cleaning the Pool," *New York Press*, 12 March 2003.
7. Michael Crowley, "Bush Eats the Press," *New York Observer*, 17 March 2003.
8. John F. Dickerson and Karen Tumulty, "The Love Him, Hate Him President," *Time*, 1 December 2003.
9. Brent Bozell, "White House Press Zombies?" *Townhall.com*, 14 March 2003, www.townhall.com/opinion/columns/brentbozell/2003/03/14/169502.html.
10. Rachel Smolkin, "Are the News Media Soft on Bush?" *American Journalism Review*, October–November 2003, 16–25.
11. Kenny Goldberg, "Good Dogs!" Letter to the editor, *American Journalism Review*, June–July 2003, 63.
12. Allan Wolper, "In Photos We Trust," *Editor & Publisher*, 9 June 2003, 26.
13. Philip J. Trounstine, "Bush's Press Slaves," *Salon.com*, 29 March 2004, archive.salon.com/opinion/feature/2004/03/29/press/print.html.
14. Tom Wicker, "Campaign Preview," *Editor & Publisher*, January 2004, 62.
15. Richard Reeves, "A Dirty 'Blowback' Campaign," *Denton Record-Chronicle*, 10 March 2004.
16. Peggy Noonan, "Unhappy Warriors," *Wall Street Journal*, 15 April 2004.
17. Bill Plante, telephone interview by author, 16 December 2004.
18. Plante, interview.
19. Michael Baruch Grossman and Martha Joynt Kumar, *Portraying the President: The White House and the News Media* (Baltimore: Johns Hopkins University Press, 1981), 8.
20. Samuel Kernell, *Going Public: New Strategies of Presidential Leadership* (Washington, D.C.: CQ Press, 1997), 77–78.
21. Ray Scherer, "The Presidential Press Conference," in *The Credibility of Institutions, Policies, and Leadership*, ed. Kenneth W. Thompson, vol. 5 of *The Media* (Lanham, MD: University Press of America, 1985), 90.

22. Steven E. Clayman and John Heritage, "Questioning Presidents: Journalistic Deference and Adversarialness in the Press Conferences of U.S. Presidents Eisenhower and Reagan," *Journal of Communication* 52, no. 4 (2002): 752.

23. William S. White, "Analyzing the 'Adversary' Relationship," in *The Presidency and the Press*, ed. Hoyt Purvis (Austin: Lyndon B. Johnson School of Public Affairs, University of Texas at Austin, 1976), 7–14.

24. Kernell, *Going Public*, 92, 96–97; quote on 78.

25. Richard W. Waterman, Robert Wright, and Gilbert St. Clair, *The Image-Is-Everything Presidency: Dilemmas in American Leadership* (Boulder, CO: Westview Press, 1999), 112, 122–123.

26. Martha Joynt Kumar, "Source Material: 'Does This Constitute a Press Conference?'; Defining and Tabulating Modern Presidential Press Conferences," *Presidential Studies Quarterly* 33, no. 1 (March 2003): 221–238.

27. Blaire Atherton French, *The Presidential Press Conference: Its History and Role in the American Political System* (Washington, D.C.: University Press of America, 1982), 35.

28. William J. Small, *Political Power and the Press* (New York: W. W. Norton, 1972), 184, 187.

29. Elmer E. Cornwell Jr., *Presidential Leadership of Public Opinion* (Bloomington: Indiana University Press, 1965), 74.

30. Thomas, interview.

31. Thomas, interview.

32. Carolyn Smith, *Presidential Press Conferences: A Critical Approach* (New York: Praeger, 1990).

33. Smith, *Presidential Press Conferences*, 80, 89.

34. Smith, *Presidential Press Conferences*, 93.

35. Smith, *Presidential Press Conferences*, 118–119.

36. Smith, *Presidential Press Conferences*, 84, 90.

37. Bill Kristol and David Gergen, interview by Greta Van Susteren, *Fox on the Record with Greta Van Susteren*, Fox News, 6 March 2003.

38. Tim Russert, interview by Katie Couric, *Today*, NBC, 7 March 2003.

39. David Frum, interview by Paula Zahn, *CNN American Morning with Paula Zahn*, CNN, 7 March 2003.

40. George W. Bush, radio address, 1 March 2003, transcript available at www.whitehouse.gov/news/releases/2003/03/20030301.html; George W. Bush, address to American Medical Association conference, 4 March 2003, transcript available at www.whitehouse.gov/news/releases/2003/03/20030304-5.html.

41. Tom Shales, "Bush's Wake-up Call Was a Snooze Alarm," *Washington Post*, 7 March 2003.

42. Kristol, interview.

43. Quoted in Mike Allen, "Bush's Distaste for News Conference Keeps Them Rare," *Washington Post*, 7 March 2003.

44. Smith, *Presidential Press Conferences*, 89.

45. Smith, *Presidential Press Conferences*, 90.

46. The press conference transcript lists 24 "Q" (question) items, but one is actually a reporter stating that she has a question to ask. Of course, if one were to count the multiple questions and rephrasings of questions asked by various reporters during their turns at the microphone, the number of actual questions would be much larger.

47. Smith, *Presidential Press Conferences*, 109.

48. Smith, *Presidential Press Conferences*, 99, 103.

49. Katrina Vanden Heuvel, interview by Howard Kurtz, *CNN Reliable Sources*, CNN, 9 March 2003.

50. Smith, *Presidential Press Conferences*, 95.

51. "'Scripted' Bush Press Conference Continues to Rankle Some White House Reporters," *White House Bulletin*, 11 March 2003.

52. "'Scripted.'"

53. Smith, *Presidential Press Conferences*, 103.

54. Crowley, "Bush Eats the Press."

55. Taibbi, "Cleaning the Pool"; Crowley, "Bush Eats the Press."

56. Wolf Blitzer, "Bush: U.S. Doesn't 'Need Anybody's Permission' to Attack," *CNN.com*, 7 March 2003, cnn.com/2003/US/03/07/wbr.permission/index.html.

57. David E. Sanger, with Felicity Barringer, "Threats and Responses: The President; President Readies U.S. for Prospect of Imminent War," *New York Times*, 7 March 2003.

58. Dana Milbank and Mike Allen, "Bush Is Ready to Go without UN," *Washington Post*, 7 March 2003.

59. "Saying No to War," *New York Times*, 9 March 2003; "The President Looks toward War," *Washington Post*, 7 March 2003.

60. Maureen Dowd, "The Xanax Cowboy," *New York Times*, 9 March 2003.

61. "Iraqi Endgame," *Dallas Morning News*, 8 March 2003.

62. Jay Nordlinger, "Impromptus," *National Review Online*, 11 March 2003, www.nationalreview.com/impromptus/impromptus031103.asp.

63. Adam Nagourney and Janet Elder, "Threats and Responses: The Poll; More Americans Now Faulting UN on Iraq, Poll Finds," *New York Times*, 11 March 2003.

64. Taibbi, "Cleaning the Pool."

65. Plante, interview.

66. Scott Sherman ("The Avenger," *Columbia Journalism Review*, July–August 2003, 44) referred to the "notorious March 6 White House Press conference," and James Wolcott ("Round Up the Cattle!" *Vanity Fair*, June 2003, 86) called the press conference a "hollow piece of absurdist theater."

67. Hutcheson, interview.

68. Plante, interview.

CHAPTER 10: NO ONE WILL DO IT BETTER

1. Bob Woodward, *Shadow: Five Presidents and the Legacy of Watergate* (New York: Simon & Schuster, 1999).

2. Richard Reeves, "A Dirty 'Blowback' Campaign," *Denton Record-Chronicle*, 10 March 2004.

3. Ron Hutcheson, telephone interview by author, 17 December 2004.

4. Hutcheson, interview.

5. G. Robert Hillman, "Writer's Access to Bush Defended," *Dallas Morning News*, 11 February 2005.

6. Sherrie Gossett, "White House Press Corps Dismisses 'Gannongate,'" *Media Monitor*, 17 March 2005, available at www.aim.org/media_monitor/2761_0_2_0.

7. Sheena Martin, "Blogger Given Pass to White House," *Columbia Missourian*, 15 March 2005.

8. Betty Houchin Winfield, *FDR and the News Media* (New York: Columbia University Press, 1994).

9. Jonathan Chait, "Calls Getting Louder for Cheney in 2008," *Columbia Missourian*, 30 March 2005.

10. Wayne Slater, interview by author, 18 August 2004, Austin, Texas.

11. See Jack Huberman, *The Bush-Hater's Handbook* (New York: Nation Books, 2003), as just one example among many of the titles in this genre. Rabid Bush haters could buy a hand-size Bush squishy toy on which to reflexively squeeze out their passion. They could also buy a toddler-size inflatable Bush punching bag, which the Dallas chapter of Mothers Opposing Bush (MOB), used to instill hatred in the next generation. See Katherine Morales, "Dallas Moms Raising Voices to Defeat Bush," *Dallas Morning News*, 14 June 2004, for a story with a picture of a toddler hitting one of those bags in a rally at a city park.

12. Evan Thomas, interview by Howard Kurtz, "Coverage of Third Presidential Debate; Should FCC Stop Sinclair from Broadcasting Anti-Kerry Film?" CNN Reliable Sources, Cable News Network, television, 17 October 2004, transcript retrieved from transcripts.cnn .com/TRANSCRIPTS/0410/17/rs.01.html.

13. Slater, interview.

14. Arnold Garcia Jr., interview by author, 17 August 2004, Austin, Texas.

15. David Broder, "Bush Gambled Big—And Is Now Paying for It," *Austin American-Statesman*, 17 August 2004.

16. Paul Burka, "Why Bush Won," *Texas Monthly*, March 2005.

17. Michael Kinsley, "The Power of One," *Time*, 21 April 2003.

18. See, for example, Carl P. Leubsdorf, "The Old 1-2-term Punch," *Dallas Morning News*, 6 October 2005.

19. "Bush's approval increases," *Dallas Morning News*, 8 December 2005, sec. a, 9.

20. Laura Rozen, "He's done," *American Prospect*, December 2005, 31.

21. Rozen, 28.

22. "Bush's approval increases."

23. James Dao, "2000 Dead: As Iraq Tours Stretch on, a Grim Mark," *New York Times*, 26 October 2005, www.nytimes.com/2005/10/26/international/middleeast/26deaths.html ?hp=&pagew.

24. Michelle Malkin, "Cpl. Jeffrey B. Starr: What the NYTimes Left Out," Michelle Malkin web site, 28 October 2005, available at www.michellemalkin.com/archives/003793.htm.

25. Office of the Press Secretary, "President Outlines Strategy for Victory in Iraq," 30 November 2005, official transcript available at www.whitehouse.gov/news/releases/2003/03/ print/20030306-8.html.

26. "President Outlines Strategy," transcript.

27. David Horowitz, "Seeing the President," *Frontpagemag.com*, 7 December 2005, available at www.frontpagemagazine.com/blog/printable.asp?ID=575.

28. "Pew Survey Finds Moderates, Liberals Dominate News Outlets," *Editorandpublisher .com*, 23 May 2004, www.editorandpublisher.com/eandp/news/article_display.jsp?vnu_ content_id=1000.

29. Jennifer Harper, "Study Finds Press Pro-Kerry," *Washington Times*, 1 November 2004, www.washingtontimes.com/functions/print.php?StoryID=20041101-122452-4025r.

30. Hutcheson, interview.
31. Hutcheson, interview.
32. Hutcheson, interview.
33. Adam Clymer, telephone interview by author, 16 June 2005.
34. Clymer, interview.
35. Bob Schieffer, telephone interview by author, 17 March 2005.
36. Schieffer, interview.
37. Hutcheson, interview.
38. Hutcheson, interview.
39. Bill Plante, telephone interview by author, 16 December 2004.
40. William David Sloan and James D. Startt, *The Media in America: A History* (Northport, AL: Vision Press, 1999), 325.
41. Ari Fleischer, *Taking Heat: The President, the Press, and My Years in the White House* (New York: William Morrow, 2005), 167.
42. "The War of Fog in D.C.," *Editor & Publisher*, 7 April 2003, 16.
43. Plante, interview.
44. Plante, interview.
45. Schieffer, interview.
46. Louis W. Liebovich, *The Press and the Modern Presidency: Myths and Mindsets from Kennedy to Election 2000* (Westport, CT: Praeger, 2001), 254.
47. Slater, interview.
48. Kent Hance, interview by author, 14 October 2005, Austin, Texas.

BIBLIOGRAPHY

Allen, Mike. "Bush Visits Worried Workers of the Rust Belt." *Washington Post*, 1 August 2004.

"Ashcroft's Press Pass." *Editor & Publisher*, 30 June 2003, 16.

Astor, Dave. "Syndicates: Good Work in Bad Times," *Editor & Publisher*, 4 November 2004, 63.

——. "Hot Toons." *Editor & Publisher*, May 2004, 50ff.

——. "*N.Y. Times* Offering 550 Cartoonists?" *Editor & Publisher*, 30 June 2003, 32.

Auletta, Ken. "Fortress Bush." *New Yorker*, 19 January 2004.

——. "Kerry's Brain." *New Yorker*, 20 September 2004.

Barnes, Fred. "Clinton's Good News." *Forbes MediaCritic* 4, no. 1 (Fall 1996): 18–21.

——. Review of *Bush at War*. *Townhall.com*, n.d., www.townhall.com/opinion/books_entertainment/reviews/FredBarnes/140584.html.

Begala, Paul. *"Is Our Children Learning?": The Case against George W. Bush*. New York: Simon & Schuster, 2000.

Billeaudeaux, Andre, David Domke, John S. Hutcheson, and Philip Garland, "Newspaper Editorials Follow Lead of Bush Administration." *Newspaper Research Journal* 24, no. 1 (Winter 2003): 166–184.

Blake, John. Interview by author. Tape recording. 7 April 2003. Arlington, Texas.

Blankley, Tony. "Espionage by Any Other Name." *Jewish World Review*, 19 January 2005. Available at www.jewishworldreview.com/0105/Blankley011905.php3.

Blitzer, Wolf. "Bush: U.S. Doesn't 'Need Anybody's Permission' to Attack." *CNN.com*, 7 March 2003, cnn.com/2003/US/03/07/wbr.permission/index.html.

Bozell, Brent. "White House Press Zombies?" *Townhall.com*, 14 March 2003, www.townhall.com/opinion/columns/brentbozell/2003/03/14/169502.html.

Brady, John. *Bad Boy: The Life and Politics of Lee Atwater*. Reading, MA: Addison-Wesley, 1997.

Brooks, Brian S., George Kennedy, Daryl Moen, and Don Ranly. *News Reporting and Writing*. Boston: Bedford/St. Martin's, 2002.

Bruni, Frank. *Ambling into History: The Unlikely Odyssey of George W. Bush*. New York: HarperCollins, 2002.

Burka, Paul. "Why Bush Won." *Texas Monthly*, March 2005.

Bush, Barbara. *Barbara Bush: A Memoir*. New York: Lisa Drew Books, 1994.

Bush, George [H. W.]. *Heartbeat*. Ed. Jim McGrath. New York: Scribner, 2001.

Bush, George W. *A Charge to Keep*. New York: Perennial, 2001.

——. Interview with Brit Hume. Fox News. 22 September 2003, available at www.foxnews.com/printer_friendly_story/0,3566,98006,00.html.

——. Interview with Brian Lamb. *C-SPAN Q&A*. 30 January 2005, available at www.q-and-a.org/Transcript/?ProgramID=1008.

Bushisms: President George Herbert Walker Bush, in His Own Words. Comp. editors of the *New Republic*. New York: Workman, 1992.

Carlson, Tucker. "Devil May Care." *Talk*, September 1999.

Chavez, Linda. "It's Debate Time." *Townhall.com*, 29 September 2004, www.townhall.com/opinion/columns/lindachavez/2004/09/29/13166.html.

Chen, Edwin. Telephone interview by author. Tape recording. 17 December 2004.

Clarke, Richard A. *Against All Enemies: Inside America's War on Terror*. New York: Free Press, 2004.

Clayman, Steven, and John Heritage. *The News Interview: Journalists and Public Figures on the Air.* Cambridge, United Kingdom: Cambridge University Press, 2002.

——. "Questioning Presidents: Journalistic Deference and Adversarialness in the Press Conferences of U.S. Presidents Eisenhower and Reagan." *Journal of Communication* 52, no. 4 (December 2002): 749–775.

Clayton, Charles C. *Little Mack: Joseph B. McCullagh of the* St. Louis Globe-Democrat. Carbondale: Southern Illinois University Press, 1969.

Clements, Ed. Telephone interview by author. Tape Recording. 11 October 2004.

Clymer, Adam. Telephone interview by author. Tape Recording. 16 June 2005.

Cooperstein, Chuck. Telephone interview by author. Tape Recording. 24 March 2003.

Cornwell, Elmer E., Jr. *Presidential Leadership of Public Opinion*. Bloomington: Indiana University Press, 1965.

Crowley, Michael. "Bush Eats the Press." *New York Observer*, 17 March 2003.

Dean, John W. *Worse than Watergate: The Secret Presidency of George W. Bush*. New York: Little, Brown, 2004.

Dickerson, John F., and Karen Tumulty. "The Love Him, Hate Him President." *Time*, 1 December 2003.

Dowd, Maureen. *Bushworld: Enter at Your Own Risk*. New York: G. P. Putnam's Sons, 2004.

Drudge, Matt. "60 Mins Planned Bush Missing Explosives Story for Election Eve." *Drudge Report*, 26 October 2004, available at www.drudgereport.com/nbcw6.htm.

Dubose, Lou, Jan Reid, and Carl M. Cannon. *Boy Genius: Karl Rove, the Brains behind the Remarkable Political Triumph of George W. Bush*. New York: PublicAffairs, 2003.

Duffy, Michael, and Dan Goodgame. *Marching in Place: The Status Quo Presidency of George Bush*. New York: Simon & Schuster, 1992.

Duffy, Michael, Matthew Cooper, and John F. Dickerson. "Collateral Damage." *Time*, 24 May 2004.

Fitzwater, Marlin. *Call the Briefing! Bush and Reagan, Sam and Helen: A Decade with Presidents and the Press*. Holbrook, MA: Adams Media, 1995.

Fleischer, Ari. *Taking Heat: The President, the Press, and My Years in the White House*. New York: William Morrow, 2005.

Fraley, Gerry. Telephone interview by author. Tape recording. 22 November 2002.

Frank, Justin A. *Bush on the Couch: Inside the Mind of the President*. New York: ReganBooks, 2004.
French, Blaire Atherton. *The Presidential Press Conference: Its History and Role in the American Political System*. Washington, D.C.: University Press of America, 1982.
Friedlander, Edward J., and John Lee. *Feature Writing for Newspapers and Magazines: The Pursuit of Excellence*. Boston: Pearson Education, 2004.
Froomkin, Dan. Telephone interview with author. Tape recording. 17 February 2004.
Frum, David. Interview by Paula Zahn. "Tough Stance on Iraq by President Bush." *CNN American Morning with Paula Zahn*, Cable News Network, television, 7 March 2003, transcript #030711CN.V74.
——. *The Right Man: The Surprise Presidency of George W. Bush*. New York: Random House, 2003.
Galloway, Randy. Interview by author. Tape recording. 19 June 2002. Arlington, Texas.
Garcia, Jr., Arnold. "Gore Capitalizes on Bush's No-show," *Austin American-Statesman*, 17 April 2000, sec. a, 11, available at nl.newsbank.com/nl-search/we/Archives.
Garcia, Jr., Arnold. Interview by author. Tape recording. 17 August 2004. Austin, Texas.
Gilles, D. B., and Sheldon Woodbury. *W: The First 100 Days, A White House Journal*. Kansas City, MO: Andrews McMeel, 2001.
Gitlin, Todd. "The Great Media Meltdown." *Mother Jones*, November–December 2004.
Giuliani, Rudolph W., with Ken Kurson. *Leadership*. New York: Hyperion, 2002.
Goldberg, Kenny. "Good Dogs!" Letter to the editor. *American Journalism Review*, June–July 2003, 63.
Goldman, Peter, Thomas M. DeFrank, Mark Miller, Andrew Murr, and Tom Matthews, with Patrick Rogers and Melanie Cooper. *Quest for the Presidency*. College Station: Texas A&M University Press, 1994.
Goldman, Peter, Tom Mathews, Thomas M. DeFrank, Mark Miller, Andrew Murr, and Patrick Rogers. "Face to Face in Prime Time." *Newsweek*, 1 November 1992.
Goldstein, Norm, ed. *The Associated Press Stylebook and Libel Manual*. New York: Associated Press, 1996.
Gossett, Sherrie. "White House Press Corps Dismisses 'Gannongate.'" *Media Monitor*, 17 March 2005, available at www.aim.org/media_monitor/2761_0_2_0.
Graubard, Stephen. *Command of Office: How War, Secrecy, and Deception Transformed the Presidency from Theodore Roosevelt to George W. Bush*. New York: Basic Books, 2004.
Greenberg, Paul. "Crazy Like Fox: Of Bounces and Non-bounces." *Townhall.com*, 10 September 2004, www.townhall.com/columnists/paulgreenberg/printpg20040910.shtml.
Greene, John Robert. *The Presidency of George Bush*. Lawrence: University Press of Kansas, 2000.
Grossman, Michael Baruch, and Martha Joynt Kumar. *Portraying the President: The White House and the News Media*. Baltimore: Johns Hopkins University Press, 1981.
Guilfoile, Kevin, and John Warner. *My First Presidentiary: A Scrapbook by George W. Bush*. Ed. Michael Colton. New York: Three Rivers Press, 2001.
Hallet, Vicky. "The Candidate to Watch." *U.S. News & World Report*, 2 February 2004.
Hance, Kent. Interview by author. Tape recording. 14 October 2004. Austin, Texas.
Hansen, Dale. Telephone interview by author. Tape recording. 31 March 2003.
Harper, Jennifer. "CBS Eyed '60 Minutes' Bush Bombshell." *Washington Times*, 27 October 2004, available at www.washingtontimes.com/functions/print.php?StoryID=20041027-123351-4664r.

——. "Study Finds Press Pro-Kerry." *Washington Times*, 1 November 2004, www.washington times.com/functions/print.php?StoryID=20041101-122452-4025r.

Hart, Patricia Kilday. "Little Did We Know . . . ," *Texas Monthly*, November 2004.

Heath, Jena. "The Brain behind the Oval Office." *Austin American-Statesman*, 21 February 2003, available at nl.newsbank.com/nl-search/we/Archives.

Hentoff, Nat. "Targeting the Fox News Channel." *Jewish World Review*, 13 September 2004. Available at jewishworldreview.com/cols/hentoff091304.asp.

Hersh, Seymour M. "The Coming Wars." *New Yorker*, 24 and 31 January 2005, 40–47.

Herskowitz, Mickey. *Duty, Honor, Country*. Nashville, TN: Rutledge Hill Press, 2003.

Hertsgaard, Mark. *On Bended Knee: The Press and the Reagan Presidency*. New York: Farrar, Straus & Giroux, 1988.

Horowitz, David. "Seeing the President." *Frontpagemag.com*, 7 December 2005, available at www.frontpagemagazine.com/blog/printable.asp?ID=575.

"Hot Type." *Editor & Publisher*, 12 February 2001, 28.

House, David. Telephone interview by author. Tape recording. 27 September 2004

Huberman, Jack. *The Bush-Hater's Handbook*. New York: Nation Books, 2003.

Hughes, Karen P. Letter to Suzanne Gamboa, October 4, 1996. Press Office, Records, Texas Governor George W. Bush. Archives and Information Services Division, Texas State Library and Archives Commission.

——. *Ten Minutes from Normal*. New York: Viking Penguin, 2004.

Hutcheson, Ron. Telephone interview by author. Tape recording. 17 December 2004.

"Impact of Ashcroft Memo Debated," *Quill*, November 2003, 41.

"Iraq, Rehnquist May be 'October Surprises.'" *New York Times*, 26 October 2004. Available at www.nytimes.com/aponline/national/AP-October-Surprises.html.

Jensen, Elizabeth. "Sinclair Airs Show on Kerry." *Los Angeles Times*, 23 October 2004, retrieved from www.latimes.com/news/nationworld/nation/la-na-sinclair23oct23,1,4024578,print.s.

Journeys with George: A Home Movie by Alexandra Pelosi. Directed by Alexandra Pelosi. New York: HBO Video, 2003.

Kernell, Samuel. *Going Public: New Strategies of Presidential Leadership*. Washington, D.C.: CQ Press, 1997.

Kessler, Ronald. *A Matter of Character: Inside the White House of George W. Bush*. New York: Sentinel, 2004.

Kettl, Donald F. *Team Bush: Leadership Lessons from the Bush White House*. New York: McGraw-Hill, 2003.

Kinsley, Michael. "The Power of One." *Time*, 21 April 2003.

Kirtley, Jane. "Keeping the Door Open." *American Journalism Review*, September 2002, 86.

Klein, Joe. "The Secrets of Reagan's Success." *Time*, 14 June 2004.

Knightley, Phillip. *The First Casualty: From the Crimea to Vietnam, the War Correspondent as Hero, Propagandist, and Myth Maker*. New York: Harcourt Brace Jovanovich, 1975.

Koring, Paul. Telephone interview by author. Tape recording. 13 September 2004.

Kristol, Bill and David Gergen. Interview by Greta Van Susteren. "Interview with Bill Kristol, David Gergen about Bush Press Conference." *Fox on the Record with Greta Van Susteren*, Fox News Network, Inc., television, 6 March 2003, transcript #030601cb.260.

Kumar, Martha Joynt. "Source Material: 'Does This Constitute a Press Conference?'; Defining and Tabulating Modern Presidential Press Conferences." *Presidential Studies Quarterly* 33, no. 1 (March 2003): 221–228.

Kurtz, Howard. *Spin Cycle: How the White House and the Media Manipulate the News*. New York: Touchstone, 1998.

Layton, Charles. "The Information Squeeze." *American Journalism Review*, September 2002, 20–29.

——. "Miller Brouhaha." *American Journalism Review*, August–September 2003, 30–35.

Ledeen, Michael. "The Hersh File." *National Review Online*, 21 January 2005, www.nationalreview.com/ledeen/ledeen200501210807.asp.

Leger, Robert. "Secrecy Compromises Safety." *Quill*, May 2003, 4.

Leo, John. "Self-inflicted Wounds." *Townhall.com*, 4 October 2004, www.townhall.com/columnists/johnleo/printjl20041004.shtml.

Lichter, S. Robert. "Consistently Liberal: But Does It Matter?" *Forbes MediaCritic* 4, no. 1 (Fall 1996): 26–39.

Liebovich, Louis W. *The Press and the Modern Presidency: Myths and Mindsets from Kennedy to Election 2000*. Westport, CT: Praeger, 2001.

Lizza, Ryan. "Flip Side." *New Republic* 231, no 13 (27 September 2004): 10–11.

Long, Rob. "My Candidate!" *National Review*, 25 October 2004, 30ff.

Loop, Travis. "Stepping Up Secrecy," *Presstime*, September 2003, 34ff.

Lo Scalzo, Jim. "Overexposed." *U.S. News & World Report*, 12 December 2004.

Malkin, Michelle. "Cpl. Jeffrey B. Starr: What the NYTimes left out." Michelle Malkin web site, 28 October 2005, available at www.michellemalkin.com/archives/003793.htm.

McKinnon, Mark. "How to . . . Sell a Candidate." *Texas Monthly*, July 2003.

McNeely, Dave. "Bush's Personal Approach Scores Political Points." *Austin American-Statesman*, 4 April 1995.

McNeely, Dave. Interview by author. Tape recording. 13 October 2004. Austin, Texas.

Mears, Walter. *Deadlines Past: Forty Years of Presidential Campaigning; A Reporter's Story*. Kansas City, MO: Andrews McMeel, 2003.

Milbank, Dana. *Smashmouth: Two Years in the Gutter with Al Gore and George W. Bush—Notes from the 2000 Campaign Trail*. New York: Basic Books, 2001.

Miller, Mark Crispin. *The Bush Dyslexicon: Observations on a National Disorder*. New York: W. W. Norton, 2001.

Minutaglio, Bill. *First Son: George W. Bush and the Bush Family Dynasty*. New York: Three Rivers Press, 1999.

Mitchell, Elizabeth. *W: Revenge of the Bush Dynasty*. New York: Hyperion, 2000.

Mnookin, Seth. "The Charm Offensive." *Brill's Content* 3, no. 7 (September 2000): 76–81, 128–129.

Montgomery, Dave. Telephone interview by author. Tape recording. 10 December 2004.

Moore, James, and Wayne Slater. *Bush's Brain: How Karl Rove Made George W. Bush Presidential*. Hoboken, NJ: John Wiley & Sons, 2003.

Morris, Edmund. *The Rise of Theodore Roosevelt*. New York: The Modern Library, 2001.

Morrow, Lance. "Triumph of the Masses," *Time*, 24 May 2004, 78

Noonan, Peggy. *Simply Speaking*. New York: ReganBooks, 1998.

Nordlinger, Jay. "A President Who Means It. What Good the Student Exchange? Straight from the Emir's Mouth—And More." *National Review Online*, 11 March 2003, www.nationalreview.com.

Novak, Robert. "Bush's Little Blooper." *Townhall.com*, 2 September 2004, www.townhall.com/opinion/columns/robertnovak/2004/09/02/12877.html.

Office of the Press Secretary. "President George Bush Discusses Iraq in National Press Conference." The White House website. Transcript, 6 March 2003, www.whitehouse.gov/news/releases/2003/03/print/20030306-8.html.

——. "President Holds Press Conference." The White House website. Transcript, 4 November 2004, www.whitehouse.gov/news/releases/2004/11/20041104-5.html.

——. "President Outlines Strategy for Victory in Iraq." The White House website. Transcript, 30 November 2005, www.whitehouse.gov/news/releases/2005/11/print/20051130-2.html.

——. "President's Radio Address." The White House website. Transcript, 1 March 2003, www.whitehouse.gov/news/releases/2003/03/print/20030301.html.

Parmet, Herbert S. *George Bush: The Life of a Lone Star Yankee*. New York: Scribner, 1997.

Peters, Charles. "Tilting at Windmills." *Washington Monthly*, September 2004, 4–7.

"Pew Survey Finds Moderates, Liberals Dominate News Outlets." *Editorandpublisher.com*, 23 May 2004, www.editorandpublisher.com/eandp/news/article_display.jsp?vnu_content_id =1000.

Pierce, Greg. "Inside Politics." *Washington Times*, 24 August 2004, available at www .washingtontimes.com/functions/print.php?StoryID=20040824-121541-9986r.

——. "Inside Politics." *Washington Times*, 13 September 2004, available at www.washington times.com/functions/print.php?StoryID=2004913-123731-69984.

——. "Inside Politics." *Washington Times*, 5 October 2004, available at www.washingtontimes .com/functions/print.php?StoryID=20041005-013053-9595r

Plante, Bill. Telephone interview by author. Tape recording. 16 December 2004.

Paulson, Ken. "Too Free?" *American Journalism Review*, September 2002, 30–35.

——. "Upon Further Review." *American Journalism Review*, August–September 2003, 60–65.

"President Announces Framework to Modernize and Improve Medicare." The White House website. Transcript, 4 March 2003, www.whitehouse.gov/news/releases/2003/03/print/20030304-5.html.

Ratcliffe, R. G. Telephone interview by author. Tape recording. 10 November 2004.

Rather, Dan. Interview by Joe B. Frantz. Transcript. 16 April 1973. Oral History Collection, Lyndon Baines Johnson Library, Austin, Texas.

Reeves, Jim. Telephone interview by author. Tape recording. 24 June 2002.

Reichert, Tom, James E. Mueller, and Michael Nitz. "Disengaged and Uninformed: 2000 Presidential Election Coverage in Consumer Magazines Popular with Young Adults." *Journalism and Mass Communication Quarterly* 80, no. 3 (Autumn 2003): 519–520.

Reno, Robert. "George W. Bush is Reagan's Heir." *Newsday*, 12 November 2002, a28.

Ringolsby, Tracy. Telephone interview by author. Tape recording. 25 November 2002.

Ripley, Amanda, with Mark Thompson. "An Image of Grief Returns." *Time*, 3 May 2004.

Rogers, Phil. Telephone interview by author. Tape recording. 18 March 2003.

Root, Jay. Interview by author. Tape recording. 13 October 2004. Austin, Texas.

Rozell, Mark J. *The Press and the Bush Presidency*. Westport, CT: Praeger, 1996.

Rozen, Laura. "He's done." *American Prospect*, December 2005, 27–31.

Russert, Tim. Interview by Katie Couric. "Tim Russert Discusses President Bush's Press Conference and Whether He Made His Case for War against Iraq." *Today*, National Broadcasting Corporation, Inc., television, 7 March 2003, NBC News transcript.

Ryfe, D. M. "Franklin Roosevelt and the Fireside Chats." *Journal of Communication* 49, no. 4 (December 1999): 80–103.

Sammon, Bill. *Fighting Back: The War on Terrorism—From Inside the Bush White House*. Washington, D.C.: Regnery, 2002.

——. *Misunderestimated: The President Battles Terrorism, John Kerry, and the Bush Haters*. New York: ReganBooks, 2004.

Sargent, Ben. Telephone interview by author. Tape recording. 20 August 2004.

Scherer, Ray. "The Presidential Press Conference." In *The Credibility of Institutions, Policies, and Leadership*, ed. Kenneth W. Thompson, vol. 5 of *The Media*, 66–93. Lanham, MD: University Press of America, 1985.

Schieffer, Bob. Telephone interview by author. Tape recording. 17 March 2005.

Schweizer, Peter, and Rochelle Schweizer. *The Bushes: Portrait of a Dynasty*. New York: Doubleday, 2004.

"'Scripted' Bush Press Conference Continues to Rankle Some White House Reporters." *White House Bulletin*, 11 March 2003.

Sharkey, Jacqueline E. "Journalism vs. Jingoism." *American Journalism Review*, April 2003, 10–11.

Sherman, Scott. "The Avenger." *Columbia Journalism Review* 52, no. 2 (July–August 2003): 34–44.

Shogan, Robert. *Bad News: Where the Press Goes Wrong in the Making of the President*. Chicago: Ivan R. Dee, 2001.

Slater, Wayne. Interview by author. Tape recording. 18 August 2004. Austin, Texas.

Sloan, William David, and James D. Startt. *The Media in America: A History*. Northport, AL: Vision Press, 1999.

Small, William J. *Political Power and the Press*. New York: W. W. Norton, 1972.

Smith, Carolyn. *Presidential Press Conferences: A Critical Approach*. New York: Praeger, 1990.

Smolkin, Rachel. "Are the News Media Soft on Bush?" *American Journalism Review*, October–November 2003, 16–25.

——. "The Crowded Bus." *American Journalism Review*, April 2003, 38–43.

——. "Media Mood Swings." *American Journalism Review*, June/July 2003, 16–23.

Spada, James. *The Bush Family*. New York: St. Martin's Press, 2004.

Spelce, Neal. Telephone interview by author. Tape recording. 8 September 2004.

Stevens, Stuart. *The Big Enchilada: Campaign Adventures with the Cockeyed Optimists from Texas Who Won the Biggest Prize in Politics*. New York: Free Press, 2001.

Steyn, Mark. "CBS Falls for Kerry Campaign's Fake Memo." *Chicago Sun-Times*, 12 September 2004, available at www.suntimes.com/cgi-bin/print.cgi.

Suskind, Ron. *The Price of Loyalty: George W. Bush, the White House, and the Education of Paul O'Neill*. New York: Simon & Schuster, 2004.

Taibbi, Matt. "Cleaning the Pool." *New York Press*, 12–18 March 2003.

Tebbel, John, and Sarah Miles Watts. *The Press and the Presidency: From George Washington to Ronald Reagan*. New York: Oxford University Press, 1985.

Texas. Governor George W. Bush Records. State Archives, Austin.

Thomas, Evan. Interview by Howard Kurtz. "Coverage of Third Presidential Debate; Should FCC Stop Sinclair from Broadcasting Anti-Kerry Film?" CNN Reliable Sources, Cable News Network. Television. 17 October 2004, transcript retrieved from transcripts.cnn.com/TRANSCRIPTS/0410/17/rs.01.html.

——, and the staff of *Newsweek*. *Election 2004: How Bush Won and What You Can Expect in the Future*. New York: PublicAffairs, 2004.
Thomas, Helen. Telephone interview by author. Tape recording. 16 December 2004.
Thomas, Helen. *Thanks for the Memories, Mr. President*. New York: Scribner, 2002.
Thomasson, Dan. "Cheap-shot Journalism." *Quill*, January 1986, 18–21.
Tittle, Mel. Telephone interview by author. 27 July 2004.
Todd, Chuck. "Air Force Won." In *Midterm Madness*, ed. Larry J. Sabato, 35–45. Lanham, MD: Rowman & Littlefield, 2003.
Trounstine, Philip J. "Bush's Press Slaves." *Salon.com*, 29 March 2004, archive .salon.com/opinion/feature/2004/03/29/press/print.html.
Tugend, Alina. "Maybe Not." *American Journalism Review*, May 2002, 50–53.
Usher, Chris. Telephone interview by author. Tape recording. 17 January 2004.
Vanden Heuvel, Katrina. Interview by Howard Kurtz. "Were White House Reporters Used as Cogs in Pro-War Machine?; What Is Life Like for Journalists on Front Lines?" *CNN Reliable Sources*, Cable News Network, television, 9 March 2003, transcript #030900CN.V50.
Waldman, Paul. *Fraud: The Strategy behind the Bush Lies and Why the Media Didn't Tell You*. Naperville, IL: Sourcebooks, 2004.
Walsh, Kenneth T. "A Case of Confidence." *U.S. News & World Report*, 17 November 2003.
——. "Hunting Quayle." *Forbes MediaCritic*, Summer 1996, 56–66.
"The War of Fog in D.C." *Editor & Publisher*, 7 April 2003, 13.
Waterman, Richard W., Robert Wright, and Gilbert St. Clair. *The Image-Is-Everything Presidency: Dilemmas in American Leadership*. Boulder, CO: Westview Press, 1999.
Weisberg, Jacob, ed. *George W. Bushisms*. New York: Fireside, 2001.
——, ed. *More George W. Bushisms*. New York: Fireside, 2002.
White, William S. "Analyzing the 'Adversary' Relationship." In *The Presidency and the Press*, ed. Hoyt Purvis, 7–14. Austin: Lyndon B. Johnson School of Public Affairs, University of Texas at Austin, 1976.
Whitman, Christine Todd. Interview by Sean Hannity and Alan Colmes. "Christine Todd Whitman Talks with Hannity & Colmes." *Hannity & Colmes*, Fox News Network, Inc., television, 27 January 2005, transcript available at www.foxnews.com/printer_friendly_story/0,3566,143440,00.html.
——. *It's My Party Too: The Battle for the Heart of the GOP and the Future of America*. New York: Penguin, 2005.
Wicker, Tom. "Campaign Preview." *Editor & Publisher*, January 2004, 62.
Williams, Herbert Lee. *The Newspaperman's President*. Chicago: Nelson-Hall, 1984.
Wilson, Joseph. *The Politics of Truth: Inside the Lies that Led to War and Betrayed My Wife's CIA Identity*. New York: Carroll & Graf Publishers, 2004.
Winfield, Betty Houchin. *FDR and the News Media*. New York: Columbia University Press, 1994.
Wolper, Allan. "In Photos We Trust." *Editor & Publisher*, 9 June 2003, 26.
Woodward, Bob. *Bush at War*. New York: Simon & Schuster, 2002.
——. *Plan of Attack*. New York: Simon & Schuster, 2004.
Woolcott, James. "Round Up the Cattle!" *Vanity Fair*, June 2003.

INDEX

ABOUT THE AUTHOR

James E. Mueller is an assistant professor of journalism at the University of North Texas. Before entering academia, Mueller worked for about 10 years as a reporter, editor, and photographer for newspapers in suburban St. Louis, Missouri. He earned bachelor's and master's degrees in journalism from the University of Missouri–Columbia and a Ph.D. in journalism from the University of Texas at Austin. Mueller has written or cowritten 3 book chapters and 15 articles on journalism and has made about 30 scholarly or professional presentations of his research. His research interests, in addition to the press and the presidency, include media management and journalism history with a special focus on George Armstrong Custer and the 19th-century press.